The United States and the Near East

THE UNITED STATES AND THE NEAR EAST

BY E. A. SPEISER

PROFESSOR OF SEMITICS
UNIVERSITY OF PENNSYLVANIA

REVISED EDITION

GREENWOOD PRESS, PUBLISHERS
WESTPORT, CONNECTICUT

MAPS PREPARED UNDER THE CARTOGRAPHIC
DIRECTION OF ARTHUR H. ROBINSON

CONTENTS

MAPS

INTRODUCTION

Before the Second World War there was no major region of the earth which to most of us here in the United States seemed more remote than the Near East. The reasons for this are obvious. The United States possessed no political interests in that great area of the world which stretches from the southern shores of the Mediterranean to the frontiers of India and from the Persian Gulf to the Caspian Sea. Commercial ties with the peoples of the Middle East were of minor importance. Our cultural interests were largely limited to the successful, but circumscribed, endeavors of a few enlightened Americans to make our educational facilities available to the people of Turkey and of the Levant, and to the work carried on by American missionaries in Iran and in a few other adjacent countries.

With the end of the war, the picture had wholly changed. American armies had occupied Morocco, Algeria, and Tunisia. American forces had been stationed in Egypt and in Iran. Agents of the American Government were constantly traveling through every portion of the Near East. Diplomatic relations between Washington and the capitals of the countries of the Near East, which had earlier been purely nominal, had rapidly acquired increasing significance.

The problem of Palestine, and the need for a just solution of the controversies which have arisen in the Holy Land, have become matters of intimate concern to many millions of Americans. Our economic interest in the equitable allocation of the oil resources of the Near East has suddenly been seen to involve questions of national security. The independence and stability of the Arab states are recognized as issues which affect the establishment of the new international order envisaged by the United Nations Charter.

Within the span of a few brief years an interrelationship between the United States and the Near East has sprung into being which would have seemed inconceivable a decade ago.

It has become evident to a great majority of the American people that in the one-world order which they wish to see established not only must the Near East become an integral part, but also, for reasons which are daily becoming more apparent, it is within the Near East that some of the present threats to the maintenance of world peace are looming ever larger.

The Near East is, of course, the scene of an immediate conflict of interest between Great Britain and the Soviet Union. Unless Great Britain can maintain intact the supremacy of her influence in the Near East, and the security of her life line to Asia through the Suez Canal and the Red Sea, Great Britain cannot long remain a major power. Russia's present efforts to obtain a preponderant control over the Eastern Mediterranean and over the Persian Gulf jeopardize that British supremacy which has been maintained successfully by successive British Governments during a period of more than a century and a half.

This clash of empires directly affects every other people of the world. Unless adequate, constructive, and lasting solutions can be found in the peace settlements still to be formulated, and through the agency of the United Nations, the peace for which the American people hope can at best be but precarious.

A clear understanding on the part of American public opinion of the present play of political, economic, and social forces within the Near East is greatly needed.

Mr. Speiser's volume on the Near East offers all of us

the means of securing precisely such an understanding. With exceptional clarity, he gives us in his book the historical background of the entire area, and a detailed survey of the major factors which are shaping the destinies of the Near East peoples. He offers us an authoritative interpretation of the trends which are determining the relations between the Near East countries, as well as the relations between the Arab World and the major powers. He has written with sympathy and with profound knowledge.

His book provides with rare lucidity the answers to many questions which have been puzzling us. It makes clear why the course of events in the Near East has become a matter of vital concern to the American people.

Sumner Welles

PREFACE TO THE REVISED EDITION

In the past three years the Near East has undergone epochal changes. A new state has arisen, the interrelations of the established countries have been transformed, and the policies of the outside powers have been markedly affected.

To do justice to all these happenings would have required, at a minimum, a separate book. And to integrate them properly with the previous account would have meant to rewrite the earlier book. This has not been possible because of limitations beyond the writer's control. But numerous changes have been made throughout and new paragraphs have been substituted for those most seriously out of date. Lastly, the major events of the past years have been compressed into one new chapter.

The one criticism of the first edition that has come up time and again derives from that book's brevity. The present version is even more vulnerable in this respect. No one could be more keenly aware of this handicap than the writer—or more helpless. As for the failure to include Turkey and Iran, it may be stated once again that this is merely a temporary defect. A separate book on these countries has been entrusted from the start to more competent hands than these.

E. A. Speiser

Elkins Park, Pennsylvania
July 29, 1949

PREFACE TO THE FIRST EDITION

What difference is there, if any, between the "Near East" and the "Middle East"? If this question puzzles the layman it is because the "experts" have been vague and confused in their use of these two terms. They have accepted the one or the other as an article of faith which absolves them from the obligation to account for their practice. The East is "Near," "Middle," or "Far" in relation to what? The British employ these designations with rather indirect reference to the British Isles. On this basis, however, the meaning would have to shift constantly as one moves eastward through Europe; and the British Isles might have to be assigned to the Near East from the vantage point of America. Actually, the traditional usage has been to equate the East roughly with Asia: thus Western Asia becomes the Near East, Central Asia the Middle East, and Eastern Asia the Far East. In following this practice Continental Europe has chosen to leave well enough alone. Neither has there been any noticeable confusion in English usage, except where modern boundaries are concerned. Yet if Syria, for instance, was securely in the Near East down to very recent times, she cannot be banished suddenly to the Middle East for some unspecified last-minute offense. The sense of continuity would become distorted, and continuity is precisely. the one all-pervasive aspect of the region's life. To be sure, all is not set and rigid where geographic and cultural concepts overlap. Egypt is geographically in Africa, but culturally she is an integral part of the adjacent portion of Asia. Our State Department reflects—unconsciously perhaps—an awareness of this problem in that it distinguishes between the Near and the Middle East, the borders of the Near East being made to coincide with the northeastern boundaries of the Arab world. For the purposes of the present book the same delimitation has been followed, and Turkey and Iran have therefore been left out of the discussion. As for the other limits, however, the definition here followed is less generous than that of the State Department. No part of Europe has been included, and of all the territories of Africa Egypt alone has come in for detailed notice. The modern Near East, then, in the present case, covers exactly the same territory that is of primary concern to the League of Arab States.

My own interest in this region is bound up with a lifelong study of the ancient Near East. In this connection I had the opportunity to conduct five archaeological campaigns in Mesopotamia, between 1926 and 1937, and I thus became acquainted at first hand with some of the problems and prospects of the region in modern times. During the war I served with the Office of Strategic Services, from 1943 to 1945 in charge of that agency's research and analysis section on the Near East and near-by territories. It was my good fortune to be associated in this task with men and women each of whom was a trained and penetrating student of the area as a whole or of some distinctive part thereof. The ceaseless yet ever constructive give-and-take of that partnership, rendered all the more productive by the urgency of wartime requirements, was an intensely stimulating and enriching experience. To all my colleagues in that enterprise I am deeply indebted. To Miss Doris E. Wrigley and Mr. J. C. Hurewitz I owe an additional debt for compiling the latest vital facts —of which only a fraction could be utilized in the text— and for reading and improving the manuscript.

My editors, Mr. Sumner Welles and Mr. Donald C. McKay, must have used much more than the normal quota of forbearance and understanding in dealing with this appreciative but long-reluctant author. Mr. Roger L. Scaife, Director of the Harvard University Press, somehow managed to make things seem worth while even during the wearisome period between the typed draft and the printed page. And Mr. Arthur H. Robinson, who did the exacting map work, was fully equal not only to the inherent difficulties of the subject but also to the shock of unfamiliar spellings.

The awkward ways of the Latin alphabet with Oriental, and particularly with Arabic, terms are fairly well known. It has been pointed out, for instance, that there are as many as thirty-six different forms on record in which the name of the founder of Islam has been reproduced in English contexts. It is customary, therefore, in technical studies to preface the argument with an explanation of the system of transliteration employed. Such systems, however, call for the use of numerous diacritical marks, something that would be highly incongruous in a book which had to dispense with footnotes. The general method which has here been followed is to apply as consistently as possible the simplest forms which will yield reasonable approximations of the original sounds; a compromise, in short, between the amiable anarchy of Lawrence and the attempted precision of the philologist. Thus, it is simple enough to use *q* instead of *k* where the Arabic indicates this distinction (as in *Iraq*, *Faruq*); to follow the Arabic in writing single (*Hasan*, not *Hassan*) or double letters (*Muhammad*, not *Mahomet*, or the like; *Hajj*, not *Haj*), as the case may be; and to reproduce adequately any of the three vowels of Arabic (hence *Muslim* rather than *Moslem*). For the same reason it was deemed preferable to use *ay* for the corresponding diphthong of Arabic, instead of the usual and indiscriminate employment of *ei* and *ai*. But once we have rejected *sheik* (which comes to be pronounced like *chic*—a most perverse association) in favor of *shaykh*, we are obliged to write also *Faysal* and *Husayn* as well as *Bayrut* and *Bahrayn* and *Kuwayt*. On the other hand, one cannot but leave the reader his *Mecca* (in place of the sounder *Makkah*); and this carries with it *Medina* and the *Yemen*. Then there are the two "glottal" consonants for which our alphabet has no ready counterparts and which are rendered in specialized works with the two respective "breathing" signs. I have ignored these consonants in all but a few instances where their omission threatened to distort pronunciation more than seemed necessary, substituting the apostrophe sign in each case. The upshot is that *Qur'an* and *Sa'd* appear to have a consonant in common which the original will not sanction. The same sign would likewise have found its way into *Sa'ud* (in reality *Su'ūd*), were it not for the fact that the conventional *Saud* and *Saudi* are now too familiar to be tampered with.

All in all, the "system" of spelling used in this book for Arabic names cannot be expected to satisfy everybody, any more than the contents can.

E. A. Speiser

Elkins Park, Pennsylvania
November 23, 1946

PART I

THE BACKGROUND

1. The Geographic Factor

1. GENERAL ENVIRONMENT

History is first and foremost the story of man meeting the challenge of his physical environment. The physical circumstances furnish the opportunity. But it is the human element, acting and interacting against the natural background, that must determine in the end how meaningful the resulting history is going to be.

Historic civilizations are distinguished by their capacity for growth and their ability to communicate to posterity the sum of their experiences. The first such progressive cultures known to man got their start in the Near East. All the other dynamic civilizations follow the Near East prelude in time and are indebted to it for much of their content. Western civilization as we know it today is in countless indirect ways the beneficiary of the pioneering achievement of the ancient Near East. The modern Near East is of course a direct representative of the same vigorous tradition. The total record of this region is thus without parallel for vitality and long-range impact. How much of this record may be attributed to geographic environment? In other words, to what extent has the Near East been favored by nature to emerge as an enduring factor in a changing world? Surely, no region is better equipped to test the everlasting interaction of environment and culture.

The evolution of the Near East into a major environmental region began well ahead of recorded history. In fact, it was this evolution that helped to usher in historic times. After a long series of preliminary steps man was at last ready to seize the opportunity which nature afforded. In this process he had the advantage of the combined features of location, topography, climate, and natural resources. Together these features influenced the formation in southwestern Asia and the adjacent strip of northeastern Africa of a naturally integrated region with common interests strong enough to offset other possible regional alignments. It is to this region that students of ancient history have given the name Near East. Since the inner unity of this area is at least as compelling today as it ever was, there is sound reason for retaining the same designation throughout.

The Near East proper includes Egypt, Syria-Palestine, the Tigris-Euphrates Valley (Mesopotamia), and the Arabian Peninsula. The whole has the shape of a rough quadrilateral with a land area more than half that of the Continental United States. Desert wastes inhibit contacts with the rest of Africa and mountain ranges form barriers in the north and northeast, towards Anatolia, Armenia, and the Iranian plateau. The Mediterranean and the Indian Ocean effectively complete the encirclement. The region itself is mostly tropical desert which is held off from a narrow semicircle of subtropical soil by the Nile, the rainfall along the Mediterranean, and the Tigris-Euphrates. The natural escape from the central desert core is towards that semicircle, the Asiatic part of which is often called the Fertile Crescent. Periods of particularly acute pressure have been reflected in spasmodic irruptions into the Fertile Crescent, with reverberations felt throughout the region and, at times, outside it. The only part of the Near East capable of relative isolation is Egypt. Yet full-scale withdrawal is never in evidence. The prevailing gravitation in Egypt is towards the Fertile

Crescent. In turn, the Nile Valley has frequently had a strong attraction for the rest of the Near East.

The whole region is thus a natural unit in spite of the considerable local variations within it. Its common interests are due largely to climate and topography. These features combine, as we shall see, with the local natural resources to facilitate the development of distinctive cultures. The fact, moreover, that principal land and water routes converge in the Near East has tended to make it a central fusing place for cultural materials from the east and the west, the focal point of three continents.

It is clear that environment has been the one constant factor in the long historic career of the Near East. Its combined and peculiar effect may have aided in, though it cannot alone explain, the continuity of the cultures which originated and matured in this region. At any rate, here was not only the geographic but also the cultural center of the Old World. Here, too, is the core of contemporary Islam, a cultural community of over three hundred million adherents occupying the vast and strategically located belt from Dakar and Gibraltar to the islands of the Indies and the vicinity of the Yellow Sea. Finally, the Near East is the home of what is today, by all cultural standards, an essentially homogeneous people, the Arabs.

It is worth observing that of the three factors just cited—environment, culture, people—the last-named is also the latest to acquire significance. The cultural pattern of the Near East, with its vitality and capacity for growth, was evolved, as we know now, not by any one race or people but by a number of diverse ethnic elements sharing the same peculiar natural equipment. In the course of many centuries the area came to be dominated by members of the same linguistic stock, the Semites. A number of distinct Semitic groups left their respective marks on the region, thereby adding to the total experience of mankind. Lastly, after the lapse of many more centuries, one Semitic group succeeded in imposing its own particular stamp on the whole of the Near East. We know that group as the Arabs. This is the situation that prevails there today. But the present cultural and ethnic uniformity is not so deep-rooted as to have obliterated the underlying differences. It is largely these differences that account for many of the conflicts now agitating the Near East. To be appreciated, they have to be viewed in the perspective of the millenniums that have gone into the making of the modern Near East. In the light of that tradition the basic factors prove to be environment and cultural progress.

2. THE INDIVIDUAL AREAS

Egypt is easily the most self-contained part of the Near East. The modern state bearing this name comprises 386,000 square miles of territory. It has the Mediterranean Sea to the north, Palestine and the Red Sea to the east, the desert tableland of the Anglo-Egyptian Sudan to the south, and the Great Sahara Desert to the west. Of this large territory—the size of Texas and New Mexico combined, or three and a half times that of the British Isles—an overwhelming proportion is itself desert. Within its enfolding mass lies the thin band of Egypt proper: the long, narrow, and cliff-bordered valley of the Nile which broadens, some one hundred miles from the sea, into the triangle of the Delta. This is the Egypt of the present century no less than of 3000 B.C., a cultivated area about one-third the size of Ohio. Into it is crowded virtually all of the country's population of some nineteen million, making it one of the most densely settled areas in the world. Particularly striking is the comparison with the Near East as a whole. For about two fifths of the entire population of the region are compressed here into one hundredth of its total area.

It would be difficult to overstate the enormous influence of environment upon the life of the country. And environment in the case of Egypt is in singular measure the product of the Nile. Nowhere else has a great civilization been molded to such a degree by a single river. The Nile—which in its course of more than nine hundred miles through Egypt receives no tributary stream—has been a basic factor in the development of the economy, the society, and the spiritual and psychological outlook of the Egyptians.

There is practically no rainfall outside the northern part of the Delta, and hence settled occupation is restricted to the reach of the river and the yearly flood of its silt-laden waters. High cliffs on either side hold down the width of the valley to a maximum of thirty miles, thus emphasizing the stark contrast between the desert and the sown, arid wastes as against the area under irrigation. Inside the valley the rhythm of life is governed by the unchanging routine of the river, so immutable as to have suggested, in remote antiquity, a method for reckoning solar time in cycles of 1460 years. The economy of the land is subordinated to this routine and is developed through coöperative effort and clannish organization. It is in the main a rural rather than industrial and trading economy. Intensive cultivation—wheat, barley, flax, more recently cotton— limits other vegetation and leaves no room for forests. The peasant's eyes turn to the river and its bed more than to the sky. It is the animals in and along the river, not the cosmic bodies, that affect most intimately his early religious beliefs and practices.

In general, then, the Egyptian environment is conducive to stability and provincialism. Yet the cultural progress made possible by this very environment prevents long-term isolation. Expanding economy creates the need for materials not available locally and leads to an exchange of goods and ideas. The resulting contacts, since the dawn of Egyptian history, have been principally with the East. In this direction are to be found the mineral resources of Sinai, the land bridge to the Fertile Crescent, and the timber of the Lebanon. The Red Sea, too, as a possible water route to Asia, is close to the Nile Valley and relatively accessible.

Thus it is that Egypt's foreign dealings—economic, cultural, and political—have since the beginning of recorded time been more with neighboring Asia than with the adjoining regions of her own continent. Recent political and technological developments have drawn attention to the potentialities of the Anglo-Egyptian Sudan as an area for southward expansion. Nevertheless, the age-old tradition is still dominant; it explains how Egypt could function as the center of the League of Arab States, although all the remaining members represented Asiatic territories. But the contrary tendency towards isolation has also left its mark. Egypt is culturally Arab, but ethnically and environmentally she remains Egyptian. She is a part of the Near East, yet within this region she has maintained her own distinctive character.

Syria-Palestine is a convenient geographic term designating the drainage areas of the eastern end of the Mediterranean Sea and the Jordan–Dead Sea rift. Economically and culturally this sector is a bridge between Egypt and Mesopotamia. Politically it has been subject to all sorts of changes throughout the course of history. Today it comprises the Palestine Sector and the Republic of Lebanon, and it includes also portions of the Republic of Syria and the brand-new Kingdom of Transjordan. Mandated Palestine had an area of slightly over 10,000 square miles and a population approaching two million: almost exactly the size of Maryland and approximately the same population density. The area of Lebanon is about 3,600 square miles and her population numbers about 1,100,000: not quite twice the size of Delaware, with more than four times as many inhabitants.

The other two states are much larger but have relatively sparse settlements. Jordan (formerly Transjordan) boasts some 35,000 square miles, but has a population of less than 400,000. Syria's 3,000,000 inhabitants occupy an area larger than that of North Carolina, but the distribution of population is very uneven, for the vast majority are concentrated along the western edge of the territory. Physiographically most of the present state of Syria lies within the drainage area of the Euphrates. The easterly portions of Transjordan likewise lean to another area, in this instance Arabia.

As an environmental unit Syria-Palestine is thus limited to a relatively narrow strip along the eastern shore of the Mediterranean. Its backbone is a plateau running from the Gulf of Alexandretta, at the base of Anatolia, to the Gulf of Aqaba, on the Red Sea, and culminating in the Lebanon range which at one point attains the height of 10,135 feet. The seaward slopes of this plateau crowd—and in parts eliminate—the shore line. Only from Mount Carmel down, towards Egypt, is there a substantial coastal plain. From the east the mountains are marked off by a continuous rift formed by the fertile Orontes Valley, the Bekaa gorge (Biq'a), the Jordan Valley, and the Dead Sea. Together these links in an elongated corridor constitute the greatest inland depression of the earth, the product of a spectacular geological upheaval which left the surface of the Dead Sea 1290 feet below sea level. With most of its course also below sea level, the Jordan drops 900 feet in the nine miles between Lake Huleh and the Sea of Galilee. Within a distance of a little over one hundred air miles the river spans the climatic zones of a continent—all the way from the coolness of the hills at its source to the tropical conditions at its mouth. These striking excesses of topography and climate in an area scarcely larger than that of a good-sized proving ground have contributed a significant share to the historic tradition of the whole region. And it is the same physical features that promise to fashion the economic future of the area—through hydroelectric power and the chemical wealth of the Dead Sea.

The mountain backbone of Syria-Palestine, as contrasted with the alluvial character of the valleys of the Nile and the Tigris-Euphrates, facilitated very early occupation. Indeed, Neanderthal man is represented on Mount Carmel, and the so-called Natufian man of Palestine, dating back to the Middle Stone Age, is believed to have been the first to attempt agriculture and the domestication of animals. In these pioneering efforts he was aided by the copious winter rains which are condensed in the hills from the same storms that sweep in from the Mediterranean. The early presence of such cereals as wheat and barley, fruits such as the date, the olive, the grape, and the fig, and the principal domestic animals except the horse and camel made possible continuous cultural progress on a provincial scale. Tillage without irrigation, and the presence of timber, notably from the forests of the Lebanon, were to distinguish the local economy from that of the emerging centers of Egypt and Mesopotamia.

The basic significance of Syria-Palestine, however—rooted in the interaction of environment and culture—is not as a source but rather as a link. Location and topography made it a natural highway between the great alluvial valleys in which urban civilization was cradled. The inland depression, in conjunction with coastal routes, afforded access to Mesopotamia as well as to Anatolia and thence to European regions. The ports along the Mediterranean coast—Jaffa, Acre, Sidon, Tyre, Byblos, and Ugarit in the past, and Jaffa–Tel Aviv, Haifa, Bayrut, Tripoli, and Latakia in modern times—have been a link with the Mediterranean basin and beyond. How vital these land and water routes have proved through the ages may be judged from a partial list of outside conquerors and campaigners who had reason to use them: Thutmose III, Ramses II, Alexander the Great, Pompey, Saladin, Richard Cœur de Lion, Napoleon, Allenby, Catroux. Thoroughfare and battlefield of nations, this narrow strip of the sown between desert and sea has retained to this day its key position within the region while giving up little if any of its traditional extra-regional importance.

Mesopotamia is the Fertile Crescent proper, a stretch of rich soil extending from the vicinity of the northeast corner of the Mediterranean down to the Persian Gulf, and comprising the piedmont and lowland drainage areas of the Tigris-Euphrates. The sheltering semicircle of the Taurus and Zagros mountain ranges inverts the whole in the direction of the Arabian Peninsula. The principal modern heir to the traditions of Mesopotamia is the Kingdom of Iraq, which comprises an area of over 140,000 square miles and has a population of between four and five million. Size, population, and sundry environmental features bring to mind the state of California, but this analogy is only roughly approximate.

The natural appeal of Mesopotamia can be gauged in part from the events, languages, and races which legend and history alike have located within her limits. It is here that mythology has planted the Garden of Eden, erected the Tower of Babel, and precipitated the Great Deluge. And solid historic facts introduce us here for the first time in recorded human experience to the Sumerians, various groups of Semites, the Hurrians, and the two main branches of the Indo-Europeans. The interplay of environment and culture yields in this case an intricate pattern. Favorable physical circumstances enabled the early settlers to develop an advanced culture. The country continued to attract other settlers, owing in part to the kind of culture achieved here by the preceding groups. In turn, the resulting composite culture reflected the hospitable character of the land. Thus the history of Mesopotamia, unlike that of Egypt, has a marked international bearing.

To concentrate for a moment on the environmental features, much of Mesopotamia has this in common with the Nile Valley: irrigation is necessary for the adequate exploitation of the rich alluvial soil. But this is about the full extent of the basic similarities between the two valleys. The Tigris and the Euphrates flow for the most part through open country. Their drainage area takes in numerous tributaries. Moreover, the entire valley has a rainy season—in the winter—and although the rainfall is slight in the lower sections, the volume increases with the gradual rise of the terrain. This means that for several months each year there is considerable grazing land beyond the cultivated stretches, so that nomad, semi-nomad, and cultivator can exist side by side. Communication with adjoining areas is never cut off for long periods of time. Even the northerly semicircle of mountains, natural boundary though it is, does not constitute a solid barrier to inter-regional contacts. From time immemorial mountaineers have been coming down into the valley following the course of the streams which enter and sustain it.

The landscape of Mesopotamia is changeable in more ways than one. Whereas the Nile is walled in by cliffs, the low and soft banks of the Tigris and the Euphrates have no such confining and stabilizing effect. In the flatlands of Lower Mesopotamia the rivers are not set in their ways, and changes in their courses have taken place within the span of written records. Even the land itself is mobile, in that it has been encroaching slowly but steadily upon the area of the Persian Gulf. Thus at the beginning of historic times, in the fourth millennium B.C., the sea approached the immediate vicinity of Ur. The Tigris and the Euphrates were to continue as independent rivers for many centuries. Today the coastline is some 150 miles farther east, the two streams have long been united, the relatively recent port of Basra has been left more than 80 miles upstream, and the Karun, which comes down from the Iranian plateau, is now but a tributary of the Shatt-al-Arab—the name for the joint course of the merged waters. The dynamic quality of the historic culture of Mesopotamia is in harmony with this mobile aspect of the Mesopotamian environment.

Flora and fauna exhibit greater variety than in the Nile Valley. The south is most noted for the date palm, while the northern foothills yield a selection of fruits, nuts, and vegetables. Oils are obtained from sesame and the olive. Citrus fruits and tobacco are successful transplantations of relatively recent date. The cereals include wheat, barley, and rice. Of the animals, the elephant and the lion are known from historic records. Jackals, hyenas, wolves, wild boars, and gazelles are still much in evidence. The water buffalo is seen in the south. Flocks of sheep and goats are among the main sources of the country's wealth. The grey-hound is attested as far back as the fourth millennium B.C. The onager (in early Sumerian times) and the ass antedate the horse and the camel.

But the greatest natural wealth of that part of Mesopotamia which constitutes the present-day Kingdom of Iraq is found underground. Iraq's petroleum resources are among the richest in the Near and Middle East. The deposits follow the foothills which extend from the Persian Gulf to Anatolia and they center about Kirkuk, north of Baghdad, and Qayyara, south of Mosul. The fields near Kirkuk had long revealed themselves to the local inhabitants in the form of ignited ground seepage which caused the spot to be called Baba Gurgur, "The Father of Flames." Neighborhood tradition identified the place with the Biblical Fiery Furnace of Daniel. Modern geologists sided with tradition at least to the extent of selecting Baba Gurgur as the site of the first shaft sunk by the Turkish Petroleum Company

—now known as IPC, that is, the Iraq Petroleum Company.

The Arabian Peninsula. This largest peninsula in the world, with an area of about a million square miles—corresponding to one-third of the United States—has today a population of considerably less than the commonly cited round figure of ten million. The preponderant bulk of this land mass belongs to the Kingdom of Saudi Arabia. In the southwest corner lies the Kingdom (or Imamate) of the Yemen with the relatively impressive figure of nearly four million inhabitants. The southern and eastern fringes of the peninsula are—with one exception—likewise independent of Saudi Arabia. They include the British Crown Colony of Aden and the various sultanates and shaykhdoms of Hadramawt and the Persian Gulf area (Muscat-Oman, Trucial Oman, Qatar, Bahrayn, and Kuwayt), all dependent in varying degrees on Great Britain. The exception is the oil-rich district of al-Hasa, south of Kuwayt, which forms part of Saudi Arabia.

Position, topography, and climate have been decisive factors in Arabia's past and present. Natural resources—more specifically oil—bid fair to transform the area's future. Arabia may thus be characterized as a highly specialized environmental laboratory on a vast scale.

The Arabs call their peninsula The Island of the Arabs. And for all practical purposes an island it is, cut off on its only land side by sand which prior to the advent of the motor car had to be traversed almost exclusively by camel, the proverbial "ship of the desert." In Babylonian writing, more than a score of centuries before the advent of Islam, the camel is designated as "the ass of the sea," thus showing that the comparison between sea and desert is a very old one. Indeed it was not until the relatively common employment of the camel set in, some three thousand years ago, that Arabia began to figure directly in the pages of Near East history. The designation of the country as an island thus proves to rest on remote pre-Arab tradition.

The ring of sea and sand around the peninsula is reinforced by an all but closed interior ring of mountains. In the southeast the mountains of Oman reach at one point a height of just under 10,000 feet. To the north there is the Najd plateau culminating in the Shammar range which sends up one of its peaks to a height of 5,550 feet. The elevation is greatest along the Red Sea coast with peaks of 9,000 feet in the north, 10,000 in the center, and 12,000 feet in the Yemen. Only along the south coast and around the head of the Persian Gulf are there extensive lowlands. In both instances the sea is receding gradually from the coast, and it is in these two areas that the impact of cultural developments was first felt on the peninsula.

Inside this doubly enclosed island an overwhelming proportion of the land consists of steppes and desert, of which a huge expanse in the southern half is aptly called The Empty Quarter. In the whole peninsula there is not a single important river which reaches the sea, nor even a navigable stream. Except in the Yemen and the coastal strip immediately to the north there is not enough rainfall to warrant systematic cultivation. Jidda in the west and Muscat in the east are among the hottest ports on earth. Apart from the coast and the mountains near by, settled life is confined to oases and sections of the Najd plateau. Otherwise the population is nomadic.

This nomadism of the occupants of the peninsula, enforced by its climate, has been a potent factor throughout the long history of the Near East. Intermittent periods of drought would at all times impose a fluid pattern on the wanderings of the tribes within the area. But events of local origin could have an effect outside the peninsula only if a sufficient part of the population was impelled thereby to break out through the northern plateau. Unusually prolonged droughts following periods of gradual growth of the population—through natural increase, invasion or infiltration by sea, or both—might well set such a movement in motion. Cultural developments could stir up the restlessness required to upset the normal pattern. Naturally, such happenings would be long in maturing. As a matter of fact they have occurred at intervals separated by many centuries. One such wave was in progress in the fourth millennium B.C., bringing to Mesopotamia the so-called Akkadians, who were the first Semitic group known to history. Another wave— more than a millennium later—introduced the Canaanites and Amorites into Syria-Palestine. Yet another, a few centuries thereafter, deposited the Arameans somewhere in Western Mesopotamia. The last great wave was the one that launched the Arabs and Islam on their joint way to the conquest of the whole Near East and the overrunning of immense areas of Asia, Africa, and Europe. The first phase of this great movement came in the first half of the seventh century. To its effects the modern Near East owes its language, its religion, and many of its other cultural characteristics.

But each of the pre-Islamic ethnic outpourings from the peninsula, though lesser in extent than the Arab one, was also to leave a deep mark on the whole of the Near East, and indirectly on other regions as well. Owing primarily to her environmental features, Arabia has in a sense been the transforming center of a catalytic force which would strike periodically in the only possible direction—to the north, either at Mesopotamia or at Syria-Palestine—thereby stirring up other forces and affecting in turn the region as a unit.

It would be a mistake, however, to assume that Arabia has always been Arab in the narrow ethnic sense, that she was necessarily the home of the Semites, or that she is racially or culturally uniform today. All these assumptions are frequently made, and all too often they find wide acceptance. A moment's reflection or consultation should make it plain that if the Akkadians, Arameans, or Canaanites (Phoenicians, Hebrews) were Arabs, then the primitive Indo-Europeans were Russians, Germans, or the like, as the case might be. The most that we can assert today about the home of the Semites is that Arabia was in all likelihood a secondary center of dissemination. And as for the ethnic or cultural uniformity of the peninsula, the present-day population of the southern fringes of Arabia and the cultural remains of that section and of the Yemen would ill accord with such an assumption. It could only blur the picture and mar the perspective of significant historic and cultural events.

A few words, finally, about the natural resources of the country. As regards vegetation, the date palm is of primary importance for the local food supply, while the frankincense tree and the coffee plant have been prominent in the export trade, the former since remote antiquity and the latter since the sixteenth century of the Christian era. The best-known domesticated animals associated with Arabia are the horse and the camel. Their place in the economy—and less directly the culture—of the country cannot be exaggerated. Yet the horse can scarcely have reached Arabia before the second millennium B.C., if that early, and there is great uncertainty as to the original home of the dromedary. Its first mention in written documents dates back only to the first millennium B.C.

Oil is manifestly the great prospective source of Arabia's future wealth and strategic significance. Some estimates place the petroleum resources of the peninsula (Saudi Arabia, Kuwayt—and including the islands of Bahrayn) higher than those of any other region of the globe. The richest deposits of the region—those of Saudi Arabia—have barely been tapped. In view of the economic changes which the presence of oil has brought about in the neighboring states of Iraq and Iran, and in view also of the size of the Saudian deposits, it is probable that what has hitherto been the most desolate and backward area of the Near East may yet become the richest and one of the most advanced.

3. GENERAL STRATEGIC ASPECTS

If individual variations and peculiarities are set aside, it is as a unit that the Near East commands today a degree of world-wide attention which it has not enjoyed since the age of Muslim conquests. The present cycle of prominence, however, is no mere revival of past glories. The main factors in the current upswing are strategic, although other considerations cannot be overlooked altogether. In moving thus into the limelight of the post-war world, the Near East has been favored by several important circumstances, some constant and others of quite recent origin.

The position of the Near East on the earth's surface has, of course, remained stable throughout historic times. Not so, however, its relation to the shifting center of gravity in a strategically conditioned global setup. In ancient times the region was both the geographic and the strategic center of a vaguely delimited orbit. That dual distinction was lost as the Roman world expanded, only to be recaptured in the early centuries of Islam. Thereafter the strategic center shifted to Europe once again, where it was to remain well into the twentieth century. It is only now, concurrently with the other changes brought about by the Second World War, that Europe can no longer be credited with a pivotal place in world affairs. Neither Russia nor Great Britain is exclusively a European power. With the United States in the forefront of the new international structure, the future strategic center of gravity is bound to be the scene of converging—and often conflicting—interests of all the major powers of today. There are several reasons why the Near East is likely to play such a part. Two of these have to be stressed in the present connection: communications and natural resources.

In the past the Near East owed much of its prominence to the fact that important land and water routes converged in that region. Today we find there a similar concentration of modern routes of transit, including air communications. The opening of the Suez Canal in 1869 marked the first step in the restoration of the onetime balance. It established or enhanced the importance of such ports as Alexandria, Port Said, Aden, Haifa, and Bayrut. Another step was the completion of trunk rail lines. Aleppo is now a key junction on the Orient Express which affords all-rail connections with Baghdad and Basra on the one hand and with Cairo on the other. The last link to Baghdad was completed just before the war, the one to Cairo after the expulsion of the Vichy troops from Syria. Finally, both Cairo and Baghdad were key air centers in the period before the war, and their importance as well as their facilities in this respect have increased very substantially since then. Thus the region is now more than ever a vital meeting place of three continents.

But in addition to being a means to further ends, the Near East has become also a vital strategic end in itself. This position is due entirely to the natural resources of the region; but not primarily such items of export as the cotton of Egypt, the grains and wool and hides of Iraq, and the chemicals of Palestine. The strategically vital natural wealth of the Near East is its petroleum, which abounds in Iraq, Kuwayt, and Bahrayn, and is stored in the reportedly fabulous deposits of Saudi Arabia, not to mention other centers which are known or believed to be commercially exploitable. Nor is the value of this asset likely to decrease appreciably in the near future as a result of the prospective development of nuclear energy. The development of atomic power to the point where it will produce mechanical efficiency at a competitive cost appears to be in the far distant future, and in any case oil and grease lubricants will always be in great demand. The Near East promises, therefore, to preserve and maintain its importance as a principal and virtually untapped source of petroleum.

Exploration and digging have given us a new perspective as to the place of the Near East in the progress of the world. Two types of explorers and excavators have accomplished this task. One is the archaeologist, whose labors have added millenniums to the known history of the region, and thus also of the world as a whole. The other is the petroleum geologist whose discoveries have a bearing on the future of the Near East as an integral part of the globe.

2. The Enduring Cultural Factor

1. PERSPECTIVE

A book which sets out to deal with some phase of the present, as an index to the immediate future, will normally require little space to sketch in the relevant background of the past. The same general proportions will be maintained in our case, though not for the same reasons. Historic background, of course, is nowhere just an academic matter. In the Near East it is even less so than elsewhere. The region may not be indeed as immutable as popular accounts would have it, but it is nevertheless, in countless subtle ways, the product of its ageless past. The fact is that the background in this instance is too vast and intricate for a balanced treatment in a discussion which sets out to analyze the current phase. You cannot get away from five thousand years of unbroken tradition, but neither can you compress that tradition into a chapter or two. Yet if you ignore it altogether, the contemporary scene will be thrown badly out of focus. The solution would seem to be to pick out of the long succession of centuries the markers that have pointed the way forward. It is the way by which the Near East has arrived at the present stage of its journey, and it is also along the same route that one must look for significant elements in the make-up of the modern Near East.

The Near East today can look back on the longest span of recorded history known to man. What is more, it knows that it can do so, and unfailingly does. For instance, a few years ago Prime Ministers Mustafa Pasha al-Nahhas of Egypt and Nuri Pasha al-Said of Iraq vied with each other for leadership of the Arab unity movement; neither they nor their respective followers could be wholly unaware of the similar conflict between the Egyptian Necho and the Babylonian Nebuchadnezzar over supremacy in the Near East more than twenty-five centuries ago. The illiterate Beduin who stands in wide-eyed amazement before a showcase in the Baghdad Museum displaying ancient Sumerian finds is moved visibly by the achievements of his remote predecessors, infidels though they were. A while later he may thrill to the sight of the latest planes without feeling hopelessly outdistanced by the civilization which produced them. And the Jew in Palestine who casts his eye on the City of David or lifts his head towards Mount Carmel can turn back with renewed gratitude to his Bible—which he is proud to have shared with the Western world through these untold years of his wanderings. All this the West must understand if it would sense the mood and appreciate the capacities of the modern Near East.

The traditional Near East persists thus as a real and living influence. The heritage of antiquity has proved enduring and meaningful. Yet our general appreciation of it is at best spotty and antiquated. A very shrewd historian of a generation ago was wont to remark that the Bible was being read with sacred inattention. In a broader sense, the region of the ancient Bible lands suffers today from a like attitude of dutiful negligence. One realizes rather vaguely that a long time ago these lands somehow played an important part in the early history of mankind. Usually that general feeling is a hangover from chapters prefaced to some history of the classical world, written a good many years before and based on second-hand information of considerably earlier vintage. All that has been achieved since then in the restless field of Near Eastern studies—where a single year may add a century to our knowledge of man's early history—is apt to remain the all but exclusive property of a handful of specialists. The result is that we either view the traditional Near East through classical eyes and with classical prejudice, or we bring to it the sort of little learning that has always proved a dangerous thing. So long as they were limited to the sphere of abstract culture, the consequences could not be particularly weighty. Today, however, the range has widened. The modern Near East has become a global center of gravity. Its roots, in turn, reach down deep into antiquity. It follows that an appreciation of that background should no longer be the sole concern of the scholar. The statesman and the man of affairs also have a stake in the matter.

There is, first of all, the question of perspective in time. Our fathers and grandfathers acquired in their school days the notion that, in matters of secular history, the Homeric age marked the dawn of civilization and that the lands to the east of Greece were essentially primitive and barbarian. We know now that what was the dawn of culture over much of classical Europe coincided with the mellow afternoon of ancient Egypt and Mesopotamia. History was being made and recorded two thousand years before the period of Homer's heroes—as many centuries prior to it as have elapsed since the time of Christ. What is more, these early cultural developments were to play a vital part in the subsequent progress of man in general and western man in particular. The history of the ancient Near East is thus in large part the historic foundation of civilized man. It has left its mark on the world of today and, especially, it enters in various direct and indirect ways into the make-up of the modern Near East.

There is also the matter of relative tempo in cultural progress. The popular idea that your Near Easterner of five or four thousand years ago—and we turn to him because he alone managed to leave us a written record of his doings—must have been a primitive creature is backed up neither by facts nor by good judgment. The armies of Naram-Sin, in the third millennium B.C., advanced no less rapidly than the troops of Napoleon. Ten years in the time of Marlborough or Metternich lasted exactly as long as a decade did in the age of Menes or Moses. We are all too often rather cavalier with centuries and millenniums as long as we affix the protective label B.C. to our reference. To do so is to let perspective take flight. The whole historic period to date is only a brief paragraph in the evolution of mankind. In art and architecture, law and literature, and—above all—in his relation to his particular social environment, your ancient Sumerian or Hebrew was no less sophisticated or progressive than is the man of today. In some respects indeed the pioneering cultures of the ancient East would seem to excel by comparison. At any rate, they had the initiative and the vision to undertake the basic work upon which modern civilization is founded. Except for the technological discoveries of our own time or of very recent memory, the fundamental difference between now and then appears to be this: Today the globe has come to be a vast geographic whole, with no major blank spots left, however unbalanced the individual regions may be in other respects. Five thousand years ago, when recorded history began, most of the world was still in deep shadow. Enlightenment was just beginning to spread from one active center. That center was the Near East. Its influence was to radiate in all directions and to stimulate many vital forces. Western civilization has never denied its debt to that source, even though the acknowledgment has rarely been more than lip service. The modern Near East, on the other hand, is a more straightforward beneficiary. To appreciate this heritage is to give due weight to the inherent capabilities of the heirs.

2. THE PATTERN OF PROGRESS

From the vantage point of today the Near East as a whole presents a vast panorama, broad and deep. The breadth results from the linking together of the several geographic areas into a large environmental unit. The depth has been built up by the progressive deposits of age upon age, unmatched in the record of history. The total is a maze of intricate detail, the subject of never ceasing inquiry. To this inquiry mankind owes much of its stock of fact and speculation. Libraries began to bulge with this collection well before the time of Abraham, and the process has been going on ever since. A Palestinian sage found out long ago that of making many books there is no end. And indeed, after more thousands of years, the end is nowhere in sight, for the subject is not of the type that can be brought to a definite close. As a factor in human progress the Near East still is very much on the march.

In boldest outline—which surely will not be taken amiss in this context—the contours in depth may be broken up into four main segments, which mark as many stages in the course of the region's development. It should be stated at the outset that in no instance is there a complete break between two successive periods, since the underlying continuity remains intact throughout. Neither do we have at any time a clear-cut separation of one environmental area from the next. While Egypt, for instance, has in some respects remained distinct from southwestern Asia, a broader unity continues to highlight the region as a whole.

The earliest of the major phases in the evolution of the Near East is prehistoric and its beginnings are therefore lost to view. What we can discern, thanks primarily to archaeology, lasted perhaps two thousand years, contributing the essential groundwork on which successors could build. With the next phase history is ushered in, roughly about 3000 B.C.

The native civilization—a product of the various local cultures—takes firm root, and the yield is abundant enough to be carried and welcomed far beyond the borders of the region. This period is commonly treated as the Ancient Near East, which is a harmless enough designation provided that it is not allowed to distort our values. The fact is that a major break does not occur until the era of Alexander of Macedon, so that this stage alone exceeds in length the total of centuries which have elapsed since, down to our own day. Such endurance is unthinkable without compelling inner strength.

The beginning of the next or third main phase in the history of the Near East finds the region overrun by the political and cultural missionaries of Hellenism. It is the first successful invasion on a large scale by a western force. The effects are far-reaching but by no means revolutionary. Before many centuries have elapsed, the conqueror succumbs to the vanquished. Rooted deeply in the Near East, though not without progressive outside enrichment, Christianity soon sets out on a course that is to lead to the eventual transformation of the West. The fourth or Islamic phase, finally, wherein older native forces reassert themselves, receives a spectacular start in the seventh century of the new era. Today, after fourteen centuries of development, Islam not only dominates the Near East with unchallenged authority but holds sway also over an enormous belt cutting across three continents and containing some three hundred million zealous adherents.

Now the composite history of this entire vast complex which we call the Near East is made up of countless component histories of peoples, states, dynasties, and individuals, some known and some obscure or altogether hidden from knowledge. Yet in retrospect the full story is more than the sum of the various separate chronicles. For through all this detail runs a thread, now slender and now stout and firm, which always marks the way ahead. Its beginnings can be made out a long way back, in the dim light of some fifty centuries ago. Thereafter this thread is never wholly out of sight. It is in fact the central theme in the over-all course of the Near East's advance. The burden of this theme is not race or nation or god-like hero. What it is instead, essentially, is a way of life: the place of the individual in the order of things.

It will be said that in this preoccupation there is really nothing novel or unique. Primitive societies will raise themselves above purely temporal concerns, and more than one advanced culture has attained glorious heights in social and spiritual thinking. All this of course goes without saying. In the Near East, however, the process starts earlier than elsewhere. It is continuous and progressive. It leads gradually—and in spite of all manner of setbacks and lapses—to a concept of society that transcends ethnic and political boundaries. The resulting civilization is not in particular Sumerian or Babylonian, Hebrew or Arab; in final analysis it is co-operative and Near Eastern. Its inherent vitality and dynamic properties may best be judged from the fact that it has produced successively three great world religions.

It may be no mere coincidence, therefore, that the first signs of the new orientation appear in the Near East at a time when prehistory is about to give way to history, conscious and articulate. The quest for a way of life which would stand the test of time is plainly a fitting theme on which to launch the history of civilized man. The Near East of today still has an abiding interest in that immemorial quest.

3. THE ANCIENT NEAR EAST

Having glimpsed the general pattern let us now examine briefly the pertinent salients at closer range. The drive and vitality which characterize the whole from a distance are still in evidence as one draws nearer. At the same time, however, there come to view various contrary trends. Peoples and cultures struggle for survival, to the accompaniment of waste and ruin, with all the fury that such a struggle can engender. Power and sovereignty shift from place to place. Yet always there seems to be a residue of ideas which have survived and can be handed down to posterity. No age is utterly resigned to its Armageddon or its apocalypse, least of all the ancient Near East which first faced these visions.

Approached from a strictly cultural angle, the ancient Near East, while sharing many features as an integrated region, is in essence the proving ground for two contrasting modes of life. The respective centers are the same that we have already distinguished on environmental grounds: Egypt on the one hand, and the Fertile Crescent on the other. The two develop along roughly parallel lines and in about the same tempo. They differ primarily—and this time fundamentally—in their approach to the rights of the individual. The difference in results would be hard to overstate. If the whole thing had been planned deliberately, as a cosmic experiment to test the effects of two opposed philosophies on the progress of civilization, the answer could not have been more convincing.

In the Fertile Crescent the foundation for all subsequent cultural advance was laid before the end of the fourth millennium B.C. by the Sumerians. Exactly how and why the process started is not known now, perhaps never will be. The Sumerians were not the only group in the land—Lower Mesopotamia—at the commencement of their pioneering activity. In all probability they were not even the first occupants of the area—there being good grounds for assuming earlier inhabitants of note. By what process of alchemy the human element and the natural environment achieved here a perfect blend remains a mystery. At all events the interaction of the two was to prove productive to an astonishing degree. Sumerian culture went on to deepen and expand even while the Sumerians themselves were dying out as an ethnic and political force. As other peoples were being drawn in, each to make its individual contribution, the co-operative enterprise gathered momentum. The Semitic Akkadians—Babylonians and Assyrians—as well as the non-Semitic Elamites and Hurrians, and the Hittites of Asia Minor, all became participants and beneficiaries. Syria and Palestine were affected in more ways than one. What had thus started out as a provincial culture developed into the vigorous civilization of a large area. Nor were the results limited to Western Asia or to ancient times. The Arabs of present-day Palestine and the Jewish settlers in that strife-torn land still employ in their respective languages the same originally Sumerian terms for "chair" and "carpenter." The dials on all our timepieces reflect to this day Sumerian concepts of time reckoning and mathematics. These are but a few of the more obvious instances of a cultural tradition which has not spent itself to date. But no sum of such details could alone convey the full significance of that tradition.

What are the specifically Sumerian contributions to this truly dynamic civilization? Briefly, they consist in a social order based on the rights of the individual, embodied in a free economy, and protected by the supreme authority of the law. The law applies to ruler and subjects alike. The king is no more than a "great man"—for this is the meaning of the Sumerian word in question—who may become the administrator of a vast empire but even then remains the servant, not the source, of the law and is responsible to the gods for its enactment. The law is the constitution which guides the ruler and safeguards the subjects. It is an instrument for the protection of the individual and a solid barrier to absolute power.

We know today that one by-product of this concept of society was the introduction of writing by the Sumerians. Emphasis on the rights of the individual was reflected—among other things—in a strongly developed sense of private property. This in turn created the need for identifying such property, in private transactions as well as in temple offerings. The problem was solved by means of distinctive markings on personal seals. The designs were eventually broadened to represent plants, animals, and objects in general. Such graphs were next associated with specific words, and the gap between picture and word was thus bridged. The following step was to use the symbols not only for complete words but also for abstract syllables. By the beginning of the third millennium B.C. the new medium had become flexible enough for any type of record desired.

Once perfected, the idea of writing could readily be adopted by other civilizations. There is strong circumstantial evidence to suggest that the Egyptians owed the idea—though not the precise form—of their own script ultimately to Sumerian inspiration. The later date of the Chinese script, coupled with the many indications of cultural contacts between the Far East and the Near, from late prehistoric times down, might again point to indirect Sumerian influence. The invention of alphabetic writing in the second millennium B.C., in the Syria-Palestine area, would be difficult to account for without prior experience of syllabic scripts. While the Canaanites were thus evolving their alphabets—one of which was to make its way to Greece and to become the ancestor of all writing in the West—lineal descendants of the Sumerian system enjoyed long and fruitful careers throughout the Fertile Crescent and its neighboring territories. They were employed for a great variety of languages, including Hurrian, Hittite, and Old Persian; and they were used also for transcriptions into Greek.

Since the question before us is not how Sumerian civilization developed but what it came to mean in terms of regional and human progress, we cannot pause here to explore the many by-products of writing. Of far from local significance, however, is the development of Sumero-Babylonian mathematics as stimulated by the employment of written symbols. One indication of the great vitality inherent in the composite civilization of Mesopotamia is the survival to this day of the old Sumerian—or sexagesimal—system of reckoning which is seen in the division of the circle into 360 degrees and the division of the hour into 60 minutes and 3600 seconds. Of course, the mere capacity to survive is not of itself proof of intrinsic merit. What gave the sexagesimal system an enormous advantage over its ancient rivals was the convenience with which it could be adapted to place-value notation, wherein the magnitude of a symbol is determined by its position. This feature of Mesopotamian mathematics has been likened to the role of the alphabet in the progress of writing. Here then is another major contribution of Sumer to modern civilization.

Yet both writing and reckoning were secondary, not basic, aspects of Sumerian civilization. Both were rooted, as we have seen, in Sumerian ideas about law and society. But writing did serve to give these primary features a permanent form, safe from word-of-mouth changes and accessible to distant generations and lands. This is how Sumerian law and its immediate descendants, and Sumerian literature—again in various elaborations—could reach out beyond their proper area and age. Other areas and ages welcomed these products because they were found to contain enduring human values. The Mesopotamian model was then modified in accordance with local traditions and needs. This happened, for instance, in the case of the Hittite law code. That code was phrased in a language closely related to Indo-European. The script was Mesopotamian. With it had come along other cultural goods. All this manifold stimulation from the

East could not in turn remain for long without some effect on the mainland of Greece to the west.

The Old Testament is another example of intensive intercultural fusion. This time the result attains to unprecedented levels thanks to the particular genius of the authors. But it does not require much probing to discover here the ultimate ties with Mesopotamia. Since the Patriarchs are linked to the Euphrates valley by origin or marriage, it is natural that their cultural background also should reflect influences from that same quarter. More significant, however, is the place of the law in the Bible. To view it in terms of a wearisome legalism is to wrench it out of its proper context. To its framers and followers it was the norm of civilized conduct, fixing the relation of the individual to society and of society to the ruler of the universe. The legacy of Mesopotamia is thus not only assimilated but also carried a mighty stride forward. God is no longer merely a local patron of a favored community or state. He is now a universal Power and all the nations are His children. His prophets are inspired social thinkers.

So far Egypt has been left out of this summary. The reason certainly cannot be sought in any relative inferiority of Egyptian civilization as compared with that of the Fertile Crescent. The attainments of both these great centers are notable milestones in the progress of mankind. But Egypt adhered to her own particular way of life and attached her own set of values to the individual, society, and tradition. Here the king was a god and as such the absolute ruler of all he surveyed. Under this concept there was no room for the all-embracing power of the law. The pharaoh was not subject to any written canon. The pyramids bear lasting and eloquent testimony to his all but limitless power.

Thus it came about that in social and spiritual ideas ancient Egypt was often in opposition to the rest of the Near

East. In the Old Testament slavery and Egypt are practically synonymous. When the advance of Hellenism
brought to a close at long last the major independent phase
in the history of the Near East, it was in adjoining Asia
that the West sought and found its most cherished prizes.
And it is likewise to the Asiatic core of the region that the
modern Near East traces its basic traditions.

4. FROM ALEXANDER TO MUHAMMAD

The conquests of Alexander the Great opened in the
Near East a new era, an age of unprecedented cultural interaction and ferment. For the first time in its history the
whole region found itself under foreign political domination. More than that, the new masters were also the carriers
of a distinctive culture, rich and pervasive. Granted that
this culture—Hellenism—had utilized in its rise substantial
elements of oriental origin: now the earlier trend was reversed. The West had come to grips with the East, and this
time on Eastern soil.

On the surface, initial honors went all to the invaders.
The political scene was completely transformed. New ideas
and customs had come in the wake of the conquering armies.
They struck root. Greek beliefs and the Greek language
overlay the traditional native products and were working
down through the topmost layers. But this penetration did
not progress far enough to prove enduring. For one thing,
the tide of Hellenism was soon to recede from India and
Iran and Mesopotamia, although the lands around the Eastern Mediterranean remained engulfed considerably longer.
Moreover, wherever Hellenism had lingered on, the native
cultures were furnishing increasing resistance from within.
Lastly, even in submission the Near East had much to teach
to its masters. In the end neither side had established cul-

tural supremacy over the other, but each had been affected by contact and conflict with the other. This relative balance, however, did not carry over far beyond the Hellenistic age. For eventually a resurgent East, allied with surviving Hellenistic elements, was to sweep on westward on a tide that could not be stemmed.

Returning for a moment to Hellenism, and bearing in mind the principal theme of this review, we find that one highly significant result of this Western venture was the test to which Near East traditions were thereby subjected. The ultimate emergence of Christianity is only a part of the answer, since it omits the intermediate steps. The critical period came earlier. Hebrew culture took up the struggle in defense of the ancient Near East tradition. The outcome was the consolidation of that culture in Judaism. The preeminent place of the law in society—an unfailing guide since the days of ancient Sumer—is given here its most emphatic affirmation. Firmly integrated with this conception is the characteristic Hebrew interpretation of history as reflecting divine purpose. These two ideas permeate the final version of the Old Testament, now given canonical form. In it is the embodiment of deathless tradition, the will of God. His Book, it is felt, is the source of all wisdom, the way of life. Indeed, untold generations the world over were to turn to it for the meaning of life.

The extent to which Christianity incorporates the tenacious kernel of the Near East's cultural experience hardly needs stressing. The goal of social good, the relationship of God and man, and the revelation of God's purpose in the chain of mundane events—all these are Jewish concepts which in turn were distilled from the cumulative social gains of millenniums. Judaism's share in this process is in full view. The earliest Christians were Jews by their own account. The Apostles fought long against admission to the Christian community of those who lacked proper appreciation of the law. And Jesus was a Jew who cannot be understood to the full save in terms of his background. But we have only begun to sense the meaning of that background.

5. THE ROOTS OF ISLAM

Islam, or the creed of Muhammad and his followers, is essentially the latest—and this time Arab—version of the traditional culture of the Near East. Here may be said to converge two main lines of descent. One is direct, leading from the ancient Near East. Arabia is environmentally an integral part of the region as a whole. At periodic intervals through the ages this area has poured wave upon wave of settlers into the adjoining lands more favored by geography and climate. We call these groups Semites, a convenient but often overworked term in which linguistic, cultural, and racial aspects are loosely combined. As part of the Semitic family, at any rate, the Arabs have had from the start a common stake in the civilization of the Near East, a civilization which sundry Semitic elements had been among the first to elaborate.

The other line of descent is roundabout. As a distinct ethnic group the Arabs have never been wholly out of touch with the various successive centers of Near East civilization. Thus they have partaken of its fruits. It was in this way that they came eventually under the influence of both Judaism and Christianity, specialized representatives of Near East tradition. Muhammad's personal relations with Jews and Christians alike are well attested. Contacts with the Jews in particular were facilitated by the fact that in those days there were many Jewish agricultural and merchant colonies in Arabia. The Jewish community in Medina, for example, enjoyed considerable prominence. In these circumstances it is not at all surprising that in numerous details early Islam should hark back to the Old Testament and the New. The very weight which Muhammad attaches to the Book is the clearest single instance of the Prophet's indirect indebtedness to the Scriptures.

Far more significant, however, is the underlying structure of Islam. It is in close harmony with the basic Near East tradition. For in the legacy of Muhammad politics and religion are so intimately blended that the one cannot be isolated from the other. Hence Islam is not only in consonance with the ideal of the theocratic state as perfected in Palestine, but it bears also an ultimate relationship to the ancient city states of Sumer whose rulers combined civil and religious authority. In each instance the law is raised into an all-embracing norm of life.

The spectacular success of Islam is surely a measure of the system's vitality. As a young and vigorous movement it catapulted its champions into world power culturally as much as politically. Arab hegemony was succeeded at length by Turkish dominance, but Islam's hold on its steadily growing number of adherents remained unimpaired. For like its predecessors Islam is basically an extra-national system especially adapted to the environment in which it was evolved. It has amply demonstrated—over a period of fourteen centuries—the same vitality that characterized the others, and a like ability to mold widely differing elements into a uniform and integrated culture. This is most evident in the case of the Arabs, the historic standard-bearers of Islam.

For the Arabs of today represent a single, closely-knit culture. They have one language—for all its variety of dialects—one religion, and a common tradition. Yet only a small percentage of the present-day exponents of Arab culture can be presumed to be the lineal descendants of the warriors who took over the Near East and the lands beyond it under the inspiration of Muhammad's teachings. The respective populations of Egypt, Palestine, Syria, and Mesopotamia were not Arab to start with. They became assimilated in the course of time. And so beneath an upper crust of relative uniformity there are other layers which bear witness to a prior diversity. In many subtle ways, and in some which are immediately apparent, your Egyptian differs from your Syrian, and the Lebanese stands apart from the Iraqi. These differences are subordinated, to be sure, to the primary forces which make for unity. In a deeper sense that was true even in the ancient Near East. But the differences exist nevertheless and they are at the root of the countless complications which keep the modern Arab world in a state of perpetual agitation.

PART II

THE RECENT NEAR EAST

3. Political Highlights Down to the End of the First World War

1. PRIOR TO THE FIRST WORLD WAR

In the early stages of Islam the spread of the new sociopolitical faith went hand in hand with the Arabization of the conquered lands. The two developments were interrelated. They were basically two aspects of a single dynamic process. Converts and conquerors blended into one community. The language of the Prophet was the language of administration and the law. Presently it became also the language of the people. The component elements were coalescing into a uniform culture. It was Arab culture spreading over Arab-ruled lands and entrenching itself among various ethnic groups whose divergencies were thereby becoming gradually reduced. The Near East was being transformed into the Arab Near East.

Beyond the borders of the region, however, Islam found itself inevitably on less congenial cultural ground. Politically and socially the movement was far from spent. In fact, Arab rule was expanding at a pace which was not to be checked for many years, and then only at prodigious distances from the home base—in Western Europe and in Central Asia. Naturally enough, Arabization in the ethnic sense could not keep up with this pace. In regions with great cultural traditions of their own—notably in the East—Arabs were predestined to remain a foreign group for all their headstart as the Prophet's people. Where such traditions were lacking—along most of the North African coast—cultural resistance was less determined. Here Arabic could assert itself and did, but the advance of the language synchronized neither with the expanding empire nor with the march of a faith. Indeed, the Berbers have not lost to this day all traces of their former identity.

On the whole, however, the progress of Arabization in North Africa was substantial enough to give this entire stretch of territory a sense of solidarity with the Arab Near East, which not only has survived to this day but even seems to be on the increase. Following along the route of Arab political penetration, Arab cultural influence carried to the limits of Northwest Africa and thence turned to Spain across the Straits of Gibraltar—leaving in the very name of the rock a solid reminder of the Arabs' passage. When the political advance was at length reversed, its cultural by-products also receded. But in retreat as in advance there was a difference in the scope and timing of the several elements which comprised the movement. The political losses were most extensive, with Europe eventually gaining footholds along the entire southern shore of the Mediterranean. But North Africa has remained culturally and ethnically Arab—even though this loyalty has proved superficial in some sections and at times rather apathetic. Islam, of course, after its withdrawal from Western Europe, was free to turn its energies to the vast hinterland of the continent of Africa.

Europe was not ready to mount a large-scale political counteroffensive against Arab lands until the eve of the nineteenth century. By then, however, the Arab Empire had long been extinguished. The decisive blow had come in 1517, with the conquest of Egypt by the Ottoman ruler Selim I. It is significant that the successor was another Islamic power; significant because the ease of the Ottoman conquest owed much to the socio-political basis of Islam. The Arab world had acquired a foreign master, to be sure, but the political change did not involve a break in the continuity of the fundamental social system. The transfer of the Caliphate from Cairo to Constantinople—if and when it was deemed necessary—could be effected without undue strain.

Within less than three centuries, however, the over-extended Ottoman Empire was the pawn of European power politics. The Arab lands found themselves involved in the process but had no voice in the matter. As Ottoman authority dwindled, pretexts for foreign intervention multiplied. Thus the expedition of Napoleon to Egypt in 1798 was for the avowed purpose of aiding the legitimate government, although his real objective was to further his own plan for world domination—and any such plan must needs involve the Near East, whoever the would-be conqueror. Britain, with a watchful eye on India, could not view this development with equanimity. The combined efforts of the British and the Turks drove Napoleon out of Egypt in 1801; the resulting Franco-British tension over the Near East has yet to wear off.

Napoleon's Egyptian venture was to have other lasting effects—not the least of which was the foundation of the science of Egyptology. In terms of subsequent Near East history the incidental results were especially far-reaching. For Mehmet Ali, a young Albanian officer with the force which the Sultan had dispatched against Napoleon, soon made himself the military master of Egypt. In that capacity he met and defeated the leader of a vigorous sectarian movement in the heart of Arabia, one Abdul-Aziz ibn Saud; the movement itself had been founded a generation earlier by Muhammad ibn Abdul-Wahhab, hence its designation as Wahhabi. Following his occupation of Syria, Mehmet Ali was well on his way to establish a new Arab empire, when European powers, led by Great Britain, stepped in. The sway of the Albanian pasha was restricted to Egypt and the Sudan, but within that sphere the rule of his line was made hereditary in 1841, under the suzerainty of the Ottoman Sultan. Today the same line constitutes the Royal House of Egypt, while a scion of the House of Saud, descendant and namesake of Mehmet Ali's antagonist, is monarch of Arabia. The two domains are separated only by the narrow band of the Red Sea. There is no like break, however, in the memory of the original conflict between the respective ruling families.

Long-range occupation by European powers began with the Arabized territories of Northwest Africa. Except for minor Spanish holdings of earlier origin, the initial penetration was entirely French. Algeria was acquired through conquest, between 1830 and 1847. Tunisia became a French protectorate as a result of the Franco-Tunisian treaties of 1881 and 1883. The occupation of Morocco, following extensive diplomatic deals with Britain and Spain, began in 1907 and was completed in 1912. Retroactive juridical sanction was accorded this move by the Franco-Moroccan Treaty of 1912, and the same instrument regulated also the status of the small Spanish Zone which began to assume shape in 1909. Since the Sultan of Morocco remained the legal sovereign of the country, he had in effect—as Toynbee so aptly expressed it—"leased the whole of his territory to France and France had subleased a portion of it to Spain with his previous sanction." For the Tangier Zone a special extra-territorial status was reserved.

In return for her assent to French expansion in Morocco, Britain was given by France a free hand in regard to Egypt. French interest in Egypt had been more than a sentimental carry-over from Napoleon's expedition. An important economic stake was created by the Suez Canal Concession of

1856, obtained through French initiative and financed by a combine in which France and Turkey were the main shareholders. Subsequently Egypt's economy came officially under the joint control of the French and the British. Disorders and uprisings inspired by this foreign interference led eventually to the shelling of Alexandria by the British in 1882 and to their military occupation of the country, France having declined to join in this particular venture. It is important to note that this development did not alter Turkey's juridical position of sovereignty over Egypt. Neither did it lessen France's interest in the country, an interest which was not overlooked in the Anglo-French Declaration of 1904 in respect to Egypt and Morocco.

The one remaining gap in the European holdings along the North African coast was eliminated in 1911 by the Italian annexation of the two Ottoman provinces of Tripoli and Benghazi. This territory, which comprised the most desirable parts of Libya, was wrested from Turkey by force of arms after Italy had assured herself of French and British acquiescence. Yet the outcome did not amount to a formal transfer of sovereignty, inasmuch as the Ottoman Sultan, in his capacity as Caliph, retained the Muslim ecclesiastical patronage of the annexed provinces; in Muslim society—it should be repeated—spiritual and temporal rights are interlocked. But separation of actual administrative authority from legal title had already occurred in Egypt. This illustrates the weakness of Turkey's political position on the eve of the First World War, but it shows also the basic strength of Islam in its ability to impede alien encroachment upon Muslim lands.

The same strength and weakness had long been apparent in the Asiatic centers of the Arab world, east of Suez. Although the political power of the Ottoman Empire was manifestly on the wane, the Sultan's key position in the Islamic world could not be ignored, nor did the West risk arousing

Muslim solidarity through concerted aggression in the Near East. Western penetration, accordingly, was wary and piece-meal. It had to wait for the right opportunity.

France got hers in Syria as far back as 1860. Druze attacks against Christian communities, which the Turkish adminis-tration was either unable or unwilling to halt, culminated in a massacre of the Christians by the Muslims of Damascus. The answer of Western Christendom was expressed in naval and diplomatic moves, with France landing an expedition-ary force in Bayrut. By 1864 Lebanon had a semi-autono-mous regime under a Christian governor directly respon-sible to the Sultan. As the protector of the local Christian communities, France had won for herself a highly privi-leged place in the Levant.

In view of her position in India, Britain marked out the Arabian Peninsula for infiltration early in the nineteenth century. Logically enough, the required moves were con-trolled from India. The port of Aden was captured in 1839 and turned into a British colony. Thereafter British penetra-tion extended eastward, towards the Gulf of Oman, where it linked up with a similar move which had begun as early as 1820 along the eastern shores of the peninsula. Except for Aden itself, the underlying purpose was accomplished by means of a series of treaties with the various local chief-tains, circumventing the nominal sovereignty of the Sul-tan. Since some of the districts involved had closer economic ties with Malaya than with the rest of the Near East, their gradual passing under British control caused little stir in the Arab world.

But the establishment of western footholds on the Medi-terranean was not viewed by the Arabs with equal calm. A sense of national consciousness was slowly emerging. Its primary target was foreign imperialism, whereas complete liberation from the Turks—brothers in Islam—could as yet be no more than a dim and distant objective. This emergent nationalism followed one of two courses. In the case of Egypt it began to assume the form of state nationalism, with the accent on Egyptian independence and the freeing of the country from foreign dominance. Elsewhere in the Near East the movement was fed by aspirations along ethnic lines. It planned and plotted in terms of Arab home rule, regardless of territorial divisions. This difference between Egypt and the other Arab portions of the Near East was due, of course, in the first place to Egypt's direct exposure to pressure by an alien power. Ultimately, however, Egyptian separatism was atavistic, nurtured continuously since the dawn of Egyptian history and conditioned by the country's natural environment.

2. THE ARAB REVOLT

On the eve of the First World War the Arab Near East was thus, in a socio-political sense, the scene of tangled loyalties. There was first of all the religious nationalism—loyalty to Islam and the Caliph. The nascent ethnic nationalism could be reconciled with it if the Ottoman constitution of 1908 was given a liberal interpretation by the authorities and was backed up with sincerity. If balked by the Turks, Arab nationalism might set its course toward complete independence, regardless of the religious complications which would ensue. Finally, the state nationalism as manifested in Egypt under the immediate impact of foreign occupation strove primarily to be rid of the intruders. Turkish rule, as a last resort, would be preferable to Western dominance.

Yet Ottoman policy in those days was not calculated to inspire confidence among the politically minded Arabs. Internally, Arab aspirations were countered with vague promises in some cases and determined repression in others. Neither did Turkey's external policy offer much encouragement to those Arab nationalists who viewed Western designs on the Near East with increasing suspicion. For Turkey appeared to be mortgaging her future to the Central Powers, thus substituting one set of European masters for another. The Baghdad Railway concession was becoming an ever more tangible spearhead of German penetration in the East. In these circumstances, the Arab nationalist movement, whatever the shade, was undecided as to its immediate course. Moreover, working underground as they must, the nationalists had limited opportunities for exchanging views and arriving at a resolute plan of action. They had the formula for setting in motion a force of great potential energy, long untapped. But there still was time to turn that force in more than one direction.

To Great Britain the general implications in this drift of affairs were plain enough. The success of Germany's eastward pressure depended on Turkish acquiescence, if not support. Since primary British interests were involved, it was essential for Britain to minimize the threat by seeking out and aligning herself with the more significant anti-Turkish elements within the Ottoman Empire. The Arabs would be a worthwhile prospect if their grievances against the Turks were to assume serious proportions; for did not Arab lands occupy by far the greatest part of the Sultan's domain? Yet in view of her involvement in Egypt, Britain could not be sure of her position in the Arab world at large. Furthermore, she was fearful lest any precipitate move upset the precarious international balance. Lastly, the strength of Arab nationalist sentiment could not be gauged adequately from the outside. All in all, Britain was cautious and hesitant. She did not alter her tactics until Turkey's entry into the war had furnished the final incentive.

Feelers from the Arab side had reached Britain early in 1914 through Lord Kitchener, who was then British Agent in Egypt. The Arab spokesman on that occasion was the

Amir Abdullah, the second son of Husayn, Grand Sharif of Mecca and scion of the ancient and noble Hashimite family. Husayn owed his office to the revolution of 1908. For years prior to that date he had been obliged to live in Constantinople—a precautionary measure on the part of the notorious Sultan Abdul-Hamid. He had returned home with no illusions about the old Turkish policy in regard to the Arabs, and his subsequent years in office as Custodian of the Holy Places of Islam in the Hijaz (the northwestern coastal sector of the peninsula) had freed him of such illusions about the new regime as he may have brought home with him. But the Sharif was just as cautious and deliberate as the British, who now began to loom as the logical ally in a contest for Arab independence under his aegis. His son Abdullah was of the same mind, whereas his third son, Faysal, was inclined toward coöperation with the Turks. And so Abdullah set out on an exploratory mission to Kitchener.

This was but the first of many steps which were to lead at long last to the proclamation of the Arab Revolt on June 5, 1916. The time taken to accomplish this purpose seems incredible and inexusable in retrospect. To be sure, both sides were cautious. The Sharifian family itself remained divided until Faysal joined the anti-Turkish camp after convincing himself of the strength of Arab nationalist feeling in Syria. But the main reason for the painfully slow progress of Husayn's negotiations with the British went much deeper. It lay in the magnitude of the stake which the Sharif—fortified by a protocol drawn up by nationalist leaders in Damascus, in May 1915, which outlined the terms of Anglo-Arab coöperation—had injected: namely, nothing less than full independence for the Asiatic Arab lands (Aden excepted). The British had commitments to the French and major reservations of their own. They were not quite ready to deal in terms of a comprehensive Arab policy. The Foreign Office had different ideas from those entertained by the India Office, which was interested in Ibn Saud, then ruler of the Najd area of the peninsula. Months went by.

As events progressed, however, Husayn's perseverance was bound to impress the British. His skill in staying out of the Holy War (Jihad) which the Sultan had proclaimed (on November 23, 1914) kept the Islamic world from uniting against the Allies. Religious prestige in Islam is never entirely divorced from political influence, and Husayn's stature as Arab nationalist leader was gaining steadily. There was thus a good chance that Arabs would heed his call to turn against the Turks. Such a move could have, all things considered, a positive bearing on the progress of the war in the East. Having arrived at this conclusion, and mindful of the risks involved in putting off a decision much longer, the British decided to accept Husayn's offer of active assistance in return for sponsoring Husayn's cause.

The foregoing account has sketched the situation in barest outline. The emphasis so far has been on Britain's approach to the problem rather than on any actual statement on her part in answer to Husayn's proposition. What the British did say is contained in a series of five letters from Sir Henry McMahon to the Sharif, which together with a like number from the Sharif constitute the so-called McMahon correspondence. Sir Henry was at the time British High Commissioner for Egypt and the Sudan, having assumed this position after Egypt had been declared a British Protectorate, on December 18, 1914. The correspondence covers the period from July 1915 to March 1916. Its contents, now available in an official British version, are a good illustration of how language can be made to obscure thought and confuse issues. Many points are vague and obliquely treated, implicit rather than expressly stated. That is why this correspondence has since become the subject of so much exegesis. It was fated to be brought up time and again for the very valid reason that, between them, the ten letters in question, together with the antecedent Damascus Protocol, constitute a general charter of Arab independence. But lawyers have seldom had to wrangle over a document more plagued by ambiguities. What made its subsequent career particularly contentious was the fact that another document—the Balfour Declaration—made explicit certain limited commitments on the part of Britain which—in the Arab view—ran counter to other commitments found to be implicit in the McMahon correspondence. Similar differences of interpretation were to come up also in connection with the Sykes-Picot Agreement of May 16, 1916, regulating Franco-British relations in the Near East.

In the summer of 1916, however, no one as yet had reason to give much thought to a detailed analysis of the McMahon-Husayn letters. The die had been cast. The Arabs were fighting openly on the side of Britain and her allies. The Revolt was on.

Just as the British were at first inclined to underestimate the potential military bearing of an Arab uprising, many have since tended to overestimate the operational significance of the Arab Revolt. It did account for something like 65,000 Turkish troops, thus freeing a number of British divisions for other tasks. It also compelled the Turks to fight on hostile soil, for all that the battlefields lay within their own legal territory. Unquestionably, the British campaign in the Near East owed much of its ultimate success to Arab aid. From the Arab angle, the culminating event was Faysal's triumphal entry into Damascus on October 3, 1918.

But it is not enough to measure the import of the Arab Revolt in terms of its military significance alone. When Faysal marched into Damascus he could not but be deeply conscious of the fact that he was entering as a conqueror the former capital of the Arab Empire. The echo of this deed reverberated throughout the Arab world. The Arab will to independence had crystallized. It was stronger than most had expected, stronger certainly than the West had allowed. Participation in the Revolt, the stated price of independence, was to become a resplendent badge of honor. Many of the participants were to furnish the leadership in the post-war struggle for self-expression. Today their list is impressive indeed. To mention only a few, Faysal proved, in many trials, to be every bit as much of a statesman in peace as he had been a leader in war. Iraq's debt to Ja'far Pasha al-Askari and Nuri Pasha al-Said—two former officers in the Turkish Army who had fought the British in the early stages of the war—can hardly be overstated. Nor did the surviving members of the Arab secret societies—the real pioneers of the Revolt—fail to leave their imprint on contemporary Arab progress. Faris al-Khuri, one of the Christian-Arab revolutionaries, who was beaten and jailed by the Turks in 1916, rose to be Prime Minister of Syria in 1945. And Shukri al-Quwwatli, eventually the President of Syria, was on one occasion desperate enough under Turkish torture to attempt suicide. The accomplishments and the spirit of these men afford some indication of how deep and real their cause has been to them and their followers.

No mention of the Arab Revolt, however cursory, can afford to omit the name of Colonel T. E. Lawrence. This is not the right place, nor is the present writer the proper person, to venture a comprehensive estimate of Lawrence's part in the events which marked an important chapter in the history of the modern Near East. This much at least seems certain: we lack the facts and perspective needed for an objective evaluation.

It is a popular misconception that Lawrence was the key personality in the Arab Revolt. It rests on the very human desire to salvage from the debris of the First World War at least one figure around whom a legend could be fashioned. Lawrence of Arabia was the man upon whom the choice fell. It was an inspired choice, what with the exotic scene of his exploits, his complex character, and the way in which the man went on to live up to the legend. There was surely something elemental and unreal about a person who, within a span of life cut short by a tragic accident, had dug in ancient ruins, roamed the desert wastes, blown up innumerable bridges behind enemy lines, injected himself into a people's struggle for independence, established a king upon his throne, and written an account of all these events in bold and earthy prose; and who followed this up with touches of superb disdain in translating Homer, refusing high rank, and taking on the lowly character of Aircraftsman Shaw. In the light of insensitive facts, however, Lawrence's connection with the Arab Revolt commenced long after the spade-work had been done and the fight begun. He had on his side the assurance of Britain's backing and the persuasive argument of British gold. Yet when this has been said, the further fact remains that Lawrence was able, thanks to a combination of rare abilities, to effect a dramatic introduction of the West to the Arabs and of the Near East to the West. Thus his detractors are confounded even as his mythifiers remain beyond the reach of logic.

It may come as a surprise to many that among Lawrence's opponents one must include today a number of prominent Arab nationalists. Yet the evidence admits of no doubt in the matter. The explanation cannot be limited to the circumstance that Britain's foreign policy fell far short of Arab expectations. For the fact could hardly have been lost on the Arabs that Lawrence's eventual retreat from prominence was largely in protest against Western treatment of the Arabs. The real reason would seem to lie elsewhere. Lawrence's attitude towards Zionism might well hold the answer. His view of the Near East could reconcile a sympathy for Zionist aspirations with a passion for a resurgent Arab world. Following another World War such a view became nothing short of treason. The issue was to reach a point where it distorted perspective and took precedence over any other problem. It grew into the dominant issue in the Near East and its repercussions were to be felt throughout the world.

4. The Period Between the Wars

1. GENERAL

The Armistice of Mudros, which terminated hostilities between the Ottoman Empire and the victorious Allies on October 30, 1918, marked for the Near East the end of one era and the commencement of another. The Empire, so long on the downgrade, was at last to be dissolved. But the shape of things scheduled to arise upon its ruins was as yet only a tentative projection into the future. And as events turned out, nothing came off according to advance schedule.

The new Turkey successfully stood off the Allies in rejecting a dictated peace and obtaining—though not before another war had been fought and won within the three following years—a settlement much more to her own liking. The Arabs, freed from their ties with Turkey, found in the post-war policies of the Western powers concerned a greater threat to their essential liberties than Turkish sovereignty had ever implied. And the intrusive powers for their part were frequently in serious conflict over past pledges and future plans.

The establishment of a juridical basis for the new order in the Arab Near East was delayed by the Turkish war of 1919–1922. This basis was ultimately provided by the abolition of the Sultanate on November 4, 1922, in virtue of which act the old Ottoman Government formally ceased to exist. The official instrument whereby Turkish rights to Arab lands were renounced was the Treaty of Lausanne, which was signed on July 24, 1923. The status of one district, consisting of the greater part of the former Ottoman Vilayet of Mosul, was to be settled separately, the Turks having refused to cede this territory outright on the ground that it was inhabited by a non-Arab "Ottoman Muslim majority." The final settlement came in June 1926, after the issue had come perilously close to upsetting the peace of the whole region. The disputed territory went to Iraq— the Arabic successor of Mesopotamia. Another adjustment, but this time in favor of Turkey, was made towards the close of the period under review in this chapter, in 1939, when the district of Alexandretta was completely detached from Syria under the press of events preceding the Second World War. The transfer was effected against the wishes of the Syrians and without reference to the League of Nations.

Of far-reaching consequence to the whole Islamic world, but in particular to the Arab Near East, was the abolition by Turkey of the Ottoman Caliphate on March 3, 1924. This move was the logical, though delayed, corollary of the abolition of the Ottoman Sultanate. In thus severing her last tie with pan-Islamism, Turkey left herself in a stronger position to pursue her chosen course of state nationalism. The Arab world, on the other hand, found itself faced afresh with the same three choices which had been close to the surface from the very beginning of the struggle for independence, but had now been placed in the foreground. One was religious nationalism under a new head, with the accent on the solidarity of all the Muslims. In this connection some elements looked for leadership to Ibn Saud, the powerful head of a puritanical sect. Another choice was ethnic nationalism, perhaps under a new Arab Caliph, with the principal emphasis resting on the unity of the various Arab groups. The leading exponent of this mode of thinking was, of course, the Sharif Husayn. The third choice was state nationalism, with the main stress on the needs and problems of the individual Arab countries. Egypt had long pursued this last course, and the new states carved out of the Ottoman Empire were also concentrating on it as the best answer to the immediate problems of the day.

Yet none of these three schools of thought was rigidly divorced from the other two, although the predominantly Islamic orientation was steadily losing ground. A clear-cut and straightforward decision, however, as between the ethnic and the provincial shades of nationalism, was rarely attempted. Each had its advantages as well as disadvantages. The ideal of over-all Arab unity had proved its strength in war and it retained its magnetism in the post-war period. But this was counterbalanced by the weight of the existing rivalries and jealousies. There was a tradition of hostility between the ruling family of Egypt and the House of Saud, and a new feud was in the making between Ibn Saud and Husayn's House of Hashim. Moreover, if Iraq or Syria emphasized pan-Arabism, then the Kurds of both these countries were immediately alienated; they had nothing to gain, but a great deal to lose, from a union of the Arab states.

The internal issues resulting from these conflicting types of nationalism have not been solved to this day. Instead, various governments would adopt the inconsistent policy of pursuing both ends at one and the same time. Inevitably they would lose out either on the pan-Arab or on the domestic issue. For some years all such differences became subordinated to the greater unifying factor of common opposition to Zionism. But the underlying divisive forces have by no means been dealt with and they are bound to come up again.

In the early stages of the inter-war period, however,

problems of more immediate urgency beset the Arab world. There was first the bitter disillusionment over the policies of Britain and France, which led to disorders and uprisings in Egypt, Palestine, Syria, and Iraq. In the Arabian Peninsula, which for the moment lay outside the reach of further Western penetration, the feud between Ibn Saud and Husayn flared up into an armed conflict, and this was followed by other clashes within the peninsula. These sectional developments call for very brief examination at closer range.

2. EGYPT

As the only Near East country occupied by a Western power prior to the First World War, Egypt did not figure in the wartime agreements and pledges in which the Allies and the Arabs were involved. These external circumstances, coupled with internal conditions rooted deep in the Egyptian environment, favored the emergence in Egypt—as has repeatedly been indicated—of a provincial brand of nationalism. In the period between the wars the political life of the country was keyed to the continuing struggle with Britain. Questions of common interest to the whole Arab world had to be relegated to a secondary position. This pattern, incidentally, was to survive, with its main features unaltered, through the Second World War and beyond. To be sure, ethnic nationalism was not to be discounted. Because of her relative social and economic advantages, as compared with the neighboring states, and by virtue of her secure status as the educational center of the Islamic world—thanks especially to the prestige of the ancient Islamic university of al-Azhar—Egypt was bound to be a factor in the evolving contest for Arab leadership. By the same token, however, she was also all the more self-reliant and militant in her relations with Britain, which called for and were accorded top political priority.

The leading figure in Egypt's initial moves against Britain was Sa'd Pasha Zaghlul. The fight for complete independence was resumed immediately after the cessation of hostilities in 1918. By 1919 Egypt was the scene of serious disorders. There were frequent attacks against British personnel in the country. A delegation (*Wafd*) was sent by Sa'd Zaghlul to Paris to lay the case of Egypt before the Peace Conference. Within a few years this nucleus was expanded into a political party which has carried the banner of Egyptian nationalism ever since. Britain attempted to meet the situation by terminating her protectorate over Egypt and proclaiming her "an independent sovereign State" in a declaration issued on February 28, 1922. It was an unsatisfactory document all around. Britain reserved for herself control of foreign affairs and of external security, as well as protection of minorities and of foreign interests in Egypt. Egypt was allowed only limited internal self-government which did not, however, include the Sudan, the vast area which had been placed under Anglo-Egyptian condominium in 1899. Thus the independent sovereignty was merely a diplomatic fiction. What is more, the declaration was unilateral and juridically faulty, inasmuch as Turkey was still at that time Egypt's legal sovereign and was not to renounce her formal rights in the matter until the signing of the Treaty of Lausanne, some sixteen months away. Small wonder then that Egypt refused to be bound by the declaration and that, anticipating the outcome, she declined to send a delegation to Lausanne.

The British move had one positive result in that the reigning Sultan, Fuad, assumed the title of King on March 15, 1922. And it has been a characteristic of Egyptian domestic politics ever since that the Palace, in seeking to safeguard its own hold on the people in the face of the growing popular prestige of the nationalist elements in power, would act independently of the dominant party while confident of the support of the divines of al-Azhar. Egyptian party politics must be viewed in terms of this political triangle. The number of formally constituted political parties in Egypt is of relatively little moment. The party that counts is the one which at the given time is recognized as the most vigorous exponent of the nationalist ideal; in other words, the *Wafd* or one of its offshoots. The other real party is the Palace, with the al-Azhar enjoying a significant balancing position.

To return to the accession of Fuad I, neither this step nor the antecedent British gesture could stop the wave of disorders in the country. Britain's first Labor Government, in the wake of a World War, was confronted with a dilemma which was to recur, under strikingly similar circumstances, after another World War and under another Labor Government. Genuine intentions for a policy of patience and conciliation in the Near East ran up against the stark reality of imperative interests of the British Empire. The local attitude was unyielding—in fact intransigent to the British way of thinking. A long series of attacks against British persons and property in Egypt culminated, on November 19, 1924, in the assassination (and this term of Arabic origin is peculiarly evocative in this connection) of Sir Lee Stack, Commander-in-Chief (*Sirdar*) of the Egyptian Army and Governor-General of the Sudan.

It fell to the lot of a new British Government to deal with this outrage, the Labor ministry having been swept out of office only one month before. The counter measures were harsh, but their immediate effect was the restoration of law and order. The basic conflict, however, remained unresolved.

In passing, it may be of interest to note the effect, whether direct or indirect, of Sir Lee Stack's murder on some of the prominent personalities concerned. In the case of two, long and distinguished careers were now drawing to a close. Sa'd Zaghlul could not continue as Prime

Minister for more than a few days, while Lord Allenby, conqueror of Jerusalem, stayed on as British High Commissioner in Egypt only six months longer. For Archibald Clark Kerr, Councillor of the British Residency, this turbulent episode in modern Egyptian history marked the beginning of a fruitful course which was to carry him, in successive stages of increasing responsibility, to Baghdad, Moscow, and most recently to Washington, as Ambassador from Great Britain. Among the Egyptian leaders charged by the British with moral complicity in the assassination, three merit special attention. Makram Ubayd, a Coptic Christian exponent of Egyptian nationalism, has remained the stormy petrel of local politics to this day. Two Muslim leaders were actually brought to trial for the crime but obtained acquittal. One of these was Ahmad Mahir, who eventually rose to the position of Prime Minister, only to become himself the victim of an ultra-nationalist assassin, on February 24, 1945, just after he had finished reading a royal decree declaring war against Germany and Japan. The other was Mahmud Nuqrashi, who was to succeed his colleague, only to be murdered in turn by a religious fanatic.

The impasse between Egypt and Britain continued throughout the reign of Fuad I, who was succeeded on April 28, 1936, by his son, Faruq I (the initial F seems to have established a monopoly in the family, since it is shared by the King's five sisters and all his daughters to date; there are no sons or brothers). On August 26, 1936, the two countries, mindful of Italy's penetration into Ethiopia, signed a Treaty of Alliance to remain in effect for twenty years. Britain undertook to end her military occupation of the country and to arrange for Egypt's admission to the League of Nations. Egypt agreed to respect British rights in the defense of the Suez Canal and also in the joint administration of the Sudan in accordance with the condominium agreements of 1899. Finally, Egypt pledged herself to stand by Britain in time of war.

These provisions, although ratified by both countries, were viewed by Egyptian nationalist circles as only a relative and slight improvement on the unilateral declaration of 1922. National pride would not be appeased by halfway measures which fell short of absolute sovereignty. Accordingly, nationalist agitation continued, and hostility to Britain sought an outlet in friendship towards other powers whose interests might clash with Britain's. But in the last analysis all of the West was potentially a hostile camp. Xenophobia was becoming indiscriminate.

3. THE ARABIAN PENINSULA

The McMahon correspondence specifically exempted from the political changes under consideration all matters which pertained to the existing relations between Great Britain and certain Arab Chiefs. This provision applied exclusively to the southern and eastern fringes of the Arabian Peninsula, where Britain, by way of India, had been exercising varying degrees of control. These relations were based on treaties most of which dated back to the nineteenth century. They embraced the Aden Protectorate and the Persian Gulf States of Bahrayn, Kuwayt, Trucial Oman, and Muscat-Oman (Qatar was added in November 1916). Only Aden proper was an outright colony (though it did not become a British Crown Colony until 1937), and was thus left out of account as a matter of course. In regard to the western coast and the vast interior of Arabia, Britain was by the end of the war on a different footing. There was here no question of protectorates, but both the Sharif Husayn and Ibn Saud had been receiving sizable subsidies from Britain, so that in one way or another the British had special interests virtually over the whole of the peninsula. In discussions with other Western powers this position could be advanced as a basis for regarding the area as part of the British sphere of influence. In general, however, it was understood that there was to be here no outside interference with the established order. And indeed, the period between the wars gave the peninsula no cause for complaints against the Western powers in so far as local affairs were concerned. It was not that far-reaching political changes were absent. No other part of the Arab world experienced greater transformation of the political scene. But these developments were due entirely to strains and pressures from within.

The story can best be summarized in terms of three leading personalities. Two of these, Husayn and Ibn Saud, have figured in this account on several previous occasions. The third was the Imam Yahya of the Yemen, the small district in the southwestern corner of the peninsula.

Just as was the case in Egypt, the end of world hostilities became the signal for settling local accounts. In this instance, however, the disputants were the local rulers whose traditional autonomy was about to be strengthened through the transfer of legal sovereignty from Turkey. Of these rulers, Husayn and Ibn Saud were the most prominent, hence their growing feud was of primary significance to the whole area. There can be no doubt that in this quarrel Husayn was the aggressor, in a diplomatic as well as a psychological sense. As early as November 1916 he had proclaimed himself, soon after the start of the Arab Revolt, "King of the Arab Countries." This move was scarcely calculated to placate the sensibilities of other Arab rulers. It was, moreover, a source of embarrassment to Britain and France, who eventually hit upon a compromise solution of the problem by recognizing Husayn as King of the Hijaz, the historic Sharifian territory, on January 3, 1917. At home, however, Husayn refused to give up the more grandiloquent title. It was a provocative practice, especially to Ibn Saud, who as ruler of Najd, to the east, not only enjoyed absolute authority over his Wahhabi territory but also had his own views about the proper custody of the Holy Sites of Islam.

The first armed clash between members of the two opposing camps occurred in 1919, at a time when—in Toynbee's words—"both combatants were receiving gold and arms from the British Government (Husayn through the Foreign Office and Ibn Saud through the India Office) and when their common patron was engaged at the Peace Conference of Paris in an attempt to restore peace to the world." British intercession prevented an immediate spread of the conflict. But after Ibn Saud had succeeded, two years later, in disposing of an older rival, to the north, and annexing the principality of Shammar, the increased power and prestige of Najd made a decisive contest with the Hijaz inevitable.

A move which helped bring on the war was the assumption by Husayn of the title of Caliph, in March 1924, just after the caliphate had been formally abolished by Turkey. The move was foredoomed to failure. It was, in the first place, impolitic in that it was backed only by a limited segment of Arab nationalist elements instead of being the considered decision of the whole Islamic world. And, in the second place, it attempted the impossible by seeking to press pan-Islamic aspirations into a pan-Arab mold. The Muslim minority in India, for instance, which alone outnumbered all the Arabs of the world, was very definitely opposed to identifying itself with Arab nationalist ideals. Nor did important Arab centers, Egypt and, particularly, the Wahhabi stronghold of Najd, take kindly to Husayn's pretensions. For Ibn Saud it was the last straw. His forces marched into the Hijaz and by October 13, in a matter of less than two months, they were in possession of Mecca. Husayn had meanwhile abdicated in favor of his eldest son, Ali, who managed to maintain himself in Jidda until December 1925. The two exiles eventually found refuge with more fortunate members of the Hashimite family, Husayn with his son Abdullah, in Amman, and Ali with his brother Faysal, in Baghdad. Ibn Saud was proclaimed King of the Hijaz on January 8, 1926, and in 1927, after elevating his hereditary seat of power from a sultanate to a kingdom, he became King of the Hijaz and of Najd and its Dependencies. On September 22, 1932, his dominions were unified into the Kingdom of Saudi Arabia.

In the meantime, the territory of Asir, to the south of the Hijaz, had placed itself, in 1930, under the protection of Ibn Saud. Wahhabi-held lands along the Red Sea coast now extended to the borders of the Yemen, a relatively populous corner of the peninsula, celebrated in ancient legend as well as in pre-Islamic and Islamic history. It was constituted as a theocratic state (imamate), and the contemporary Imam was the already elderly Yahya, leader of an old branch of the Shi'ite sect. On religious grounds alone Yahya would have been disposed to suspect and fear the ruler of the fanatical Wahhabis. These misgivings were strengthened by political considerations. During the war Yahya's separatist leanings had caused him to side with the Turks, hence against both Husayn and Ibn Saud. Now the more dreaded of the two rivals had become master of all but the Yemenite corner of the peninsula. A long-festering issue had come to a head.

Open warfare commenced in the early part of 1934. It was all over within two months. Ibn Saud dictated the peace, which was concluded on May 20, 1934; but his terms were moderate and statesmanlike. Neither the sovereignty of the Yemen nor the integrity of her territory was disturbed. The victor had gained added renown in the Arab world and prestige in international councils. The vanquished retired to his own corner to brood and plot. Henceforward he was to be more receptive to outside urgings, particularly those from quarters not directly allied with Ibn Saud. Italy, embarked on an expansionist program of her own which leaned heavily on the Red Sea area, was a highly interested party. Japan was another. Japanese imperialism was making a concerted effort to arouse the Islamic world against the West, and Japanese propaganda was beginning to penetrate the Near East on a tide of cheap Japanese goods and of gratuitous promises to liberate enslaved Muslims from Western oppression. There were credulous audiences everywhere, but especially in socially backward communities. Hence, when in 1938 Tokyo was celebrating the opening of a mosque with much publicity and political fanfare, one of Yahya's nine sons was prominently in attendance. But the shrewd and seemingly imperishable Imam must have sensed the failure of his policy soon after the British victory at al-Alamayn.

4. THE MANDATED TERRITORIES: GENERAL

The part of the Near East sometimes known as the Fertile Crescent has always been a rich source of perplexities to the student of human events. A crossroads since the dawn of history, it has never enjoyed peace and tranquility. As settled and transient mingled and clashed through the ages, each generation would add its own particular design to the over-all pattern, ever more and more intricate. With each period there would be an increment of diverse yet interlocking elements, and new factors would come up, some divisive and others unifying. In the long perspective, one might discern in all this ferment some significant trend toward human dignity and freedom. But, at short range, the turmoil would express itself in the narrow terms of exclusive freedoms—religious, ethnic, nationalist—making for suspicion, quarrels, and conflicts.

The First World War and the period immediately thereafter marked no departure from this age-old pattern. On the contrary, inherent tendencies were intensified and new complications were added. The Arab Revolt came as the dramatic revival of a long-dormant force. The upsurge of Zionism gave new direction to another traditional striving. That these two movements ran head on into each other was due, however, in part at least, to extraneous causes. For each was, or believed itself to be, supported by promises and commitments from the same outside quarter. In allying herself with two dynamic forces which bid fair to prove mutually incompatible, Britain had sought to protect her vital interests in the Near East by whatever means seemed ready to hand. The strained relations between France and Britain shortly after the signing of the Armistice, with the Near East as their source, were proof that British anxiety about the region had been justified. For her part, France had problems in Syria, as did Britain in Iraq, which were at the start unconnected with the Zionist problem. They were compounded of past history, current local tensions, and broad ambitions for the future. Truly, the Fertile Crescent is a soil luxuriant with thick and tangled growth.

The post-war settlements concerning this troubled area—Palestine, Syria, and Iraq—attempted compromise solutions of issues that could not be readily compromised. Some were too deep and involved and others as yet too inchoate for rule-of-thumb treatment. On each side there was more to the situation than the opposing side realized. The West underestimated the extent and strength of the Arabs' determination to reap their reward promptly and in full. As for the Arabs, they had neither the patience nor the understanding for realities on an international scale. Nor did they appreciate sufficiently, in the excitement of the moment, that genuine independence and sovereignty cannot be achieved overnight through grants and agreements alone and without the due process of gradual evolution. Their passion for self-government was in itself no guarantee that they were ready for it. Confronted with obstacles for which it had not allowed in advance, Arab nationalism tended to overreach itself.

On the whole, the Allies—that is to say, Britain and France, the powers most directly concerned—viewed the entire situation far more realistically than the Arabs did, or could be expected to do. The Anglo-French Declaration of November 8, 1918, sought to assure the populations of the liberated Arab territories that the necessary period of transition would not be detrimental to local interests. But in the interpretation of this document, which hints at the Arabs' need for outside assistance in their progress toward self-government, the two powers had to be guided also by previous commitments made under the pressure of wartime conditions: Britain by the McMahon correspondence and the Balfour Declaration, and France and Britain jointly by the Sykes-Picot Agreement. The fact that these three obligations were yet to be reduced to a common denominator acceptable to all the parties involved added considerably to the existing difficulties. Furthermore, since France was a party to only one of these commitments—the Sykes-Picot Agreement—and was disturbed further by the possible effect which Near East developments might have on her North African possessions, she was inclined less favorably than Britain to the Arab cause.

This being the background, the newly arrived-at formula of mandates appeared to offer the best solution. At that, much preliminary work remained to be done. Under the Sykes-Picot Agreement, France was to be given supervision over the Mosul district and a hand in administering Palestine. Britain now felt, however, that such allocation of responsibility ran counter to her own interests and conflicted with her other commitments. After protracted negotiations, and in return for certain balancing concessions, France finally consented to leave Mosul and Palestine to a proposed British sphere of influence while contenting herself with

Syria and Lebanon. Meanwhile, Faysal, acting on behalf of the Kingdom of the Hijaz, had been prevailed upon to sign, in January 1919, an agreement with Dr. Weizmann, on behalf of the Zionist Organization, looking forward to "the closest possible collaboration [between Arabs and Jews] in the development of the Arab State and Palestine." In a postscript written in Arabic, Faysal made the fulfillment of this agreement contingent on the satisfaction of the Arab demands for independence.

The mandate formula, devised for the territories taken from Germany and Turkey at the end of the war, recognized in principle the right of these territories to eventual independence. In practice mandates were to be classified as A, B, and C, according to their relative readiness for self-rule. All the occupied Arab lands in the Near East, and only those, were to be placed in Class A, to signify that the period of outside tutelage was to be relatively brief. Nevertheless, the hastily elected Syrian Congress, assembled in Damascus on July 2, 1919, passed a set of resolutions which vigorously opposed any mandatory status for Syria and Iraq, demanded immediate and absolute political independence for Syria—Palestine, Lebanon, and Cilicia included—and rejected categorically the Zionist claims to Palestine.

Concurrence of Arab nationalist circles in the proposed settlement was thus out of the question. The Damascus Resolutions sounded a clear warning that unless the Allies gave in, peace could not be expected. Undoubtedly, the Arabs were bitterly disappointed. That extraneous considerations and interests had played a part in the kind of solution which the Allies envisaged is no less plain. Vague and ambiguous promises and secret agreements entered into during the war had contributed their share to the general tension. It cannot be said, however, that the prevailing Arab attitude did anything to offset the feeling in the West that the area in question—which, as enemy-occupied territory, it was the

Allies' responsibility to administer—was not fully prepared for self-government. The resolutions were intransigent in tone and immoderate in at least some of their demands. Thus the indicated annexation of Cilicia could not be viewed as anything other than aggression based on faulty ethnography. Just so, the insistence on the inviolability of Greater Syria was poor history. As delimited in the resolutions, such an area had never constituted an integral and independent state in all the many centuries of its recorded history. The designation of Palestine as "Southern Syria" is no more defensible—or no less—than the corresponding Zionist practice of referring to Transjordan as "Eastern Palestine."

Mention must be made in this connection of one other document, namely, the report of the so-called King-Crane Commission. This commission was sent to Palestine and Syria by President Wilson in order to ascertain the wishes of the local populations. Originally it was to have been a larger Allied body, made up of two representatives each from Britain, France, Italy, and the United States. When the other three powers failed to act, the American members were instructed to proceed alone. They arrived in Jaffa on June 10, 1919, and their mission was completed within less than six weeks. The report was submitted on August 28.

Since the document had no official standing it was never acted upon. But it is an interesting document just the same, for several reasons. One is that it embodies the results of an inquiry undertaken at the request of the President of the United States to obtain a broad sampling of public opinion in the Near East. Whether or not the methods were adequate or the time spent sufficient, the report remains the first instance of American concern, at the top level, with basic information about the area independently obtained. Another reason for the continuing significance of the King-Crane report is the frequent use which is made of it in Arab and Zionist circles. Because the report recommended a greatly reduced Zionist program, the Arabs have not ceased to extoll it, and the Zionists to condemn it, even though the basis on which the recommendations were made was vastly different in 1919 from the conditions which obtain today.

But more important than its views on Zionism are the report's conclusions regarding two of the Damascus Resolutions (although these are not mentioned by name). The need for mandatory supervision is never questioned. The problem is only as to which power should be entrusted with the mandate. As to the Arabs' claims to Cilicia, these are dismissed as unjustified. In other words, the basic contention of contemporary Arab nationalist circles— namely, that the area was ready for self-rule and had no need for foreign tutelage—is not borne out by a report which the same circles have since been praising as fair and just. The Allied decision to establish mandates in the Near East cannot therefore have been the act of unrelieved iniquity that the Arabs make it out to be. This much at least must be said for the other side.

At any rate, on April 25, 1920, the Principal Allied Powers, at the San Remo Conference, assigned the mandate for Syria and Lebanon to France and the mandates for Palestine and Iraq to Great Britain, subject to approval by the Council of the League of Nations. The subsequent history of these countries during the period now under review will be sketched very briefly in the succeeding sections. In one respect the San Remo decisions had the same effect in all the mandated territories of the Near East. They led to serious outbreaks of violence, terrorism, and rebellion which were followed in due course by corresponding concessions on the part of the respective mandatory powers. While the pattern thus established was unfortunate—particularly since it reflects the whole situation only in a superficial sense—no room for doubt was left concerning the strength of the underlying Arab desire for complete independence. The problem which France and Britain came to face was how to meet this urge without jeopardizing their own fundamental interests. Although considerable progress toward solving this problem was to be made in the course of time, a complete answer is not yet available.

5. PALESTINE AND TRANSJORDAN

Of all the Class A mandates, Palestine remained longest under official foreign control. And, indeed, in no other part of the Near East have the conflicts of interests been as serious and widespread as in this case. The controversies arising from the mandates over Iraq or Syria-Lebanon were primarily two-way problems—between the mandated territory and the mandatory power. The Palestine question, on the other hand, was from the start a three-way issue—involving Britain, Arabs, and Jews. Furthermore, the other disputes were mainly of a local nature. But the Palestine issue could not be localized in a like manner. It soon spread to embrace, in one fashion or another, Jews and Arabs far beyond the borders of the country, together with substantial numbers of ardent sympathizers with either side. Britain, too, came to be more acutely conscious of Palestine than of the other portions of the region. It was not that the importance of the Suez Canal or of the Near East's oil resources could be matched by any direct advantages that Palestine had to offer. But the time could be foreseen—and it was in fact nearer at hand than the conferees at San Remo had reason to anticipate—when Egypt and Iraq would disengage themselves from the British Empire. In Palestine, therefore, just as in the Levant or in Iraq, extraneous interests of the mandatory powers took precedence over any strictly local considerations. But, unlike the other territories, Palestine was fated to provide those interests with their last line of defense. To appreciate, then, the Palestine issue in all its complexity, one must

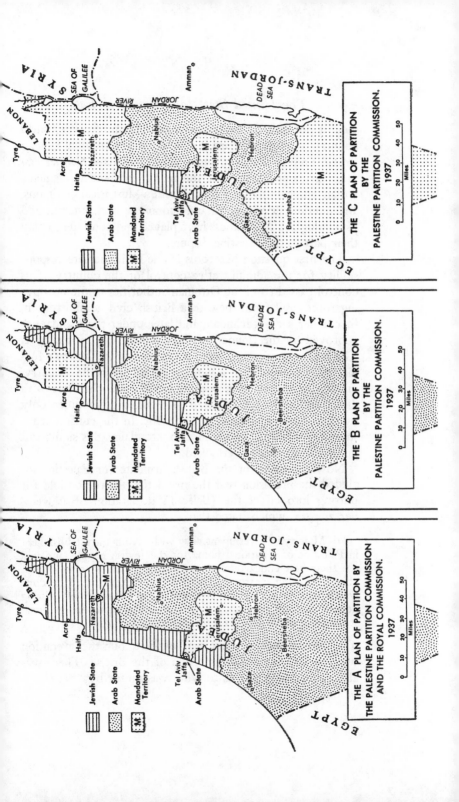

view it not only as the indigenous problem of a very small country; one must regard it also as a grave regional issue, a British Empire problem, and a world problem. Neither can one leave out of account the many component elements which enter into the larger question—historical, religious, and political; legal, social, and economic; humanitarian and psychological. All of these have played and continue to play their part in the Palestine dispute.

The first question before us is one of immediate responsibility for the administrative control of the country. This control passed from the Ottoman authorities to the occupying forces and from these to a British civil administration, first under a draft mandate and later under the mandate as approved by the Council of the League, on July 24, 1922. The legal requirements were completed with Turkey's formal surrender of her sovereign rights over the country, under the Treaty of Lausanne. Britain was thus left with direct authority, which could be revoked or modified only by the League or its proper successor. In the confusion resulting from all the claims and counterclaims this significant point is sometimes overlooked.

Now the terms of the British mandate for Palestine included the provision that the mandatory be responsible for putting into effect the (Balfour) declaration of November 2, 1917, which stated that

His Majesty's Government view with favour the establishment in Palestine of a national home for the Jewish people, and will use their best endeavours to facilitate the achievement of this object, it being clearly understood that nothing shall be done which may prejudice the civil and religious rights of existing non-Jewish communities in Palestine or the rights and political status enjoyed by Jews in any other country.

The general commitment was explicit, but the execution was left largely to the discretion of the British. There was also room for debate as to what was meant by "the establishment of a national home for the Jewish people." Although the mandate did not tie the hands of the mandatory in this respect, it went on to provide for the recognition of an appropriate Jewish agency to advise with the administration in the matter of establishing such a home. Furthermore, Jewish immigration was to be facilitated under suitable safeguards. All in all, Britain was allowed considerable latitude in interpreting as well as in implementing the terms of the mandate. What she did subsequently, up to the adoption of the White Paper of 1939—which document was questioned by the Permanent Mandates Commission but could not be acted upon either way by the Council of the League owing to the outbreak of the war—could not be assailed on juridical grounds, however doubtful such acts may have appeared in other respects.

The Arab opposition to the mandate was aimed chiefly against its moral basis. The Balfour Declaration and the mandate which proceeded from it were said to be in flagrant contravention of prior commitments as contained in the McMahon correspondence. McMahon's note of October 24, 1915, had placed "portions of Syria lying to the west of the districts of Damascus, Homs, Hama, and Aleppo" outside the borders of the proposed Arab state. It is clear that the geographical terminology of this letter lacks the precision of documents drawn up in state chancelleries. At any rate, the British have always insisted—and McMahon himself personally confirmed it—that Palestine was included in the excepted territory. The Arabs, on the other hand, have been equally constant in their assertion that the exclusion of Palestine from the area reserved by the British was implicit in McMahon's written statement. Here again the legal honors in the case go to the British. But this cannot lessen in any way the bitterness and resentment of those who regard themselves as the injured party.

That Britain did not wish to be charged with repudiation

of the McMahon commitments—as she understood them—
may be seen from her actions with regard to Transjordan.
This territory, which clearly lay within the limits of the
state that had been promised to Husayn, was first assigned
to the Provisional Arab Government which had been set up
by the Amir Faysal in 1918 with Damascus as the capital.
After the overthrow of Faysal by the French in 1920, Transjordan became administratively part of Palestine. When Faysal's elder brother, the Amir Abdullah, later threatened to
stir up trouble for the French in Syria, the British negotiated with him an agreement whereby he was to be installed
as administrator of Transjordan, "with the condition that
any action hostile to Syria must be abandoned." Standing
debts—to the French as well as to Abdullah—were thus paid
off and fresh difficulties avoided. A special status for the
territory was approved by the Council of the League in
1922, in the form of a Note to the Palestine Mandate expressly exempting Transjordan, though still part of the
Palestine mandate, from the provisions relating to the establishment of a national home for the Jews. This time it was
the Zionists' turn to oppose the action of the mandatory
power. But Britain, once more, was able to point to her
previous commitments—not to mention authorization by the
League—as proper grounds for her policy.

In 1923 the British announced their willingness to recognize the existence of an independent government in Transjordan, under the Amir Abdullah, provided that certain
specified conditions were first met. Although Abdullah lost
no time in proclaiming the independence of his territory, the
Anglo-Transjordan Treaty was not signed until 1928. Under
it the Amir was granted a measure of legislative and administrative authority, but all external relations of Transjordan
as well as effective internal controls remained in the hands
of the British High Commissioner, who would hencefor-

ward act simultaneously for Palestine and Transjordan, under the British Colonial Office.

To return to Palestine proper, the delimitation of a separate state by that name was modeled officially on the Biblical frontiers "from Dan even unto Beersheba," subject to marginal adjustments. While this meant going a long way back in search of a title, the fact remains that there is no later record of an independent sovereign Palestine ruled from within. In post-Biblical times Palestine was governed from Damascus, Baghdad, Cairo, and from farther afield, but then only as a portion of some larger political entity. The Latin phase during the Crusades was a brief interlude of Western, not Arab, rule from within. No plausible case could thus be construed in favor of Palestine as a separate and independent Arab country, or of a distinctive Palestinian Arab nation. The only time when Palestine was both separate and independent was under Israelite domination. This is not to press the historical argument but merely to present that argument in its proper historical perspective.

The history of Palestine under the mandate is a record made up of achievement and violence, evasion and indecision. The achievement is overwhelmingly Jewish. The violence, until the outbreak of the Second World War, was almost entirely Arab; later on radical Jewish elements were to make the frustrated hopes of the Jewish community an excuse for terrorism and outrages. The British cannot escape the charge of protracted evasion, relieved only rarely by samples of the now familiar policy of too little and too late. Much can be said for each group and not a little against each. But the composite picture remains confused and disheartening.

The achievement of the Jewish settlers has been described too often to need elaboration. One of the most neglected and backward areas of the Near East has been turned into a center of social, economic, and cultural progress. The Valley of Esdraelon, once marshy and malarial, is now covered with healthful agricultural settlements. Hillsides have been cleared of rock and planted with vines. A modern city was created on a strip of sand, and the maritime plain, nearly desolate a little over a score of years ago, is now a populous and flourishing province. Education at all levels, from nursery to university, has made great strides. Health and living standards have been transformed, social institutions advanced, industries promoted. The Jordan and the Dead Sea have been enlisted in the task of recapturing the land's inherent promise. And the idealism pent up since Biblical times has been released to transfigure the workers in pursuit of that task.

The total achievement has benefited primarily the Jewish community in Palestine. But while the gap between Jews and Arabs remained great all through the mandate, the Arabs of Palestine became healthier, more advanced socially, and ever more prosperous—as the result, whether direct or indirect, of the Jewish effort in the country. The charge is often heard that the Jews had acquired the best land in Palestine. As pointed out, however, in a note to the Palestine Partition (Woodhead) Report of 1938, the truth would seem to be "that much of the land now in possession of the Jews has become the best land." At that, the amount of arable land obtained by the Jews—at highly inflated prices—represented only a small proportion of the total. But all such arguments are a poor weapon in the face of political antagonisms.

These antagonisms are not now, nor were they at the beginning of the period under review, limited to conflicts between the three principal groups. From the start there were serious differences of opinion within each party to the dispute. The Jews increased in number from some 55,000 in 1918 to about a half million at the outbreak of the war.

The diversity of opinion among them grew proportionately. The great mass of the Jewish settlement (*Yishuv*) falls within the Zionist orbit. But there are extremist elements both to the right and to the left. The small group to the extreme left are communists who not only are outside the Zionist fold but even have coöperated at times with Arab nationalists. To the extreme right, and again outside the party proper, are ultra-orthodox elements on the one hand and ultra-nationalist Jewish elements on the other. Both these rightist groups have often been in opposition to the regular Zionist program: the ultra-orthodox body on the ground that the program was political in nature, and the ultra-nationalists, or Revisionists (in 1945 about 5 per cent of the Yishuv) on the ground that it was not political enough. The Revisionists withdrew from the World Zionist Organization in 1935 and have been acting independently ever since. They were the first to throw over the Jewish Agency's policy of self-restraint and to resort to acts of retaliation against the Arabs during the outbreaks of 1936–37. Their ideological off-shoots included the Irgun Zvai Leumi (National Military Organization) and the so-called Stern Group, both of which bodies were to figure in the British White Paper of July 24, 1946. Nor was their activity to be confined to Palestine. Their propaganda was not infrequently confused in the United States with the releases of the Zionist organization proper, with the result that Zionism has been identified with moves to which it is actually opposed.

But even the Zionists themselves are not, and have never been, of one mind on practically any question. A large segment of the Zionists stood long for coöperation with the Arabs and a smaller segment has favored a bi-national state. These together represent the moderate Zionist wing. The Zionists within the party, however, who held out for a Jewish state, have always been in the majority and they went on gaining ground under the impact of reactionary developments abroad and the Yishuv's growing distrust of Britain's policy in Palestine.

The politically minded Palestine Arabs were likewise split several ways. All were united in their opposition to Zionism. Beyond that there was considerable disagreement as to methods and aims. The Muslims, who constitute almost 90 per cent of the Arab population, were divided into two main groups. The Husayni faction, headed by the Mufti of Jerusalem, desired an independent Arab Palestine, and was thus not only the implacable foe of Zionism but also strongly anti-British. It represented an extreme form of state nationalism. The other group reflected the ethnic type of Arab nationalism. It favored a united or federated Arab state and leaned to Britain as the power most friendly to that idea. Christian Arabs, finally, were no less hostile to Zionism than the Muslims, but would seem, on the whole, to regard some form of outside supervision as the best guarantee of their own ultimate safety.

Of all these Arab groups, the Husayni party was by far the strongest. It had long been dominated by Hajj Muhammad Amin al-Husayni, the best-known member of the influential Husayni family. The office of *mufti* ("expounder of the law") had been in the family for two generations and it came down to him in 1921 on the death of his half-brother. Since there is no religious hierarchy in Islam, the title Grand Mufti has political rather than theological significance. Far more valuable to him in a practical sense was the presidency of the newly created Supreme Muslim Council to which he was appointed in that same year. For, in addition to placing him in control of sizable funds, it first drew the Mufti to the attention of the Arab world and of broader Islamic bodies as well.

Arab opposition to Zionism and the Balfour Declaration led first to the Easter riots in Jerusalem in 1920 and the Jaffa riots in May 1921, with a toll of more than a hundred killed and over four hundred wounded. The Churchill White Paper of 1922 sought—unsuccessfully, it developed—to conciliate Arab opinion by drawing a distinction between a national home and a national state. After a period of relative quiet, extensive pogroms occurred in 1929. The British met this trouble with the Passfield (Sidney Webb) White Paper of 1930, which brought a further redefinition of the mandate. The next wave of disorders began in 1936 and grew into an organized rebellion. The victims included not only Jews— Zionist as well as non-Zionist, and even pro-Arab—but also British officials and mere transients, and finally Arab victims of Revisionist retaliation. This time the complicity of the Mufti was plain enough to compel the British to depose him as president of the Supreme Muslim Council, in October 1937. Other Arab nationalist leaders were deported to the Seychelles. In taking this relatively firm stand the British were prompted by the rejection on the part of the Arabs of the Peel Report, published on July 7, 1937, which recommended partition of Palestine into Arab and Jewish enclaves. Eventually the plan was shelved and, with the rebellion spreading and world war threatening, the (MacDonald) White Paper of May 17, 1939, was substituted as a new instrument of policy. It amounted to the abrogation of the mandate. Jewish immigration was to cease, unless the Arabs approved, at the end of five years, and Jewish land purchases were severely restricted. Since the elected assembly, as envisaged in the White Paper, would be two-thirds Arab, the kind of state that it would recommend would be bound to be an Arab nationalist state. Under the circumstances, the Permanent Mandates Commission could not but question the validity of the document. The League Council had no opportunity to pass on the subject.

In last analysis, inter-Arab differences on the subject of Palestine have been minor, and the differences among the Jews largely marginal. British opinion, too, has been divided from the start, but in contrast to the others these disagreements have been fundamental. British experts on the Near East questioned the wisdom of the Balfour Declaration, and liberal British elements were dubious of its propriety. The decision was pressed by the Foreign Office for reasons of broader policy. It was not the first time that the reasoning of the Foreign Office proved to be something of a mystery to colonial officials and to groups outside the government. Similarly, the India Office has more than once been at odds with the central authority on Britain's foreign affairs; notably so on matters of policy concerning Arabia and Iraq. However, the Foreign Office prevailed. Its conclusions in this instance were approved by the Allied powers, embodied in the League's mandate, and adopted in the Anglo-American Convention of 1924. The mandate was a specific encouragement to the Zionists, who proceeded on that basis to pour into Palestine an enormous amount of energy and treasure. As a result, that country became in the middle thirties vastly different from what it had been in 1917.

The implementation of the terms of the mandate fell to the lot of the Colonial Office. Its initial misgivings on the subject could only be underlined by later developments. Many of the colonial officials were distinctly hostile to the project and their hostility increased as time went on. In the words of the Peel Report of 1937, the Palestine Jews are "a highly educated, highly democratic, very politically-minded, and unusually young community. It is conceivable, though we think it improbable, that it would acquiesce in a dictatorship if the dictator were a Jew of its own choice; but it can never be at ease under an alien bureaucracy." Especially so, it may be added, when that bureaucracy has been nurtured in a climate of superiority toward natives. The majority of Palestine Jews are not natives in either sense of the term. Confronted with the average colonial functionary they had no cause to feel inferior. And the higher type of British official

—the type that commands respect and admiration—was not very conspicuous in Palestine. The prevailing type, on the other hand, faced with unprecedented problems, found in the Arab position a welcome means of escape and self-defense.

To the Foreign Office, too, the scheduled policy on Palestine proved to be a source of grief. The strength of Arab nationalist sentiment had been badly underestimated. As Arab unity was crystallizing—however negative the basis, as it certainly was in the case of Palestine—the advantage of united Arab support came to outweigh other considerations. This became more and more apparent as the world crisis progressed. Before that, the traditional imperialist practice of divide and rule—the same practice that was attempted by the French in the Levant with reference to Muslims and Christians, and by the British themselves in Iraq with reference to Arabs and Kurds—had been in evidence in Palestine. The country was advancing too rapidly. The Jews were becoming too strong. An understanding between Jews and Arabs would not be an ideal solution in so far as basic British interests were concerned. This feeling was certainly one of the reasons, though by no means the only reason, for British evasion and indecision in Palestine. A deep sense of obligation in regard to past commitments was never absent from the councils of the British Government. The White Paper of 1939, for instance, was opposed by such men as Amery, Morrison, Sinclair, and most vehemently and eloquently by Churchill. Yet its immigration and land provisions were firmly carried out by a later government in which all these men were included.

British foreign policy, whatever the group in power, is not dedicated to the purpose of liquidating the British Empire. Palestine had slipped into a key opening in the defenses of the Empire. Extraneous considerations, therefore, must take precedence over local and regional problems. But the devious processes of foreign policy are seldom allowed to come out in the open. A forthright course from the very start would have gone a long way toward relieving tension, if not feelings. At least, the tension would have remained localized. Time came when piecemeal remedies would not suffice. Yet forthrightness on each side might still help in retrieving some of the lost ground.

6. SYRIA AND LEBANON

The Syro-Lebanese territory, also known as the Levant States, was designated as a French mandate by the San Remo Conference on April 25, 1920. This draft mandate was approved by the Council of the League on July 24, 1922.

After the Armistice of October 30, 1918, the coastal regions had been placed under Anglo-French occupation while the interior had formed part of the Arab National State, under the Amir Faysal, with its capital at Damascus. Following the withdrawal of the British troops to Palestine in 1919, Franco-Arab tension flared up, and the French used this as an excuse, upon receiving the draft mandate, to drive Faysal out and occupy the Arab-held part of the territory.

In the pursuit of her long-standing plan to entrench herself in the Levant, France sought to make use of the existing parochial differences which in this area are unusually profuse, even for the Near East. There is here a bewildering array of minorities, religious and ethnic, splinters or survivals of once larger bodies: Christian minorities, like the Maronites, Greek Orthodox, Gregorian Armenians, four Uniate groups, and several others; and Muslim or pseudo-Muslim sects, like the Druzes, the Ansariyah or Alawites, Ismailis, and Shi'ites proper. Taking the territory as a whole, the Sunni Muslims constitute a large majority. In Lebanon, however, the Sunnis are outnumbered by the Maronites. The French had intervened on behalf of the Maronites as far back as 1860, with the result that the district was given a semi-autonomous regime, under a Christian governor. France thus had a traditional claim to Maronite sympathies. She was hopeful of strengthening her position by uniting the Christian groups into a political bloc while emphasizing the existing inter-Muslim divergencies. The scheme was not to enjoy unqualified success. Various Christian bodies, jealous of the influence of the Maronites, refused to join them in political matters and even sided against them with the Muslims. And the Muslim religious divisions were not nearly as profound as was their solidarity on nationalist questions.

The move which made clear the French intentions and solidified nationalist sentiment was the enlargement of Lebanon through the addition of neighboring districts containing large Muslim groups, by order of the French High Commissioner in August 1920. Subsequent administrative and economic steps intensified anti-French feeling in Syria. Repressive measures in the Druze district led to the Druze rebellion in 1925. Hostilities spread to Damascus, and the city was shelled by the French in October of that year. Though order was gradually restored in the city, the psychological damage to France's position in Syria was never repaired. In the Druze district the rebellion was not terminated until 1928.

French policy now fell back on fresh attempts to foment and underline Lebanese separatism. The Syrian nationalists, for their part, continued to press for the unification of the whole territory, the establishment of normal Franco-Syrian relations under a treaty, and the admission of Syria to the League of Nations. France declared her willingness to consider the gradual liquidation of the mandate for Syria, but not the one for Lebanon. Lebanon obtained a constitution in 1926, but Syria had to wait for hers until 1930.

After much wrangling back and forth, France finally agreed to negotiate treaties with Syria and Lebanon. The drafts represented instruments of alliance to which were attached significant military conventions. France was granted the right to an extensive military occupation in Lebanon and to a restricted use of airport facilities in Syria. The Druze and Alawite districts were to remain autonomous within the general framework of the Syrian state. The treaties were to come into force three years after ratification, at which time the two states would become fully independent as members of the League of Nations. However, although Lebanon ratified her treaty with France in November 1936, and Syria in the following month, the French parliament refused to follow suit. The mandate system was reëstablished and, after prolonged unrest, the constitutions were suspended in 1939.

Extreme nationalist elements in Syria, led by the Syrian Nationalist Party, were not displeased by the French refusal to ratify the respective documents. They had been opposed to the treaties on the ground that the splitting up of the territory was thus being perpetuated and the objective of a unified Syria indefinitely delayed. Another source of Syrian grievance was the district (*sanjaq*) of Alexandretta. Originally part of the mandated area, this district—specifically exempted in the McMahon correspondence from direct Arab control—was slated for a special regime under the Franco-Turkish Treaty of 1921, in view of its large Turkish minority. In 1937 the Council of the League adopted a Statute and Organic Law for the Sanjaq, making it into a separate state. The Syrian nationalists demanded the return of the area to their country. But in 1939, when Turkey's good will was a prime objective, France consented to Turkish annexation of Alexandretta (designated as Hatay by Hittite-conscious Ankara) in a treaty signed at Ankara on June 23. Yet the matter is not a dead issue to the nationalists and it is certain to be brought up again. Like the Jewish Revisionists, rightist extremists in the Levant have often been accused of fascist philosophy and methods. At any rate, Lebanon was to feel obliged, in July, 1949, to execute Antun Saadi, long a leader of the extreme nationalists.

7. IRAQ

In common with Palestine and the Levant States, Iraq was assigned to a mandatory power—in this case the British, who proved in many individual instances to be stubbornly attached to the old term Mesopotamia—at the San Remo Conference. There are certain additional points of similarity, in background and in subsequent developments, between Iraq and the other mandated territories. The pattern of anti-Turkish feeling and corresponding Arab nationalist sentiment was much the same in all three instances, as was likewise the aftermath of hostility toward the intrusive Western power. On closer examination, however, the course of events in Iraq cannot be described as paralleling by and large the history of the other mandated lands of the Near East.

Iraq gravitates physically towards the Indian Ocean and away from the west and the Mediterranean. It points the way to Farther Asia. Western expansionism used this natural route under Alexander and sought to use it under Wilhelm II. Islam followed it on its march eastward. By the same token, the strategic defenses of the Asiatic interior reach out to Iraq. It was here that Britain, as an Asiatic power, took precautionary moves against Napoleon, and it was here, too, that a British expeditionary force arrived from India in 1914. Symbolically enough, the capital of Iraq is today the contact point of two significant rail systems: the famous Baghdad Railway from the west, and another one from the head of the Persian Gulf, built with Indian resources, manned initially by Indian personnel, and using a special gauge.

But Iraq's cultural contacts have long been with her western neighbors, and it is from that quarter that Iraqi Arab nationalism got its inspiration. Pulled thus in two opposite directions, the country could not avoid various forms of dual influence. Iraq is the only Islamic country where the two major Muslim groups, the Sunnis and the Shi'ites, are almost evenly divided. Since the main strength of Shi'ism is concentrated in non-Arab lands, while its principal Holy Places are in Iraq, either Islamic or state nationalism will carry a greater appeal with this sect than does militant ethnic nationalism. When they joined the Sunni Arabs in fighting Britain it was more because Britain was a non-Muslim power than because she stood in the way of Arab nationalist strivings.

Neither did British policy in Iraq escape the effects of the prevailing local dualism. The Indian school of thought, which came in with the occupation forces, would have preferred to treat Iraq as an outpost of India. They saw in the draft mandate a serious danger to their plans. But the Foreign Office school, mindful of British commitments to the Arab nationalists, viewed the mandate as the only possible compromise between Arab aspirations and the interests of the Empire. The pro-Indian orientation eventually lost out.

To the Iraqi nationalists, however, a British mandate was scarcely preferable—if at all—to Turkish dominance. Indeed, the Shi'ites regarded it as a change for the worse. Only the Kurds in the north of the country, who as Sunni Muslims were torn between their solidarity toward fellow Muslims and their antipathy for Arabs as such, remained on the sidelines. Eventually a rebellion broke out in 1920, in June in the Mosul district and a month later in the south. It lasted until October and its cost ran into thousands in killed and wounded and into tens of millions in pounds sterling. It aroused also a popular clamor in London for the abandonment of "Mesopotamia" by the British.

The British Government could not retreat that far, but

it was obliged to make concessions. A Provisional Arab Government was established in Baghdad on November 11, 1920. The joint efforts of Winston Churchill, in his capacity as Colonial Secretary, and T. E. Lawrence resulted in the enthronement of the Amir Faysal, whom the French had in the meantime forced out of Damascus, in Baghdad on August 23, 1921. The next move was to negotiate a treaty with the new kingdom. The Iraqis wanted it to be an instrument of alliance. The British sought to safeguard under it such controls as they believed to be essential for their purposes. British pressure won out over nationalist opposition and the document was ratified on October 10, 1922.

The next few years witnessed continued nationalist agitation for complete independence and progressive British assistance toward the partial achievement of that goal. Steady advance was registered in various departments of government and community organization. Administrative personnel was being trained, and there was gradual progress in the development of the financial, judicial, educational, and health systems. Agriculture and commerce were stimulated, but industry in general remained in a rudimentary state. The opening up of the rich Iraqi oil fields brought to the country badly needed capital. By 1930, when a new treaty was being negotiated, both the Iraqis and the British could look back upon the intervening years with considerable pride and satisfaction. Except for the persisting political impasse the retrospect was gratifying indeed.

The most important clauses of the new treaty, which would terminate the mandate and gain Britain's support of Iraq for membership in the League of Nations, were as follows: The two parties would consult with complete frankness on external matters affecting their common interests. Each party was to aid the other in the event of war, the aid required of Iraq being limited to facilities within her own territory, including the use of railways, rivers, ports, and airfields. To safeguard British communications in the common interest of both contracting parties, Britain was to maintain three air bases in Iraq. The treaty would remain in force for twenty-five years.

The new agreements were concluded on June 30, 1930. The League of Nations was informed that Britain was recommending unconditionally the admission of Iraq as member of the League in 1932. In the hearings which followed considerable doubt was expressed as to the extent of the country's administrative, political, and social progress, as well as its ability to insure the future of the various minorities in Iraq. In the end, the Permanent Mandates Commission yielded to British persuasion. The Council agreed to the admission of Iraq to the League, provided that she furnished a declaration guaranteeing minority rights and the observance of proper standards of law and justice. This declaration having been submitted, Iraq became a member of the League of Nations on October 3, 1932—the first Arab country to gain that distinction.

Nevertheless, nationalist circles remained dissatisfied. The more extreme elements among them were claiming that Britain had succeeded in freeing herself from international responsibility under the mandate while assuring herself of all the desired privileges through the expedient of an alliance with a member state of the League. The charge was obviously exaggerated, but so are also certain aspects of Iraqi nationalism. Self-conscious as a result of internal difficulties and schisms, Iraq has been inclined at times to seek reassurance in extremes. To the powerful Kurdish minority, in a state of local rebellion for periods of years and in a state of disaffection throughout, the central government would stress its basic interest in the state. In dealing with other Arab states, however, Iraq would emphasize her pan-Arab orientation. In ruthlessly suppressing the Assyrians in 1933—a few months after having assured the League on the subject of the minorities—Iraq may have had reason for taking stern measures, but certainly not for a massacre. Yet the officer responsible for the outcome won acclaim and promotion, while the more sober elements in the administration did not dare to impose checks on the ultra-nationalist fervor. Progress in Iraq had indeed been considerable, but only in a relative sense.

Faysal I, who throughout his reign strove valiantly to steer a middle course in the face of mighty pressures from without and turmoil within his young country, was succeeded, on September 9, 1933, by King Ghazi I. Lacking his father's broad political background and experience, the new ruler was impetuous where his predecessor had been determined but statesmanlike. On his death on April 4, 1939, as the result of an accident, his four-year-old son took over the reign as King Faysal II. Ghazi's cousin, the Amir Abdul-Ilah, has been serving as Regent.

It was a time when Iraq needed a mature ruler more than ever. Extreme nationalism was spreading, owing in part to the arrival in Baghdad of the Mufti of Jerusalem. The government granted him a substantial subsidy. German and Italian agents were making appreciable inroads. The British Consul in Mosul was murdered in a riot which was subsequently traced to incendiary leaflets printed by German groups in Baghdad. And within two years a pro-Axis Iraqi government was to wage a full-scale war against the British.

5. The Period of the Second World War

1. GENERAL

The twenty-five years between the outbreak of the First and the start of the Second World War had thus been a period of marked and rapid change in the Near East. Four centuries of stagnation under Ottoman rule had come to a formal close. Such successor states as Saudi Arabia, Iraq, Egypt, and the Yemen had become sovereign and independent in the internationally accepted meaning of these terms. To be sure, foreign dominance was still licensed in the two mandated territories of Palestine-Transjordan and the Levant. But throughout the region, and particularly in the areas lying outside the Arabian Peninsula, great progress had been made in administrative, social, and economic matters—although the most advanced of these states still had a very long way to go to approach average Western standards. Most important of all, Arab national consciousness had developed into a unifying force strong enough to outweigh the existing divisive factors.

In the earlier war the nationalist sentiment had been a source of aid and comfort to the Allies. In the inter-war period, however, the same sentiment proved to be a cause of acute discomfort to the intrusive Western powers. Locally, nationalism was a versatile weapon in the hands of the respective leaders. It had won important foreign conces-

sions for all the Arab states, notably the emancipation of
Iraq and Egypt—the two traditional centers of Near Eastern
progress. At the same time, nationalism remained throughout
the Near East the surest means of controlling the masses,
thereby diverting their attention from domestic affairs which
continued to suffer from mismanagement and corruption.
Hence, whether it deserved it or not, the West was habitually
blamed for most of the local ills. And the West in this
case meant Britain and France.

Thus it came about that the late war, unlike the previous
one, found the Near East as a psychological liability to the
Allies. Many Arabs believed—especially in the critical early
stages—that the Axis would win. Various elements made no
secret of their hopes that the Allies would lose. It was not
that these groups necessarily sympathized with Axis ideals.
The Allies were "inside"—in one form or another—not only
in the Near East but also in the richest portions of North
Africa and along most of the Islamic belt, all the way to the
interior of China and the outer reaches of the East Indies.
Germany, Italy, and Japan were out. They bid fair to dis-
lodge the Allies and therefore they had an initial hold on the
sympathies of most of the local populations. This advantage
had been skillfully exploited before the war and it was being
constantly pressed with the spread of hostilities. Added to
this was the long string of military successes which Berlin,
Rome, and Tokyo lost no time in converting into the most
telling kind of propaganda throughout the Islamic world.

Whether all these circumstances combined would have
sufficed eventually to draw a majority of the Arab states
into the war on the side of the Axis powers is a matter for
speculation. The issue was certainly not as clear-cut and
compelling as had been the argument in favor of the Arab
Revolt. On the other hand, Arab opinion is relatively easy
to inflame, given a plausible incentive and demagogic leadership. Be that as it may, there was no opportunity for a

pronounced anti-Allied trend to develop, owing to the presence of British garrisons in Egypt, Palestine, and Iraq, and of strong French contingents in the Levant. But the British had to take resolute measures in Egypt and to fight a war in Iraq. As against this there was Palestine's substantial contribution to the Allied cause—thanks largely to Jewish efforts—and the part which the troops of Transjordan, ably led by the British, played in the victory over the Iraqi insurgents.

2. THE MILITARY PHASE

In the First World War the Near East was involved in military operations throughout the contest, Turkey remaining a factor until the signing of the Armistice of Mudros in October 1918. In the late war the contestants were extraneous to the region. That they fought there at all is proof of the outstanding importance which the Near East had attained in the intervening years as a strategic center on a global scale. But the actual fighting was intermittent and limited to the early part of the war. For the Axis powers, control of the Near East would have meant the last stage but one on the way to complete victory. As long as the Allies remained in occupation, their cause was not yet hopeless. Germany sought to envelop the region by a gigantic pincers movement, one arm of which was to close in by way of the Caucasus and the Caspian while the other was to sweep from Libya, past Suez and Arabia, to the head of the Persian Gulf. Britain, fully alive to the danger, managed to reinforce her Egyptian garrison at the very time that the British Isles were facing their darkest hour following the evacuation at Dunkirk. Under the circumstances it was a heroic act in a struggle for the highest stakes. Eventually it was to pay handsome dividends. Indeed, the turning point of the war was signalized by Montgomery's defeat of

Rommel at al-Alamayn (el-Alamein), on Egyptian soil and at the very gates of Alexandria.

At the beginning of the war France had a large army in the Levant under the command of General Weygand. But the broad strategy which called for the presence of this force in the Near East, as a threat to the enemy's position in Eastern Europe, never could be acted upon. In a matter of a few months Weygand himself was to lead the French home armies in a losing battle. After France fell, the Levant States passed under the control of Vichy forces commanded by General Dentz. This gave Germany a convenient base for intensified subversive activity, pending the development of her ambitious operational plan. Nazi agents in Syria could now count on no worse than acquiescence on the part of the French authorities in any undertaking which might be ordered by the German Legation in Baghdad, the headquarters at that time for Axis under-cover work in the area.

Serious trouble in Iraq was foreshadowed early in 1941, when Prime Minister Nuri al-Said was replaced by Rashid Ali al-Gaylani. Both had established themselves as ardent nationalists. But whereas Nuri, disciple of Faysal and Ja'far al-Askari, sought to further the interests of his country through hard bargaining with the British, Rashid Ali's personal ambitions would not be satisfied by so orthodox a course. Neither was in a position to ignore the promptings of the Mufti of Jerusalem who was now sojourning in Baghdad. Nuri, however, would not follow the plotter into the pro-Axis camp. Rashid Ali did. Having conspired with a small group of colonels headed by the notorious "Golden Square," the new Prime Minister waited for the first excuse to place the country at the disposal of Germany. He did not have to wait very long. The British, alarmed by the happenings in Vichy-controlled Syria, had landed additional troops in Basra and began moving them up into the interior in accordance with the explicit terms of the Treaty of 1930.

When Rashid Ali threatened to block these troop movements, and the British insisted on their treaty rights, all
further pretense was abandoned. Iraqi troops laid siege to
the British Embassy in Baghdad and attacked the British air
installations at Habaniyyah. For a few weeks in May and
June 1941 the British were hard pressed. But Rashid Ali
had erred in his timing. The Germans had not been able to
assemble in Syria sufficient reserves of personnel and supplies.
Prompt intervention on the part of the Transjordan Arab
Legion helped to put down the uprising. The instigators,
headed by the Mufti and Rashid Ali, fled to Iran. This
brought them only a brief respite, however, since that
country came shortly thereafter under joint Russo-British
occupation. Eventually the four colonels comprising the
"Golden Square" were apprehended, tried as traitors by the
reconstituted Iraq Government, and executed. But no such
punishment was to be meted out to the prime instigators of
the coup. Both the Mufti and Rashid Ali managed to find
their way to Germany, whence they proceeded to broad-
cast to the Arab world the releases of the Berlin propaganda
doctors. Nor did their luck run out following the defeat of
their patron. Rashid Ali turned up, in the best picaresque
tradition, at the court of Ibn Saud, where his personal safety
was assured by ancient Arab custom and modern political
considerations. Not to be outdone, the Mufti, after a period
of thoughtful detention by the French—carried out without
benefit of Arab custom but with due regard to other political
considerations—made a spectacular trip by air, in June 1946,
to Cairo, where he was welcomed as a national hero by
the Arabs, to the accompaniment of unconvincing protestations of helplessness on the part of the British.

Disorders in Iraq continued for some time after the suppression of the Rashid Ali coup. With the return of the boy
King, the Regent, and the loyal members of the Cabinet to
the capital, which they had been obliged to leave to the

mercy of the insurgents, normal conditions were gradually restored. To enhance the position of the pro-Allied elements in the country, Iraq declared war on the Axis powers on January 16, 1943, the first Muslim country to take this step. Iran followed in September of that same year by declaring war on Germany, but her declaration of war on Japan did not come until early in 1945, at which time the rest of the Near East joined in the formalities as the necessary preliminary to membership in the United Nations.

Restoration of order in Iraq was followed by the expulsion of the Vichy forces from the Levant. Their collaboration with the Nazi agents in Syria had been flagrant enough to prompt several battalions of French-led soldiers to secede to the British and Fighting French forces stationed in Palestine. The Allies now had ample justification for advancing on Syria and Lebanon, and the occupation of these states was completed, after several weeks of fighting, in July 1941, under the command of General Catroux. The British assumed responsibility for maintaining security in the liberated territory. The resulting dual control with the French was to lead, however, to added Franco-British friction, especially in the crises of November 1943 and May-June 1945.

Palestine remained throughout the war securely in Allied hands. As a mandate she could not make an independent declaration of her sentiments, but her contribution to the war effort was nevertheless very noteworthy. This is true particularly—and for more than one reason—of the Jewish share. Although recruitment had to be on a voluntary basis, the small Jewish community produced over 25,000 volunteers to the British pool, whereas the much larger Arab community, double in size, furnished less than half that number. Nor did Palestine industry, the most advanced and diversified in the Near East—and this time almost exclusively Jewish—play a negligible part. On the other side of the ledger must be listed the increase in illicit arming, by Jews as well as

Arabs, which was made possible by the presence of large armies in the region. Another source of perplexity was the agitation for a separate Jewish army, easily understandable under the circumstances, but pressed beyond the dictates of sound reasoning by various Revisionist elements both in and out of Palestine.

Egypt was bound by the terms of the 1936 treaty to come to Britain's aid in the event of a war. But that treaty lacked from the start the backing of nationalist elements, which were grouped around the *Wafd* and were led, at the outbreak of the war, by Mustafa Pasha al-Nahhas. The Palace, for its part, was endeavoring to gain popularity by steering an independent course, diverging from the policies of the anti-British nationalists and yet uncongenial to the British. Its attitude, in short, was discreetly pro-Italian. In the execution of this balancing act the King relied on a succession of Cabinets of his own choosing. The strain was evidently severe, for one Prime Minister, Hasan Sabri, suffered a fatal heart attack while reading the speech from the Throne on November 14, 1940. Meanwhile, some of the leading officials were making no secret of their pro-Axis leanings.

But Britain, sobered by her recent experience in Iraq and deeply involved in the desert where the battle was swaying back and forth across Egypt's western borders, was for once in no mood for temporizing. Early in February 1942 the British requested in no uncertain terms that King Faruq dismiss his premier and substitute one approved by themselves. After a tense interval of two days the King yielded to pressure. The British choice fell on Nahhas Pasha. While his past record could scarcely be construed as pro-British, he had in his favor the fact that he was the leader of the country's most influential political party and, further, that he would not be likely to fall in with the Palace. The wisdom of this resolute move was borne out by subsequent events. Although Nahhas' ministry, which maintained itself in power till October 1944, had a turbulent domestic career, the British had no grounds for complaints with respect to its conduct of foreign affairs.

3. FOREIGN RELATIONS

So long as the Near East was preoccupied with military operations the political life of the region remained on a day-to-day basis. All was dominated by the immediate requirements and consequences of the war, which left little room for long-range objectives. By the end of 1942, however, the operational phase had passed. Although the emergency was far from over, those areas from which the battle had receded could now get a sampling of the many complexities of the post-hostilities era. Old struggles were thus resumed and new problems added. And the same powers that were united as allies in the West were lining up as rivals in the Near East.

The period just concluded, as a result of the battle of al-Alamayn, had brought out most emphatically the outstanding strategic importance of the region and the immensely enhanced value of its natural resources. These facts were now fully appreciated by all concerned; not only by Britain and France, who had long been involved in the Near East, or by Russia, whose interest dated back just as far—despite the temporary interruption—but also by the United States, the one newcomer on the scene. While joined for the moment in a common cause, each of these powers was thinking also in terms of the day after tomorrow. As regards the Near East, their respective plans added up to some agreements of interests and not a few conflicts. Then, too, the native populations of the region were very much of a factor. They in turn had agreements and conflicts of their own. On each major issue, therefore, there would be inevitably diverse alignments and combinations. A complex and fluid pattern was plainly in prospect. It was equally apparent that the full force of its component elements would not be brought into play until the moderating influence of the war had been superseded by the relative liberties of peace.

The most serious conflict during the period under review centered in the Levant States. The basic issue was the release of Syria and Lebanon from mandatory supervision by France, the local countries pressing their demands with steadily increasing vigor and the supervisory power resisting the pressure by every conceivable means. Before the crisis passed its peak, however, other powers were drawn in—fresh proof that the new Near East had become an international center of gravity. In this case, relations between France and Britain came dangerously close to the breaking point and both the United States and Russia found themselves involved. In the end France was on her way out as a Near Eastern power. But the other three—the Big Three—could not abandon a region where so many of their respective interests converged and often clashed. Their mutual problems, in conjunction with those of the local states, would remain to be transformed—in the Near East as much as elsewhere—into a design for the post-war world.

A tentative sectional draft of such a design was attempted in the De Gaulle-Lyttleton agreement of August 7, 1941, which was to the effect that France and Britain pledged themselves to the independence of Syria and Lebanon, but that among all the nations of Europe the position of France in the Levant was to remain one of special privilege. In other words, the mandatory system in the Near East was outmoded, but special foreign privileges and spheres of influence were still on the agenda. Whatever the merits of the plan, it proved unworkable in its application to the Levant. Syria and Lebanon objected to its second provision and France proved reluctant to carry out the first.

It will be recalled that the two Levant countries had rati-

fied the draft treaties of 1936 whereby France recognized
the independence of these states while retaining her preeminent position in the area. But owing to the opposition of
various French elements—military, commercial, and ecclesiastical—France had declined to approve the documents. The
De Gaulle-Lyttleton agreement was in essence a promise
of belated ratification by France of the treaties which she
had failed to approve five years earlier. It was, accordingly,
a conservative move, careful in its insistence on the preserva-
tion of special privileges inasmuch as their renunciation by
France would entail parallel concessions by Britain in Iraq,
Egypt, and Palestine. Anglo-French concurrence in the
matter was calculated, moreover, to balance the expected
Russo-American opposition to the maintenance of unilateral
advantages. It was all the more urgent, therefore, that France
carry out her part of the understanding. Yet the French were
repeating the history of 1936 all over again, in spite of the
fact that even a genuine desire by France to honor the
promises of 1936 would no longer satisfy the local states.
Britain had thus ample reason to feel annoyed with her
blundering partner. And France proved herself no less human—after her short-sighted policy had eventually come
to grief—in shifting the blame not only to native intransigence but also to British interference.

The immediate cause of the difficulties was the refusal
of France to surrender her mandatory rights in the Levant
States. This refusal was based on the nice legal argument
that, since the League of Nations could not be convened
in wartime, there was no properly functioning body to re-
lieve France of her responsibilities under the mandate. This
technicality could easily have been overcome by declaring
the mandate as being in liquidation *de facto*. The real reason
for the French tactics, however, was the unwillingness of
the local governments to give France the kind of treaties
she wanted. Tension mounted after the first Lebanese elec-

tions since the outbreak of the war had resulted in a victory
for the nationalist—and hence anti-French—element in the
one part of the Levant where France had counted on native
gratitude for past favors. The critical stage was reached
when the French arrested the country's Christian President
and its coalition Cabinet, on November 11, 1943. The British,
who were ultimately responsible for wartime security in the
area, took an unequivocal stand against the French action,
on the ground that their own endorsement of the 1941
promises of independence had amounted to a guarantee.
This determined position, effectively backed up by the
United States, brought the November 1943 crisis to a conclusion favorable for the Lebanese. The French officials
who had ordered the arrests were removed and a conciliatory
gesture by De Gaulle temporarily relieved the strain between the two Western powers. But the Franco-Levant impasse continued.

The British then reverted to their earlier understanding
with the French, namely, that the two should jointly uphold
their stand on special foreign privileges in those Near East
countries whose independence had been recognized. As was
anticipated, the Soviet Union expressed its disapproval of
this stand by recognizing unconditionally the independence
of Syria and Lebanon, in the summer of 1944. When the
United States and China promptly followed with parallel
moves, the international lines were sharply drawn. This disagreement was partly resolved with the extension on March
28, 1945, of an official invitation to the Levant States to take
part in the San Francisco Conference. While Syria and
Lebanon, as participants in a conference of the United
Nations, could thus no longer be regarded as mandated territories, the formal termination of the French mandate still
must await the signing of the requisite treaties between the
two states and France. It was an ambivalent position which

could not continue very long without leading to fresh trouble. The inevitable crisis reached a climax even as delegations from the countries concerned were attending the charter meeting of the organization which was to seek ways and means to forestall violence in international disputes. The Levant outbreaks of May-June 1945 made those of November 1943 appear as an anemic rehearsal. Once again it was a three-cornered conflict, in which France found herself opposed by the local states as well as by Britain. This time, however, with the hostilities in Europe just ended and mankind's hopes centered on universal peace, the events in the Levant could not escape the full glare of world publicity. Hence the added sensitiveness, bitterness, and suspicions which characterized the 1945 crisis.

The fundamental issues had not changed since the earlier flare-up. Conscious of her inferior position in international affairs, increasingly jealous of Britain, and worried about the concurrent troubles in Algeria, France was more anxious than ever to salvage something out of her cultural, political, and economic investment in the Levant. Since no other means were now possible, France wanted to obtain by treaty the same kind of rights that Britain enjoyed in Iraq and Egypt—not to mention Palestine. But this time the local states, irked by France's alleged opposition to their participation in the San Francisco Conference, were unwilling to discuss treaties while foreign troops were still on their soil. And they categorically opposed the granting of special privileges to any power.

After protracted efforts Britain finally succeeded in persuading Syria and Lebanon to enter into treaty negotiations with France. But just at the time when the subject of foreign troops had become an explosive topic, France made another of those psychological blunders for which she had become notorious in the Levant. She chose that dangerous juncture to reinforce her local garrison. Neither British remonstrances nor the strong local protests could dissuade her from so provocative a course.

The events which followed were beyond the power of the Syrian authorities to cope with. Local attacks on the scattered French garrisons led to reprisal shellings of open and crowded cities: Homs, Hama, and—most unfortunate of all—Damascus, which still bore the scars of the shelling of a score of years before. In the capital alone casualties amounted to hundreds in killed and a proportionately larger number in wounded and injured. The British were compelled to take stern measures if they would prevent an explosion which might rock the entire Arab world. Quite apart from their own far-flung interests in the region, communications with the Far East had to be protected in that decisive stage of the war with Japan. Churchill did not hesitate. The French were handed an ultimatum calling for the withdrawal of their troops and civilians from Syria. They had no choice but to comply. It was more, however, than French pride could bear. De Gaulle angrily placed the blame for the basic difficulty in the Levant on British machinations and interference, arising from Britain's selfish motives to displace the French in the Levant.

For the space of a few short weeks the international rift was hard to repair. Sensing that France had lost her last chance to retain a foothold in the area, De Gaulle was determined to embarrass the British to the utmost by requesting the three remaining major powers to look into the problem of the Near East as a whole. He got little encouragement, however, inasmuch as the United States backed up Britain diplomatically while Russia chose to remain on the sidelines. China, of course, had other problems of more immediate concern to herself. In the end wiser councils prevailed and Anglo-French relations regained their proper balance.

The Near East phase of these relations still remained to be clarified. For a period of several decades the region had been witnessing an alternating succession of conflicts and agreements of interests between these two powers. According to this rhythm of events a fresh agreement would now be in order. But the intervening years had also gradually reduced the range within which foreign interests could continue to operate. The local states themselves had become an increasingly influential factor. In the present instance the French mandate was dead in fact although it had not yet been formally extinguished on paper. Foreign troops in the Levant, British as well as French, were real enough, but their days were plainly numbered. The latest developments, and particularly the second shelling of the ancient Syrian capital within the space of twenty years, left France with no prospect of salvaging anything at all in Syria; Lebanese parochialism, however, continued to favor France to a very limited degree. As for Britain, it was distinctly to her advantage that a power with an imperialist history and ideology parallel to her own should not be eliminated from the area. She needed France's support—moral if not much more than that—in the forthcoming contests with the native states and in the indicated competition with the United States and Russia. All such considerations, therefore, would have to enter into the new accord on the Levant between France and Britain.

The agreement was long in coming. It was announced finally on December 13, 1945. In it the signatory powers promised the evacuation of all their troops from Syria and Lebanon, but they provided also for mutual consultation and support on all Near East questions and for non-interference in each other's established interests in the region. France was thus confirming, at long last, the complete independence of Syria and Lebanon. But neither France nor Britain was as yet prepared to forswear special privileges.

The reaction in the Levant to the Franco-British accord was one of disappointment, primarily because a final date for the departure of the much-resented foreign troops had not been set. Nor was the stated reason for their temporary retention—namely, that they were needed to guarantee security—calculated to appeal to local pride. On February 5, 1946, Syria and Lebanon addressed a joint note to the United Nations Security Council requesting it to recommend the "total and simultaneous evacuation" of the British and French garrisons in the Levant. The Council was of a mind to vote such a recommendation but was prevented from doing so by Russia's veto—the Russians having insisted on the use of stronger language inasmuch as the sovereignty of members of the United Nations was involved. On May 3, 1946, France and Britain formally notified the Council that their troops had been withdrawn from Syria and that the evacuation of Lebanon would be completed by the end of the year. A new era was ahead for both states, an era which neither was facing with quite the assurance that each had displayed in the long struggle for independence.

Outside of the Levant, the foreign relations of the Near East during the period under discussion cannot be described as eventful. Such major moves as were being attempted were in preparation for the uncertain future rather than in fulfillment of past obligations or in answer to the demands of the present. This is true in particular of the treaty between Britain and Transjordan which was published on March 22, 1946, and led to the crowning of the Amir Abdullah as King of Transjordan on May 25. It is true also, though in a different degree, of the slowly unfolding rivalry in economic matters between Britain and the United States, as witnessed especially in Saudi Arabia and Egypt. It was because of the growth of this rivalry that Britain was in no way displeased by the widespread Arab protests against the 1944 platforms of the two major political parties in the

United States, which mainly for reasons of domestic politics went on record as favoring the Zionist stand on Palestine. That direct American interest in the Near East was not wanting and that it would not be limited to the economic sphere was dramatically illustrated by the fact that President Roosevelt, in February 1945—barely two months before his death—went out of his way to meet with Arab leaders in the vicinity of Suez.

Russia, too, served notice that she meant to reëstablish herself as a factor in Near Eastern affairs. Diplomatic relations with Egypt were resumed in 1943 and ministers were exchanged with Iraq and the Levant States in 1944. In 1945 Patriarch Sergius of the newly reorganized Russian Orthodox Church made a pilgrimage to Damascus, Jerusalem, and Alexandria. The previous year Muslim pilgrims from Russia had appeared in Mecca and their visit had been publicized in the Russian press. Similar methods had enabled Czarist Russia to gain much prestige in the Near East. Now the Soviet Union was repeating the old tactics while holding new weapons in reserve. Small communist parties were in existence in Palestine, the Levant States, and Iraq. The victories of the Russian armies had made a strong impression on the Arab world. And opposition to Western penetration gave Russia a psychological advantage in the Near East. None of these factors would be neglected, but each would be exploited to the fullest advantage, once the post-war struggle for position had begun in earnest.

4. REGIONAL AFFAIRS

The one major problem of internal policy which agitated the Arab Near East during this period concerned the broad question of Arab unity. The general principle of inter-Arab coöperation had been given concrete expression in the Arab Revolt of 1916–1918. But wide differences as to scope, form, and procedure were bound to develop between the individual Arab countries, each faced with its own particular domestic problems. Provincial traditions and the pretensions of the local leaders stood in the way of a concerted regional policy. The Near East's kaleidoscope of minorities was another divisive influence. Lastly, the competing Western powers were naturally disunited on an issue which must needs affect their respective interests. And foreign motives had a way of influencing local politics.

As against these potent disruptive factors, there were two important unifying forces. One was positive, arising from the common cultural and economic interests of the Arab world. The other was negative, based on the Arabs' opposition to Zionism. Of these two, the negative factor has been the dominant one so far. It played a decisive role in the formation of the League of Arab States and it constituted the main single reason for that body's initial cohesion. Whether this entente, powered largely by a common hostile impulse, could find the inner unity needed for long-term constructive purposes, remained for the future to decide.

The beginnings of the recent stage of the Arab unity movement are traceable to British inspiration. By the end of 1938 Britain's prestige in the Near East had reached a low ebb, owing to effective German and Italian propaganda. Convinced of the need for winning Arab good will by furthering popular Arab desires, Britain availed herself of the opportunity afforded by the Palestine Conference in London in February–March 1939 to initiate a movement looking to an Arab world united in friendship towards herself. Although this involved changes in earlier British plans—especially in regard to the Kurds in Iraq and the Jews in Palestine—the British adhered to their sponsorship of Arab unity, and the movement became the keystone of British policy in the Near East.

In the implementation of this policy Britain could count

on effective support by Iraq. Ethnic nationalism has often been Baghdad's cure for many of the country's internal ills —quite apart from appealing in its own right to some of the most influential local leaders. It afforded a welcome distraction from the perennial difficulties with the Kurds, the smoldering feud between Shi'ites and Sunnis, and the chronic economic and administrative troubles. Now Iraq's leadership in a prominent cause could not be allowed to go unchallenged by her ancient rival on the Nile. In the ensuing contest between Nuri of Iraq and Nahhas of Egypt the unity movement proved to be the principal beneficiary. Britain's investment in this enterprise bid fair to pay handsome dividends when all Arab countries but one had shown themselves willing to shelve the Palestine question until after the end of the war. There was even the possibility that the Arabs might take a moderate stand on the Zionist issue. Yet that single veto was to prove decisive. For the dissenter was Ibn Saud.

Modern Arab politics is conditioned by leaders more than by political issues. In inter-Arab relations it is the ruler or head of state who personifies his country to the sister states. Hence the traditional tension between the Royal House of Egypt and the House of Saud, and the recent feud between Ibn Saud and the Hashimite family, interposed barriers not only between the personalities concerned but also—though to a less pronounced degree—between the respective countries in question. Ibn Saud was cool towards Egypt and plainly suspicious of Hashimite-ruled Iraq and Transjordan. The Levant States, being constituted as republics, were essentially neutral in this clash between royal pretensions. But they were sought after all the more by the respective contestants. Ibn Saud in particular was anxious to win Syria over to his side, since he wished to prevent the oft-threatened establishment of a Greater Syria—which would comprise the two Levant States, Transjordan, and possibly also Iraq and Palestine—under a Hashimite ruler. The Amir Abdullah had been campaigning periodically for such a merger and the British had expressed interest in the project. Inasmuch as prominent Syrian leaders were opposed to Hashimite over-lordship, they looked for support to Egypt and Saudi Arabia, but especially to Ibn Saud himself, whose prestige in the Arab world was beyond all danger from competition. With Syria on his side, Ibn Saud could now inject himself into the thick of inter-Arab politics. Finding in the Palestine issue the one subject on which all Arabs could achieve unanimity most readily, Ibn Saud took up the defense of Palestine independence with a zeal and an intransigence which he had never before exhibited in political matters.

If the Saudian position caused any embarrassment to Britain, it was not what the King had aimed for. His primary purpose was to block his Arab rivals from gaining too much political ground. For analogous reasons, Rashid Ali, fugitive from Iraqi justice and radio orator on behalf of Germany, was later to find asylum under Ibn Saud's roof. The one solution, therefore, that the Saudi ruler would view with favor was a League of all the independent Arab states; under it no single country could gain supremacy, while his own prestige would assure him personal preëminence. Accordingly, an Arab League became the prime objective of Arab policy, with British support indicated in advance. Britain might have occasional misgivings as to whether the movement which she had nurtured so carefully had not become altogether too robust. But no substitute course was feasible any more, and —after all—the development was not out of harmony with Britain's plans in the Near East. Her backing of ardent Arab nationalists would improve her standing in the whole region—not to mention other Islamic areas—strengthen her hand in dealing with the French in the Levant, and leave her in a favorable position for the anticipated competition with the United States and Russia.

While discussions were in progress regarding a definitive charter for the proposed league, King Faruq of Egypt visited Ibn Saud near the port of Yanbu, in Saudi Arabia, in January 1945. This meeting symbolized the new trend toward mutual coöperation between the two countries while signifying at the same time a corresponding decline in Hashimite prestige. Nor could Iraq take comfort from the fact that she had been omitted from the discussions between Ibn Saud and President Roosevelt in February of the same year, and from the separate sessions between the Saudi ruler and Prime Minister Churchill, whereas President Shukri Quwwatli of Syria had been included. That sundry ultra-nationalist elements were still active on their own was demonstrated by the assassination of the Egyptian Prime Minister, Ahmad Mahir, on February 24, following his reading of a royal decree containing Egypt's declaration of war against Germany and Japan. It was an anti-Allied move in the narrow tradition of state nationalism. As such it was out of step with the new pan-Arab orientation in which broader issues were at stake and to which Britain had given her blessing. The tangible result of that orientation was the formulation of the Pact of Arab States, which was signed in Cairo on March 22, 1945.

The signatories comprised Egypt, Iraq, Saudi Arabia, Syria, Lebanon, and Transjordan. The Yemen was listed among the states participating in the Pact, but her delegation, dependent for its every move on the whims of the aged Imam Yahya, arrived too late for the signing. Membership in the League was declared open to all "independent Arab states." At the time of the signing Transjordan was still a mandated territory although enjoying a measure of self-government. Since ratification of the document by Transjordan could not be effected without British consent, the fact that this state was included made it apparent that Britain was already considering the treaty which was to convey the formal independence of Transjordan one year later. No such prospect existed, however, in the case of Palestine. Yet Palestine could not very well be ignored. At the same time Britain must not be antagonized or international law disregarded. The dilemma was resolved by the adoption of a resolution which was annexed to the Pact. The Annex stated that the independence of Palestine was implicit under the Covenant of the League of Nations and that extraneous circumstances alone had prevented that country from exercising the attributes of her independence. The Council of the Arab League was requested, therefore, to appoint an Arab representative from Palestine to sit in with the official delegates from the other states. It was strictly a symbolical move since the Palestine representative could not create obligations binding on the mandatory regime. Other dependent Arab states could join in the work of the economic, social, and cultural committees to be set up under the Pact, but they could not take part in the political activities of the League. The way was thus left open for the eventual admission of such Arab territories in North Africa as might qualify in due time. For the time being, however, the League was strictly a regional organization, intent on cementing its position in the Near East before risking a trial of strength elsewhere.

The objectives of the League, expressed in general terms, were set forth as follows: coördination of the policies of the member states; the guarding of their independence and sovereignty; and a general concern with the affairs and interests of the Arab states. The Council of the League was set up as its executive organ, each state to have one vote in it. No state would be bound against its own will by majority decisions of the Council. In the event of aggression or a threat of aggression, whether affecting two member states or a member state and a third power, the Council would determine the measures necessary to repulse the aggressor. The nature of such measures was not specified. The member states remained free to conclude treaties with other states, and existing treaties were upheld.

It is clear that the terms of the Pact had been made sufficiently flexible to allow the signatories unhampered participation in the world body which the forthcoming San Francisco Conference was to set up. Care had been taken not to embarrass established foreign interests. While the result was thus agreeable to Britain, and incidentally also to France, it fell far short of the expressed wishes of the dominant nationalist groups throughout the Arab world. The ambiguity of some of the Pact's provisions, however, left room for considerable latitude in interpretation. It remained to be seen whether this instrument was sound enough to stand the dual test of local needs and international requirements at one and the same time, particularly in the troubled and uncertain years at the beginning of the post-war era.

5. THE ECONOMIC SITUATION

The economic life of the region up to the end of the last year of war need be considered only in so far as it affected general relations between the local states and the interested outside powers, or had a bearing on the interrelations of the foreign powers concerned. The question of oil, which looms so large in the general position of the Near East, need not for the present be gone into at length. During the late emergency petroleum constituted a very vital aspect of the broader strategic and political problems centering in the Near East, and as such it has been adverted to occasionally in the discussion so far. And since the cessation of hostilities and the onset of the subtler emergencies of peacetime, the local oil resources have come to underlie more prominently than ever many of the region's problems of the present and the future, problems which will be taken up in the concluding part of this book.

In the San Remo agreement of April 1920, Britain granted France a one-fourth interest in the Mosul oil fields and paved the way for the laying of a British-controlled pipe line to Haifa and its French-controlled outlet to Tripoli, in the Levant. This accord, which formed part of a comprehensive settlement of various outstanding issues between the two powers, was opposed by the United States as a violation of equal economic rights for all the Allies in the territories subjected to mandatory regimes. Eventually the United States was granted a 23.75 per cent share in the fields, which was confirmed by the Iraq Government in 1925. In subsequent years American oil exploitation was extended to Saudi Arabia (1933), Bahrayn (1936), and Kuwayt (1938).

A further consequence of the American protest against the economic provisions of the San Remo Conference was the signing of treaties with Britain and France which guaranteed the United States equality of economic treatment in the Near East. In practice, however, the mandatory powers found ways to circumvent these treaties to their own benefit. This was particularly true of the areas in the British sphere, most notably after the conclusion of the inter-Empire trade agreements of Ottawa in 1932. On the eve of the late war, therefore, Britain stood first by a wide margin in the import and export trade of Iraq, Palestine, and Egypt, while in the Levant States France was second to Britain in regard to imports, and to Palestine in regard to exports. Moreover, the two European powers had placed the local currencies on their own respective standards of exchange: Britain pegged the Egyptian pound, the Palestinian pound, and the Iraqi dinar (which had been preceded by the Indian rupee) to the pound sterling, and France pegged the Syrian pound to the franc. All of these Near East countries (the Levant in

1942–44), came thus under the sterling bloc which gave Britain substantial control not only of the local economy but also of economic ventures from the outside.

This control proved to be an increasingly important weapon as the United States, owing to the wartime stoppage of other sources of supply, began to move up as supplier of imported goods in the Near East, exclusive of Lend-Lease shipments. Owing to the large expenditures by Allied forces stationed in the region, the local countries accumulated large sterling balances. Virtual cessation of normal commercial relations during the war prevented these balances from being invested in imports. Accordingly, these holdings were placed in the sterling pool which by 1945 contained an estimated 450,000,000 pounds to the account of Egypt, Palestine, and Iraq. So long as these amounts, which were in the form of credits to London, could not be unblocked for the purchase of dollars, such trade as was possible remained under the effective supervision of the British.

Meanwhile, the critical supply situation prompted the British to set up in April 1941 the Middle East Supply Center, which had the task of allocating import quotas on the basis of available shipping space. In March 1942 the United States became a partner in this enterprise. Competition gave way to coöperation on a scale necessarily limited as to time and extent. While even within these limits a certain amount of friction was unavoidable, the Near East owed substantial benefits to this joint arrangement. Yet in spite of the Center's assistance, inflation made alarming progress. By the end of 1944 the price indexes in the region were from three to six times as high as the price levels of 1939.

The area in which, and over which, British-American economic competition was perhaps at its highest was Saudi Arabia. Here the immediate requirements of the day could not be entirely overshadowed by the high stakes which the near future held in store. In general it was understood that

Britain was not to be interfered with in this country on political matters, just as the United States was to have a free hand in economic affairs. But the two spheres are sometimes difficult to separate, especially in the Near East. Both powers needed the good will of Ibn Saud, and the King needed outside economic assistance, now that the pilgrimage to Mecca, one of the country's main sources of revenue, had been sharply reduced under wartime conditions. The result was a joint British-American subsidy to Ibn Saud, under the Lend-Lease formula, the United States share amounting to several million dollars a year in 1943–44. This move affords an excellent illustration of the close interaction of the various interests in the area: strategic, economic, and political; American, British, and Arab. It affords also an insight into the problems which remain to be faced today.

PART III

PROBLEMS OF THE PRESENT AND THE FUTURE

6. Strategic and Economic Problems

1. STRATEGIC QUESTIONS

The Near East introduced history to the world. By recording his daily doings man was made aware of himself as part of a universal community. The moving stylus forged imperishable links which bound region to region and period to period. Out of this collective experience of unity through change, there began to evolve, five thousand years ago, the concept of One World.

Ever since that fateful initial stage the Near East has held a central place in mankind's historic evolution. For many centuries the region retained its position as the geographic and cultural center of an as yet limitless earth. This dual role was eventually lost as a result of cultural diffusion and geographic discoveries. There was left, however, a spiritual focus, the legacy of millenniums of social progress reflected in dynamic religious systems. The youngest of these systems, Islam, succeeded briefly in restoring to the Near East its ancient cultural supremacy, in concert with a process of political expansion on a hitherto unprecedented scale. When this phase was over, the political center shifted, as it had once previously, to the West. But the accession of Islam enhanced the position of the Near East as a spiritual center, and the region regained also much of its old-time cultural leadership by establishing itself as the heart of the vigorous and steadily expanding Islamic world.

Meanwhile, geography had accomplished its task of exploring the limits of the globe. The now finite world called for a regrouping of the various forces intent on the control of its surface spaces and the exploitation of its subsurface wealth. The era of strategic thinking on a global scale had begun. And it was thanks to this new orientation that the Near East—the world's cultural and political center on previous occasions—was fated to regain also its long-held distinction as the central crossroads of the world. One cycle has thus been completed and a new course, of uncertain design, is now in progress.

That global rivalries must either be composed or come to a head in the Near East is the inevitable consequence of geographic environment. Here is the natural meeting place of three continents—Europe, Asia, and Africa. In this region converge the main intercontinental land routes and the shortest water routes. The modern age favors the same strategic area for yet another purpose, the very vital one of central air communications. Control of the Near East, therefore, has always been a prime requirement for world power. It was sought and briefly held by the land forces of Alexander and Pompey. Another would-be world conqueror, Napoleon, sensing the coming role of naval power, hoped to further his plans in the Near East by taking advantage of the opportunity afforded by the Isthmus of Suez. But his land forces met with defeat before his engineers could get started on the project which was to link the Mediterranean with the Red Sea. All these were European attempts at expansion into Asia. When Britain and Russia commenced, at the turn of the nineteenth century, their long rivalry which came to focus on the Near East, they did so primarily as Asiatic powers, each striving to protect its own particular interests on that continent. Britain's world empire did not become a reality until she had made herself the preëminent foreign influence in the Near East. To accomplish this end, however, she had to occupy and hold Egypt in order to protect the new strategic waterway provided by the Suez Canal. Henceforward, any challenge to Britain's intercontinental supremacy would necessarily gravitate toward the Near East. It was so in the case of Germany, whose Baghdad Railway project was a plain portent of war. In the period between the wars, Italy and Japan served notice of their respective challenges by intensifying their activities in the region, to be joined, shortly before the outbreak of the Second World War, by a strenuous propaganda drive directed from Germany. It is scarcely a coincidence, therefore, that one of the decisive turns against the Axis—perhaps the decisive turn in the sense of global strategy—should have come with the British victory over Rommel's Italo-German armies at al-Alamayn.

Nevertheless, until the late war the Near East was a secondary rather than a primary political battlefield. The world's political center of gravity was still in Europe and the contest for world supremacy was essentially a contest between European powers. That the center was shifting, however, could be seen from the fact that the breeding ground for wars had moved to southeastern Europe—the Balkans. But the conflicts that were nursed there were largely conflicts of European powers at odds over mutually incompatible European interests. And the eventual solutions brought temporary respite from European tensions, without drastically affecting the situation on the other continents.

One of the most far-reaching effects of the late war has been Europe's radically changed position in world affairs. Powers with predominantly European interests—notably Germany and Italy—have ceased to be potent factors in world politics. The emergence of the United States as a highly interested party, which can no longer afford to trust to isolationism, has meant a further decrease in Europe's long-time political leadership. World power today is balanced among states which have vital interests in more than one continent. Neither Britain nor Russia is an exclusively European power, and the United States has never been one at all. The place where the interests of all three converge, and often clash, is the Near East. This is due primarily to the geographic factor of the region's location on the face of the globe; but the number of converging and conflicting interests is increased in no small measure by the further strategic factor of the local petroleum resources—a subject reserved for separate treatment in the section which follows. Thus, Russia's western boundary region, where she runs up against British influence, may or may not be of greater importance to her than are her common frontiers with Iran and Turkey—two border states in which she has to contend with British influence reaching out from the countries of the Arab world. Britain might view her position in India as one of greater urgency than her present status in Arab lands. The United States, for her part, cannot but look upon the Pacific area, where relations with Russia require constant attention, as a sector demanding higher priority than the coastal areas of the Persian Gulf or the Red Sea. Similarly, United States agreement with Britain over Italy or Germany might take precedence at the time over conflicts with the same ally concerning Palestine or Saudi Arabia. But in no other part of the globe is the problem of long-term relations affecting all three powers at one and the same time—and not just any two of these—as acute and delicate and fraught with danger to world peace as it is in the Near East and its borderlands. The place where peace might be upset most readily is where the number of interpower frictions is greatest. That is precisely why the Near East is in the process of replacing Europe as the world's center of gravity and breeding place of fresh conflicts.

The casual follower of world affairs may have wondered at times about the reasons behind this seemingly sudden prominence of the Near East. The fact of such prominence, however, could not have escaped him. It became generally apparent during the later stages of the recent war and it has been underlined with repeated emphasis since the cessation of hostilities. The military campaigns in the Caucasus and the Egyptian desert, both converging on the Near East; Russia's recognition of the insurgent Rashid Ali regime in Iraq in the spring of 1941; President Roosevelt's declaration that Saudi Arabia was vital to the defenses of the United States; his detour to Egypt in February 1945 to meet with Arab leaders; the United Nations' first test case over Iran, an area having close geographic, historic, cultural, and economic connections with the Arab Near East; the bitter Anglo-French conflict over the Levant in 1945; the perennial crisis over Palestine; the British Labor Government's renewed stress on the vital importance of the Near East to Britain; and President Truman's reference, in his Army Day address of April 1946, to "the Near and Middle East" as an area which "presents grave problems . . . contains vast natural resources . . . lies across the most convenient routes of land, air, and water communications . . . might become an arena of intense rivalry among outside powers" which rivalry "might suddenly erupt into conflict"—these are but some of the unceasing indications that the Near East has indeed erupted into the persistent limelight of world politics. It has become, in short, a sensitive barometer of the problems and prospects of the post-war era.

There is one final major strategic consideration which gives the Near East an importance that extends far beyond the borders of the region itself. It concerns the central position of the Near East within the broad reaches of the whole Islamic world. As the homeland of the Prophet and the seat of the Holy Places of Islam, Arabia is the heart of the world-wide community of Muslims, possessing the one spot to which each communicant turns from all other points of the compass in his daily prayers. Arabic, as the language of Muhammad and his Sacred Book—which the orthodox, whatever his own tongue, will not touch except in the original—is above all other languages the most honored in that polyglot community. Just so, the Arabs, as the Prophet's own people, occupy a place in Islam which no other Muslim people can rival. Although the Arabs of the Near East do not exceed forty million in number, they command nevertheless a solicitude which may vary among, but is never altogether absent from, the nearly one hundred million Muslims of India and Pakistan, the seventy million Muslims of the Netherlands Indies, the twenty-five million Muslims of Russia, the twenty million Muslims of China, not to mention other Muslim communities in Africa, Europe, and the Americas. The annual pilgrimage to Mecca serves not only to strengthen Islamic solidarity but also to furnish an impressive reminder of the Arabs' preëminent position in the body of Islam.

Now it is a curious coincidence that much of the Eastern Hemisphere's wealth in natural resources—and particularly in petroleum resources—is concentrated along the extended stretch which is often called the Islamic belt. Not only the oil fields of the Near East and Iran, but the petroleum deposits of the Caucasus and the Netherlands Indies—in other words, the overwhelming bulk of all the oil reserves outside the Americas—are situated in territories occupied by Muslim peoples. The same is true of the Eastern Hemisphere's strategic waterways: Gibraltar, the Dardanelles, the Suez, and Malacca (Singapore). Accordingly, friendly relations with the Arab world mean more than just the good will of the dominant element of a single area. They may have a bearing —in varying degrees—upon the attitudes of populations in a whole group of strategic areas. This point should neither be overlooked nor yet overemphasized in an analysis of a given power's policy in the Near East.

2. THE QUESTION OF ARABIAN OIL

In addition to its immemorial function as the central cross-roads of the world, the Near East has the very recent distinction of being one of the earth's richest petroleum centers —if not indeed the richest. The strategic value of the region's oil reserves—centrally located as they are and as yet virtually untapped—can scarcely be overstated. This was amply demonstrated in the late war; not only by the use which the controlling powers made of the local supply, but even more strikingly by the desperate efforts which the opposing powers, lacking adequate deposits of their own, exerted in a vain attempt to gain access to the oil fields at the head of the Persian Gulf.

The post-war era has not taken the pressure off the inherent strategic problem; it has only added fresh complications of an economic and political nature. Interests now in control of the local oil-bearing areas are in competition among themselves. Other interests are eager to obtain concessions in districts not yet blanketed by such grants. The local states want larger royalties and hence look askance at any check on maximum production. At that, a sharp increase in production may not be far away. For with the indicated decline in the productive rate elsewhere—especially in the United States, where known reserves have been dwindling steadily and new fields are becoming more and more difficult to find—greater effort will be directed to the practically virgin territory in the Near East. In the words of E. DeGolyer, a ranking petroleum geologist, "The center of gravity of world oil production is shifting from the Gulf-Caribbean area to the Middle East—to the Persian Gulf—and is likely to continue to shift until it is firmly established in that area." And this cannot but aggravate the existing strategic and political conflicts.

The major oil fields of the Near East, exclusive of lesser

ones in Egypt, are covered by four basic concessions, which
are operated by a varied combination of companies. The interests of some of these interlock, while those of others
compete with one another. The concessions extend over
several different countries and principalities. But if a rectangle is drawn to enclose the outermost points of the
Arabian Peninsula, it will be found to envelop all four of
the concessionary areas in question. Included in it will be
also the district under exploitation by the Anglo-Iranian Oil
Company (AIOC), which first drew world attention to the
petroleum deposits of the Near East. To some extent, therefore, the Iranian field which the British are operating con-
figurates with the oil-bearing areas in Arab countries. As
though to underline this relationship, the population inside
the British concession in Iran is largely Arab and thus ori-
ented toward the rest of the Arab world, and not in the
direction of Tehran. All four concessions, therefore, may be
said to lie within the Arabian oil area. Only a rough semicircle formed of the east-central part of Saudi Arabia makes
a substantial break in the continuity of the concessionary
rectangle.

To list now the four concessions and their respective
ownership, the Iranian holdings are operated by the AIOC,
in which the British Government is the majority shareholder
—not as an official body, however, but as a private corporation. This nice legal distinction is not always followed
through. Labor disorders, for instance, in the company's
territory—believed to have been inspired by leftist political
circles in Tehran—caused Britain in the summer of 1946 to
land a British-Indian force at Basra, within sight of her concessionary area in Iran. A flexible legal device thus had to
be suppressed in favor of the harsher political-strategic
realities.

The Iraq Petroleum Company (IPC) holds the fields of
Iraq and Qatar, as well as concessions in Syria, Palestine, and

Trucial Oman—at the lower end of the Persian Gulf. The ownership of this company, except for 5 per cent of the holdings, is divided in equal parts among four groups: the AIOC, Royal Dutch-Shell (also British-controlled), the Near East Development Company (Standard of New Jersey and Socony-Vacuum), and a French group. The remaining one twentieth is owned by "one individual," as the financial statements sometimes put it—and in their effort to be strictly factual provide the stuff of which legends are made—the reference being to one Calouste Sarkis Gulbenkian.

The rich field in Kuwayt and the concession covering the whole of this little principality (shaykhdom) are owned by the Kuwayt Oil Company, half of which is financed by the AIOC and the other half by a subsidiary of Gulf Oil Corporation.

Lastly, the fields and concession in Saudi Arabia are held by the Arabian-American Oil Company (Aramco), and the field in the Shaykhdom of Bahrayn (Bahrein) is operated by the Bahrein Petroleum Company. Both these companies are the joint property of Standard Oil of California and The Texas Company, being thus the only holdings in the Arabian oil area which are wholly American. The Kuwayt interest and IPC are half-British, and AIOC is entirely so.

The strong British position is even more favorable than appears on the surface. Of the four areas just listed, Britain is wholly in control of the first, while American interests have a financially unchallenged stake in the fourth. But British political influence in the peninsula and near-by territories, which is backed up by military installations and agreements covering various Arab lands, makes even the wholly American holdings dependent, in ever so many intricate details, on British favors. In the event, for instance, of serious disorders in Saudi Arabia—a threat which can never be entirely disregarded in view of the no-man's land character of much of that vast and wild and thinly inhabited country

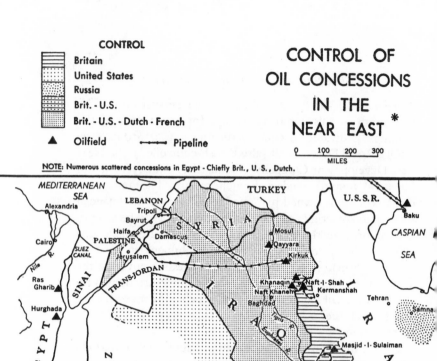

CONTROL

Britain
United States
Russia
Brit. - U.S.
Brit. - U.S. - Dutch - French
▲ Oilfield   ⊷ Pipeline

CONTROL OF
OIL CONCESSIONS
IN THE
NEAR EAST *

0   100   200   300
MILES

NOTE: Numerous scattered concessions in Egypt - Chiefly Brit., U. S., Dutch.

MEDITERRANEAN
SEA
Alexandria
TURKEY
U.S.S.R.
Baku
CASPIAN
SEA

LEBANON
Tripoli
Bayrut
Haifa
PALESTINE
Jerusalem
Damascus
SYRIA
Mosul
Qayyara
Kirkuk

Cairo
SUEZ
CANAL
Nile R.
Ras
Gharib
SINAI
TRANS-JORDAN

Khanaqin   Naft-I-Shah
Naft Khaneh   Kermanshah
Baghdad
Tehran
Samna

Hurghada
EGYPT
RED SEA
HIJAZ
IRAQ
Euphrates R.
Tigris R.

Masjid - I - Sulaiman
Basra   Haft - Kel
Abadan
IRAN
Gatch Saran

Medina
SAUDI
KUWAYT
Burgan
Abu Hadriya
Ras Tannura
Dammam
PERSIAN
GULF

Mecca
Riyad
Bahrayn
(Am. Conc.)
N

ARABIA
TRUCIAL OMAN

ERITREA
YEMEN
OMAN

ETHI-
OPIA
FR.
SOM.
Jibuti
ADEN
GULF   OF   ADEN

* As of 1946.

and the insecurity which would be caused by the problem of succession to the aging and ailing Ibn Saud—in such an event British protection could be of incalculable value.

Yet even in the second and third of the above concessionary holdings, where American interests are in partnership with the British, this association does not imply proportionate rights for the Americans. Restrictive cartel arrangements have thus far prevented Gulf Oil from shipping a single barrel out of the Kuwayt field, although the company owns one half of this field. It goes without saying that the American one-quarter share (or rather 23.75 per cent, to be precise) in IPC does not carry with it a corresponding right to a voice as to marketing and distribution, such policies being rigidly controlled by the so-called Red Line Agreement, which is wholly anglocentric.

In order to appreciate the full bearing of this situation on the world oil problem, it is necessary to glance at a few comprehensive figures which afford a comparison of the Arabian petroleum reserves with the major oil deposits elsewhere in the world (as of 1946).

Of the total world oil production to date, the Western Hemisphere has contributed nearly 78 per cent, and the United States alone some 63 per cent. This enormous drain has cut sharply into estimated ultimate resources. The United States is believed to have an ultimate balance of about 30 per cent, and the Gulf-Caribbean area a balance of not more than 13 per cent of the world's total. Yet our consumption exceeds by a wide margin the total consumption of the rest of the world combined. The time cannot be far distant, therefore, when this country will be forced to import oil instead of continuing to regard this commodity as one of our principal items of export. Of the other large oil-producing centers, Russia is said to have access to about 8 per cent of the world's total—or about as much as her foreseeable needs. The only remaining large center is the Arabian oil area, with some 45 per cent of the ultimate world resources. It is from here, then, that future needs must be supplied—not only those of the Eastern Hemisphere exclusive of Russia, but also the prospective United States deficit.

Specific estimates of Near East oil reserves, as proved by developed fields and indicated by fields already discovered but not yet fully explored, are listed by DeGolyer as follows: 9 billion barrels for Kuwayt, 6 to 7 billion for Iran, 5 billion for Iraq, 4 to 5 billion for Saudi Arabia, and 1 billion for Qatar. Yet these great discoveries are the result of very meager exploration. There is a substantial number of known prospects that await drilling, and vast areas are still to be explored. On this basis, the reserves of Saudi Arabia alone have been estimated at anywhere from 20 billion barrels upward. The usually cited figure for proved reserves in the United States is slightly over 20 billion barrels. Yet the oil field in Kuwayt alone—a principality of less than 2,000 square miles and with a total population that could be seated comfortably in Yankee Stadium—is now known to have proved reserves of 11 billion barrels, or about one-half of the latest figure for the whole of the United States.

It may be noted in passing that the Arabian crudes yield good gasoline and fuel oil, but that the lubricating fractions are of inferior quality.

Faced thus with the sobering fact of her rapidly dwindling oil reserves, the United States cannot but view the Arabian deposits with increasing concern as well as interest. The concern derives primarily from Britain's petroleum policy. Although we hold a very substantial share of the oil concessions in the Near East, our full exploitation of these holdings has been hampered by British cartel restrictions. The prospects for the future are dimmed by virtue of the fact that in countless political details our position in the region must long remain under the shadow of Britain. And Britain, by relying largely on the oil of the Western Hemisphere, has so far left her Near Eastern reserves virtually intact. It would seem to be imperative for the United States to establish a more equitable balance of distribution.

By 1944 the gravity of the situation had become plain enough to those of our government departments which were most directly concerned—Navy and Interior—to inspire plans for unprecedented measures. Accordingly, the three American oil companies with holdings in the Near East, namely, Standard of California, Texas, and Gulf, arranged with the Government Petroleum Reserves Corporation that it finance and operate a $165,000,000 pipe line from the fields on the Persian Gulf to the Mediterranean. This would have given the three companies an increased outlet for their oil at lower costs and—what is more—the very important advantage of the official backing of their government which, by financing and operating the pipe line, would have become a full-fledged partner in the enterprise. For it is precisely this kind of tie-up between government and business—with the government acting as a commercial concern for business purposes and as an official body in political matters—that has given Britain the dominant position she now enjoys with regard to Near East oil.

Nevertheless, however justified this attempt may have been on grounds of national United States policy, it was foredoomed to failure for two reasons: the opposition of rival business interests in this country, and the political complications abroad. Competing American oil companies invoked the always awesome specter of ultimate government control of the oil industry. Further, the government agencies involved had failed to take into account the full strength of British opposition to this move, for political reasons as well as economic, and the extent to which the success of the plan would be dependent on Britain's acquiescence if not active support, owing to that country's headstart in the Near East. The plan had to be abandoned. But the very fact that an independent American oil policy in the Near East had proved impracticable made the need for an equitable agreement on the subject with the British all the more imperative and urgent.

After protracted negotiations in Washington, representatives of the two countries, led by several Cabinet members on each side, reached an agreement in the summer of 1944 looking forward to international controls of the production and consumption of the world's petroleum. Since the matter involved relations between nations, President Roosevelt decided to handle it as a treaty. Accordingly, the draft was sent to the Senate for ratification in August 1944.

The same interests, however, which had been responsible for the suppression of the pipe-line plan, proved too much of a stumbling block in this instance as well. The American oil industry as a whole, fearful of federal controls at home, was insensitive to the urgent need for official sponsorship of oil operations abroad. Since the treaty faced certain defeat in the Senate, it was withdrawn in January 1945, and the burden of redrafting the document was transferred to the industry itself. A new agreement was eventually reached and duly signed in London on September 24, 1945. Like its predecessor, this document, too, envisaged an international petroleum body; but unlike the other, this one called only for a commission vested with powers of study and recommendation, instead of mandatory directives. Its eventual approval was further assured by the overwhelming backing of the oil industry.

Since 1946 important changes have been effected to bring the main concessionary parties closer together. Standard of New Jersey and Socony-Vacuum, already members of IPC, obtained interests in Aramco totaling 40 per cent, and agreed to purchase substantial quantities of crude oil from AIOC. For its part, IPC was guaranteed increased production and means of transport. The capital expenditure of Aramco alone is to exceed half a billion dollars during the next five years. Investment in Near East pipe lines is expected to reach $800,000,000. Lastly, a new combine, the American Independent Oil Company, was granted in July 1948 a concession in Kuwayt's half interest in the neutral zone which lies between Kuwayt and Saudi Arabia.

3. ECONOMIC QUESTIONS

The Near East is the victim as well as the beneficiary of its unparalleled environment. Location has made it a central crossroads. The countless groups who since the dawn of civilization have converged on it, in transit or for settlement, have left the region with a rich and vivid history which has dominated and haunted each of its successive occupants. But so strategic a center cannot long be abandoned to its own devices. It will be condemned and expropriated for public use by the powers that be. Hence the Near East has seldom had real privacy and it cannot expect much of it in the future.

Of a sudden the region finds itself fabulously rich in treasures for which the whole world has been searching. It cannot hope to enjoy this boon by itself. There is too much of the treasure for its own needs and too little available elsewhere. Moreover, the needs of the Near East cannot be satisfied without outside help. All-around self-sufficiency is seldom a feature of an ever-busy crossroads. The place is far too dependent on extraneous services.

With history-haunted peoples such a sense of dependence can readily become an obsessive influence. Freedom must be won back at any cost. Now, after two-score years of single-minded effort, the goal appears attained. Virtually the whole region enjoys the outward symbols of sovereignty and independence. But the victory is far from complete. However independent the Arab states may be in a political sense, they are a very long way from the less tangible goal of economic independence. Their economic resources are badly unbalanced. The countries are oversupplied in some respects and critically deficient in others. Their economic machinery is outworn and outmoded. In the race for political emancipation, the economic well-being of the region has been all but neglected. Dependence on foreign interests remains a stark reality, and the local states are as yet too inexperienced and unskilled in such matters to effect a sound balance between politics and economy, and between their great wealth and their equally great needs. It has been said of the Arab lands that they are too poor to afford wealth. When applied to the disproportion between their political liberation and their continued economic dependence, this statement will be found to come close to the mark.

To say that the Arab Near East—so long in the British sphere of influence, and in political matters still tied to Britain more effectively than to any other foreign power—is part of the United Kingdom's economic empire would not be as much of an overstatement as might seem at first. Both the export and import trade of the region are chiefly with Britain. As part of the sterling area, the Near East accumulated in London the equivalent of some two billion dollars in sterling securities. What happens to this huge stake, how it is to be liquidated, will be determined in London and not in Cairo or Baghdad. In the meantime, Britain is in an excellent position to enhance her financial and commercial ascendancy in the Near East. The fact is that the Near East is in urgent need of outside economic assistance. Britain happens to be on the ground floor to furnish it. This form of collaboration is termed exploitation by some and development by others. Under the circumstances the two designations refer to one and the same thing. The local states may choose to place the accent on the exploitation, and the outside power would doubtless stress the resulting development. At any rate, an extreme nationalist approach to the problem could accomplish little in the way of the necessary cures. A common denominator for the two terminological opposites just cited can of course be found in equitable coöperation, which would involve a united Arab economic front and such outside powers as can best insure the desired results—in free and open competition—to the greatest mutual advantage of all concerned. Until this has come about, the economic position of the Near East will remain unsound and a barrier to the balanced progress of a sector which the world cannot bypass.

A step which should lead to a curtailment of Britain's economic imperialism in the region was taken in July 1946, when the Anglo-American Trade and Financial Agreement was finally approved. Under it the British, in accepting the principle of liberalized international trade policies, undertook to abolish within one year the dollar pool of the sterling area as a whole whereby imports from outside this area were rigidly controlled by London. In addition, Britain agreed to settle as promptly as possible her indebtedness to the sterling-area countries and to unblock any of such sterling balances as were thus released. The effect of this commitment remains to be tested in practice. Since both the time and the nature of the envisaged settlement were left open, the discriminatory trade practices which it is to eliminate are likely to persist for a long time. And so long as the restrictions remain operative, anti-foreign agitation in the local states will have an added argument to feed upon. State nationalism cannot, on the whole, have a salutary effect on the economic life of the Near East, at least not until the region has acquired the skills and the experience which will enable it to dispense with foreign participation. Yet Egypt, for example, is in a mood wherein national valor is deemed superior to discretion. In her progressive xenophobia she would grant foreigners only temporary or provisional right of residence; prohibit purchase of real estate by foreigners; stop the formation of foreign corporations, and take steps to liquidate foreign-owned property and business concerns already established in the country; and, finally, set up restrictive duties on foreign imports. Even if so extreme a program is delayed in part until the country is in a healthier economic state than at present, the forces that press for it are gaining strength all the time.

The fundamental unsoundness of the present economic structure of the Arab Near East may be highlighted by the following illustration. Egypt's principal export is cotton, mainly of the long-staple variety, accounting for 70 to 80 per cent of the country's total of exported goods. The principal imports are manufactures, chiefly textiles. In other words, Egypt must pay a heavy premium, in processing and two-way transportation costs and profits, for goods made of her own raw materials. The greatest sufferers are of course the peasants (*fellahin*), who constitute some three fourths of the country's population. Theirs is indeed a depressed class. Symbolically enough, the term "fellah" is one of social derogation.

True, the precise anomaly just cited does not recur in the other Arab lands. But in all of them exports are weighted overwhelmingly with agricultural products—grains, raw wool, skins and hides, dates and citrus fruits—while imports, aside from including tea and sugar, without which the Near East would be a very unhappy place, range over the whole field of manufactured goods. The commodities which the region sells must often face stiff competition in world markets, and also the hurdles of various tariff policies (the Arab must frequently wish that his language had not contributed the word "tariff" to the international dictionary). On the other hand, the Near East cannot readily replace its essential imports from within its own resources; apart from textiles, it needs iron and steel manufactures, machinery and apparatus, automobiles and tires, wood, and drugs. In the event of a world emergency, there is no cushion against a breakdown in normal communications.

During the war certain specialized local surpluses, notably the citrus crop of Palestine—which in pre-war years approached 75 per cent of that country's total exports—became an all but total loss. The unbalanced local agricultural economy caused by such top-heavy concentration on a single exportable commodity aggravated the already serious food shortages. Inflation, stimulated by many factors, soared. Following the end of the war, this condition, coupled with the drawbacks implicit in the sterling-area restrictions, placed the export trade of the Near East at a further disadvantage, because of the great disparity between the local price levels and those of the countries which normally buy from the Near East.

The solution obviously lies in a far more diversified economy. There are considerable inherent opportunities for the achievement of such a goal. New exports can be developed and promoted—for instance, the manganese of Egypt and the immense chemical deposits of the Dead Sea, which are said to be capable of incredibly easy production and to include enough potassium alone to supply the needs of the world for a thousand years. Great stretches of potentially valuable land remain to be reclaimed. The way has been pointed by the Jewish colonies in Palestine which—in the words of Walter Clay Lowdermilk—"are showing the most remarkable devotion to reclamation of land that I have seen in any country of the New or Old World. The result of their efforts thus far is an inspiration and splendid achievement. Unknown to themselves, these colonies have laid the foundation for a Greater Palestine and have shown the way for the resurrection of the Near East as a whole." An enormous addition to the land already reclaimed could be made through the translation of the singular possibilities of the

Jordan into the proposed Jordan Valley Authority. Furthermore, the potential water resources of this area and of the adjacent territories could be converted into power and thus enable the region to make a substantial start toward industrialization, perhaps its greatest current economic need.

For the present, various political factors prevent the Near East from finding its proper economic level. In 1947 Egypt withdrew from the sterling bloc in a move which owed more to nationalist pressures than to a careful balancing of the economic consequences. For this show of outward independence did not free Egypt from the need for negotiating with Britain a viable financial agreement, which was obtained at last in January 1948. In the same month Syria left the franc bloc, thus divorcing her currency from that of Lebanon and interposing countless practical complications in the normal intercourse between two intimately related states. For reasons that are likewise political in origin, but this time on the initiative of the foreign power concerned, Palestine left the sterling area in February 1948. Technically, this withdrawal took with it Transjordan, which had a common currency with Palestine; but the Arab state promptly applied for readmission. Settlement of outstanding sterling balances, amounting to some hundred million pounds, is one of the major issues confronting the new state of Israel.

The Palestine war and the emergence of Israel will inevitably have a profound effect on the economy of the whole region. The task of absorbing huge numbers of immigrants—in proportion to the settled population—will tax Israel's powers for years to come. The Palestine war, moreover, which drained the treasuries of all the combatants, has deposited in its wake the pressing problem of hundreds of thousands of Arab refugees—a staggering economic problem as well as a moral obligation. In short, the economy of the entire region is due to undergo a profound transformation in the immediate future.

The significance of the region's oil reserves should not, of course, be ignored in this connection. Neither should it be overstressed. The Near East can use only a very small fraction of its total petroleum production. The industry is preëminently a foreign enterprise. It remains to be integrated with local needs. The beneficial effects on native economy which it has had so far have been incidental rather than direct. The oil interests have been responsible for the building of the Kirkuk branch of the Iraq Railways and for minor agricultural and social improvements in Saudi Arabia. They have contributed also sorely needed royalties to the budgets of the producing territories, even if the average contribution has thus far been well below 20 per cent of the annual total. But it should be remembered that the interests in question are intrusive, and that their very magnitude makes a balanced regional economy all the more difficult of attainment.

7. Social Problems

1. PSYCHOLOGICAL QUESTIONS

To have prefaced this discussion of the Near East today, and of the problems which loom ahead, with a summary of basic strategic and economic questions is in no way a concession to traditional economic determinism or its more recent strategic counterpart. As was stated at the outset, geographic environment and cultural developments in the broadest sense of the term are interacting factors in the progress of history. Physical circumstances furnish the opportunity, but it is the human element that determines the use to which this potential shall be put. The necessary background—physical and strategic as well as historical and economic—has been sketched. The Near East of tomorrow will be forged, in final analysis, out of the passions and pressures, the gains and the losses—in short, out of the conditions and the aspirations—of human beings acting and interacting against that background.

The central factor in this mobile pattern must obviously be the group which is in the forefront of the stage, the dominant ethnic element of the region. Will the Arabs retain their present outward prominence when all the backstage forces have been brought into play? What will be their part in the international trial of strength as focused on the Near East? To these questions there can be no confident and uniform answer. But a brief analysis of the underlying social factors should at least help to clarify the inherent probabilities.

Of these factors, perhaps the most normative is the one which is rooted in the never-ceasing interaction of the East and the West. Can the indigenous culture draw on sufficient inner reserves to stand up to the West with dignity and self-respect, or will the present-day exponents of that culture be panicked into a headlong course which can lead only to waste and retrogression? And what of the leadership required at this critical juncture to meet the various impulses from without and the stresses from within? It is a complex problem; and at its core is this question: can the Near East and the West arrive at a common tempo? In a matter of this kind, which comes down ultimately to the human element, the activating forces are undoubtedly psychological.

The Near East is acutely conscious of its pioneering role in the cultural history of the world. Such an awareness can be a two-edged instrument. It may mean added confidence, but it may also mean self-consciousness. When the region was a cultural and spiritual center, and especially at such times as it enjoyed political supremacy, its relations with the world outside gave little cause for inner strain. But in its relatively static intervals, when other regions forged ahead, the remembrance of past glories made its current dependence a bitter pill to swallow. Four centuries of Turkish dominance and neglect left the Near East far behind the West in social, economic, and scientific progress. The impact of two world wars has done one thing primarily: it has restored the proper geographic balance. But under this restored balance only the physical rapport between the East and the West has been fully reëstablished; not the free cultural interplay of their respective civilizations. For tradition has stepped in to interpose a solid block.

The Near East has been straining to close up the existing

gap between itself and the West. It has sought to do so practically overnight. Western concepts and Western institutions have been brought in wholesale. They have been put to work hastily, with little time allowed them to become acclimated to the local soil. Instead of the needed adaptation, keyed to absorptive capacity, there has been indiscriminate imitation. Inevitably, the whole process has proved too superficial to strike root. Superficiality has become the curse of the modern Near East. Further, native tradition, a growth rich and long established, had not been reckoned with sufficiently. It was not to be shoved aside without ceremony by a mere interloper. And so, instead of a meaningful blending of native and imported elements, we find in the Near East an incongruous association of the two, which often leads to serious collisions between them. The modern Near East cannot do without the West; it is far less able to dispense with its own age-old traditions. Where the dilemma cannot be resolved immediately, tradition wins out and reaction against the West sets in. But because the need for bridging the gap persists, and shotgun solutions promptly prove their inherent fallacy, failure is made to masquerade as virtue: the Western innovations failed because the native institutions were superior. Yet inwardly the Near East goes on envying the West with a growing sense of its own inferiority. The block which tradition has interposed is thus essentially a psychological block.

The psychological overtones in the present meeting of the Near East and the West are sharpened by a further factor. The chief custodians of Near East tradition today are the Arabs. But they are not its only custodians. The Kurds of Iraq and Syria have their own version of the region's ancient heritage. The Jews of Palestine have theirs. Nor is that heritage uniform among the Arabs themselves. The Christian Arab groups of Lebanon, Syria, and Palestine, and the Copts of Egypt, differ from the Muslim Arabs in regard to religious tradition, a most significant cultural feature in the Near East. Other Christian groups in Arab lands, notably the Armenians, the Chaldeans of Iraq, and the Nestorians (Assyrians), are marked off from the neighboring Muslim groups by their employment of separate languages or dialects, apart from religious differences. These ethnic and religious minorities aggravate the situation in that, by testifying to the existing divisions, they introduce a shrill and self-conscious note into the resulting protestations of unity.

Moreover, the Muslim Arab's lack of national self-assurance shows itself in yet another way. His backward political status under Turkish rule led him to seek solace in the much more gratifying record of the antecedent Arab caliphates. But he does not stop there. Because the Near East is overwhelmingly Arab today, this condition is naively extended to cover just about all of the region's history. The Arabs, he reasons, are Semites. So were also the Canaanites and Arameans, and the Babylonians and Assyrians. All had come originally from Arabia proper. They were, in short, Arabs. The whole contribution of the Near East to world culture was thus the work of Arabs. In this unsophisticated process the reasoner is aided and abetted by the eclecticism of the Qur'an. Jesus, Elijah, and Moses were—in effect—Arab prophets. And Abraham was the revered patriarch of the nation. Hence his tomb in Hebron is hallowed ground which must not be profaned by the presence of unbelievers. If you are still unconvinced, modern Arab scholars will adduce you etymologies which will settle the point beyond any shadow of doubt. They have done so in otherwise competent studies on the history of the Arabs, as if that history did not speak for itself, without any need for the compilers to go so far afield—and astray.

In such a climate will flourish many strange ideas, strange not because they are fantastic but rather because they are based on half-truths or wish-fulfillment. Iraq views herself as the lineal heir of an ancient state the integrity of whose borders is traced back to remotest antiquity. But Babylonia and Assyria and their respective predecessors were no less hostile toward one another than are the Arabs and Kurds of today. On the eve of the San Francisco Conference the Egyptian press was hopeful that Arabic would be recognized as one of the official languages of the conference. It was also stated that Egypt would present a project for future world organization which would surpass anything heretofore suggested. The opinion was expressed likewise that Egypt would be a natural place for future international meetings and that Cairo or Alexandria might well replace Geneva as an international center. There is, of course, nothing illogical about any of these suggestions emanating from Egypt. But the underlying feeling of local superiority is disquieting. It suggests the nervousness of one whistling in the dark.

On the surface, then, the general atmosphere in the Arab states is one of unreality. The governmental structure is shaky because it was put together out of imported parts, by artisans having a very superficial acquaintance with the design and materials. At the same time, the native materials and designs and skills are being squandered, either through disuse or hybridization, instead of being husbanded through unhurried selection and integration. The resulting sense of insecurity is compensated for by an inflated feeling of political self-importance, which is enhanced by a variety of circumstances: the heady experience of new-born freedom, a slanted and subjective interpretation of the past, and the ingratiating tactics of the interested foreign powers.

Not far from the surface, however, there are very different stirrings: a desire for the indigenous product, deeply rooted in the soil; an impatience with the superficial manifestations of freedom while the people remain helpless pawns in the hands of incompetent local leaders and powerful foreign interests; a genuine will to coöperate with the outside world on an honorable basis, and a conviction that the Near East has the ability and the moral fiber to take its place as a full-fledged and valued partner in such a common enterprise; and with it all, a sense of despair of ever attaining this goal. These subsurface trends may well coalesce into a groundswell. It would be futile to speculate at this time about its possible ultimate effect.

The region needs resolute yet statesmanlike leadership, far-seeing and unselfish. Thus far it has pitifully lacked such leadership. Provincial overlords have not had the stature or the freedom from parochial ties to commend them to the Arab world as a whole. Ibn Saud's fanatical sectarianism has inspired fears in the various heterodox communities. At present he is an old and ailing man and his own state faces a period of political uncertainty and social insecurity. Faruq has against him his inexperience, his narrow local interests, and—above all—his non-Arab family background. The Hashimite princes have done little to remove the prevailing suspicion that they are intent primarily on their personal aggrandizement. Iraq's Faysal I alone had the requisite attributes of background, personality, training, and wisdom to make him acceptable as the helmsman of the Arab Near East. But his premature death cut short his career of service at a time when he was needed most. The one prospect is that the present crisis will bring up leadership from the ranks and introduce direction to a nation plagued by illusions and drift.

Of the many needs which confront the Arab world today, and will test the Arab leadership tomorrow, the most urgent need beyond doubt is a way to come to terms with the West, psychologically and culturally as well as politically and economically. Tradition and Westernization must be made to coöperate instead of working at cross-purposes, as heretofore. A Westernized Arab who turns his back on tradition is soon revealed as neither Western nor Arab. He has forfeited his own priceless heritage, while assimilating only the outward forms instead of the inner content of the other culture. The dinner jacket which he has put on in place of his flowing robes often proves to be a straitjacket. Freed from its encumbrance at last, the wearer is apt to retain a phobia toward all else that came from the same quarter. And so he proceeds to discard the useful together with the needless.

Most of the new Arab states have adopted Western constitutions, codes, and techniques without an appreciation of the mental processes that went into their creation. The states have not been operating well. Corruption is rampant, social inequalities have been accentuated, and the unity that was achieved in 1944 derived from a negative impulse and failed to inspire genuine confidence. The present leadership shifts the blame for a situation which its own incompetence has brought on—at least in part—to the source of the institutions that fell short of a panacea—the West. But it adheres to one peculiarly Western concept—under an artificial native pedigree, to be sure—nationalism, a concept raised into an obsessive force by the local incongruities which persist. The resulting reaction goes to one of two extremes. On the one hand is religious fundamentalism, centered mainly in the older generation. The Egyptian "Muslim Brotherhood" (*Ikhwan al-Muslimun*) is one example; attacks on the women of Damascus attending a cinema, on the ground that they had fallen for a foreign allure, are another instance. These groups subscribe to nationalism, but with them it is the old pan-Islamic nationalism which they somehow confuse naively with pan-Arabism, and equate, with no greater clarity, with the genuine socio-political basis of Islam.

On the other hand you have the political extremists who draw their strength from among the youth of the region. In this category you find "Young Egypt" (*Misr al-Fatat*)—

whose members planned and executed the assassination of Prime Minister Ahmad Mahir, in February 1945, because at the eleventh hour he had gone through the motions of placing his country on the side of the Allies; the Syrian People's Party; and the paramilitary youth organization (*futuwwah*), which flourished in Iraq until recently and brought its leaders medals from Hitler and Cabinet posts at home; lately this organization has been planted in Syria and Palestine. All these youth groups share a contempt for democracy and its Western sponsors and a predilection for activist, if not totalitarian, ideologies and techniques. On the fringe which they occupy they rub shoulders with, but maintain a distrust for, the compact communist groups which are animated by a like hostility toward the democracies. The fanatical nationalism of the activists and the slanted internationalism of the local communists yield thus mutually suspicious neighbors, who join occasionally in an uneasy partnership against the constituted authorities.

Between these extremes is crowded the large majority of the population—undecided, groping, and as yet voiceless. A small element among them can at least give a name to the things they want and the things they fear. They know that something is radically wrong, but they are uncertain as to which way they should turn. They want direction. Vaguely they realize that their own latent strength must be made articulate. They sense also that the tempo of the Near East must be synchronized with that of the West. They want friendly assistance but would balk at paternalism as much as at outright exploitation. Their admiration for the scientific and technical excellence of the West does not blind them to the fact that outsiders too need to strike a healthy balance between their institutions and their practices. Accordingly, they address the West without the strident overtones of their present leaders or of the elements on the fringe. They feel that they have much to learn and acquire, but they know also that they have something to offer in return. It is genuine coöperation they seek, and it is this kind of co-operation which the West must be prepared to offer them. Without it the Near East cannot achieve strength and stability. And if the Near East remains weak and unstable, the world which camps at its gates cannot enjoy peace and security.

2. COMMUNAL QUESTIONS

Today, however, the Arab lands are as yet a long distance away from their goal of strength and stability. Their social structure is top-heavy, and such essential instruments of society as public health and education, or press and public opinion, are backward even by minimum Western standards. It is this unconcealable backwardness that shocks the ordinary visitor to the Near East. Wendell Willkie carried away with him a strong impression of this shock, and when Arabs read about it later they found it extremely difficult to forgive the author for telling the truth. What the casual visitor fails to get, on the other hand, is the inherent richness that is veiled by the unprepossessing, even squalid, exterior. The Arabs of the Hadramawt, for instance—as was pointed out by one of the greatest European masters of Arab lore—can leave their singularly barren and forbidding homeland with but a few rags and proceed on some primitive freighter to India or Malaya. It does not take them many years to establish themselves in their adopted land and to make full use of their latent abilities. They will construct cosmopolitan hotels or run influential newspapers. Having made their mark, some will come back to their native desert and build roads and swimming pools. In brief, the present-day Arab, as an individual, is but a short stride removed from modernism, because he is the product of a mature yet vigorous culture. A somnolent interlude in his comings and goings should not deceive one as to the life and energy which constantly stir inside.

Yet much of this inner vigor and ability is prevented from emerging to the fore by the medieval social structure which still prevails in the Near East. Abject poverty is the melancholy lot of not less than three fourths of the population. The cultivator who harks back to his nomadic past, or the shepherd who has remained semi-nomadic, may not have quite the same attachment to land and property that characterize agricultural communities elsewhere. But he has the same basic needs which cannot long go unfulfilled without lowering the level of the community as a whole. Yet the fellah continues working, under trying climatic conditions, for an absentee landlord who often pays him barely enough to make three meals a day out of a flap or two of barley bread, with rice and vegetables a rarity and mutton a semi-annual luxury. This is not the norm to be sure, but the average standard of living is not appreciably higher. Small wonder, therefore, that the average Arab's social and political horizon does not extend beyond his village or town and seldom includes his particular country, let alone the neighboring lands. The relatively favored one fourth of the population are worldly by comparison. But they in turn are too engrossed with the domestic political and economic problems to have much time for regional, not to mention international, affairs. And they pay no more than lip service to the basic needs of the half-starved majority. There is as yet no labor movement to speak of, which might wage a war against serfdom. And so, when the outside world hears today about the desires and aspirations of the Arab world—always excepting Palestine—the voice that is heard is the voice of a small minority—or rather that of the thin layer of the well-to-do which overlies that minority. The rest can be easily incited to disorder, and often are. Their action, however, is not so much the result of an inner impulse as it is the reflection of the will—or the confusion—of their masters.

Some improvement in these social and economic conditions in the Arab Near East is bound to take place as the general level of the communal services is gradually raised. But here, too, the distances to be covered are prodigious. Let us take, for instance, the question of public health. The region is still described as disease-ridden, and rightly so, although gratifying progress has already been made in this field, thanks primarily to the assistance and enterprise of Westerners. But the bulk of the native population still suffers from eye disease, is feverish with malaria, and carries permanent scars of the same widespread affliction which perverse provincial pride insists on calling the Baghdad boil, the Aleppo or the Jericho button, and the like. Dysentery, typhoid, and tuberculosis take a heavy toll. At times of particular economic stress, or when government attention is relaxed for one reason or another, some of these plagues result in a staggering rate of mortality. Thus in 1943–44 malaria alone took hundreds of thousands of Egyptian lives. Infant mortality in Iraq was as high as 318 per thousand in 1927–33, dropping to 227 in 1938–41. In Egypt the figures for comparable periods were 224 and 203 respectively. This contrasts with 173.8 for India, 141.8 for Latin America, and 62.6 for the United States and Canada.

In literacy and general education the situation is roughly similar to that which obtains in regard to public health. Considerable progress has been made since the end of the First World War, when the spread of Western political and economic interests brought the region within closer view of other systems and methods. Yet there was so much lost ground to be made up at the start that many additional years will be required before minimum Western standards can be approached. In few Arab states can the level of literacy among Muslims over the age of seven be said to exceed

25 per cent. For the most part it is lower, especially in Saudi Arabia and the Yemen. Much of the schooling is stopped somewhere in the lower grades. Secondary education is proportionately rare and colleges are few. Except for a single theological college, Saudi Arabia has no real institution of higher learning; the whole educational system of the Yemen is primitive and minute. Conditions are more promising in those countries which have been exposed to foreign influence. The French have done very substantial work in the Levant, and the influence of the American University of Bayrut is felt among circles scattered throughout the Near East. Several Western countries have been active in cultural ways in Egypt and Palestine. Iraq has benefited from her American secondary schools. Yet all this activity is confined to a very small segment of the community. Iraq, for example, has not a single university, although sundry specialized colleges have been established. Egypt has several institutions listed as universities—aside from her celebrated traditional center of al-Azhar; but the general work of these institutions cannot in all candor be termed first rate. Allowing for the difficulties which each of these relatively new states has had to face, the conclusion is nevertheless inescapable that none of them has made an adequate investment in the health and intellectual progress of its people. Furthermore, politics has invaded the local schools to a degree that is plainly alarming. If students of a medical college stay away on strike for whole semesters, for political reasons, they are just as likely as not to receive full credit for the time they have lost, once their strike has been settled. No one will compensate the future patients for the losses which they are certain to suffer as a result of such curious doings.

Nor is domestic politics alone a retarding influence in the progress of contemporary Arab society. Much as the Arab states may appreciate the West's superiority in certain aspects of this broad field, they remain suspicious of the outsiders' motives in extending them the necessary assistance. They remember that French culture—which they continue to admire—was used as the spearhead of French political penetration, and they are now doubly shy of welcoming other foreign aid. Not all of this myopia—whether rooted in nationalism or religion—can be brushed aside as utterly baseless. But a way must be found to reach common neutral ground. Today local standards are far behind those of the West. This is true not only of the culturally inhospitable areas of the peninsula but also of such a place as Palestine, where Western usages and methods have been put into intensive operation by the Jews. For while the Muslim Arabs of Palestine may be ahead of the population of the neighboring countries in regard to health and living standards, they still are far apart, on the same counts, from the Jewish community in Palestine. The report of the Anglo-American Committee of Inquiry paid considerable attention to this sharp disparity. And in so doing it placed the accent on the basic problem of communal inequality, between Arabs and Jews and between the Near East and the West, which romancers at home and abroad are all too apt to gloss over. This gap must be narrowed before the other problems can be attacked with any prospect of enduring success.

Just as Arab politics, owing to its neglect of fundamental domestic issues, is not a true mirror of the region's many problems, so likewise the Arabic press fails to provide a representative index of the thoughts and feelings of the people. For the local press is keyed to politics in a most single-minded fashion. And because Arab politics is dominated by party leaders rather than by the political parties, the average newspaper will usually be the personal mouthpiece of the given politician. There are of course exceptions. The two leftist papers of Iraq and Lebanon respectively were, when not banned, stable as to ideology and did not idealize personalities. Incidentally, these two were also among the best-edited dailies in the whole region. Parochial papers, especially in the Levant, favor their particular ecclesiastical interests. Christian Arabs own and edit many of the newspapers throughout the Near East, far out of proportion to the actual number of the Christian elements within the Arab community. This is due primarily to the long history of contacts between these groups and the West, which gave them an early acquaintance with the European press.

The number of daily and periodical publications ranges from one in the Yemen to a dozen or more in the Levant and Iraq. In the last-named instances the diversity of the local minority and sectarian interests accounts for a corresponding variety of newspapers. By the same token the whole of Saudi Arabia boasted until recently but a single daily. A second was added only at the beginning of 1946. As regards circulation, Egypt has one Arabic paper which prints about 100,000 copies daily and another which averages about 25,000. These two can lay claim to a show of political independence, always however within the limits of the ruthless censorship which prevails throughout the Near East. The other dailies run from a few hundred to 3,000 copies. A paper suppressed one day may reappear the next day under a different masthead. This is why the character and orientation of the press are difficult to follow—most notably so in Iraq.

In these circumstances public opinion in the Arab Near East cannot readily be gauged from its press. Nor does the press in turn contribute its due share to the enlightenment of the public. It exercises an inflammatory and disruptive rather than a moderating influence. Our own *Time* magazine would probably characterize the Arabic press as hyperthyroid. Except for Egypt, at any rate, the average Arabic newspaper lacks the devotion to genuine public service which other countries expect of their news organs, and frequently get. The impression of volatility and constant excitement which is thus conveyed reflects in considerable measure the instability and lack of balance which pervade social life and institutions in the Arab Near East.

3. QUESTIONS OF GOVERNMENT

It remains to round out this discussion with a few essential details concerning governmental machinery and practices in the Arab countries. In this respect the differences among the several states are as marked as the unbalance of the social and economic structure within each individual state. For we find here two absolute monarchies, three limited constitutional monarchies, two republics—one of which just suspended its democratic institutions—not to mention a whole array of petty sultanates and shaykhdoms. There is, of course, a corresponding disparity in executive and legislative functions. The judicial field, moreover, reflects the underlying depth in social and historical stratification. Religious law operates alongside tribal law, national courts coexist with mixed tribunals, and the civil codes in general—in so far as their operation is not circumscribed or altogether excluded by traditional law—have a French framework in some instances and an English framework in others, while important Ottoman features have survived throughout. It is plain, therefore, that no branch of government in the Arab Near East is in more urgent need of integration and reform than its judicial machinery.

Saudi Arabia is an absolute monarchy which remains split into the two kingdoms of Najd and the Hijaz. A constitution applicable to the whole population is yet to be introduced. The King's eldest son and heir apparent is Viceroy of Najd, while another son, who combines the functions of President of the Council of Ministers, Minister of Foreign Affairs, and Minister of Interior, also acts as Viceroy of the Hijaz during his father's absence. The Law of Islam is the common law of the land and is administered by the religious courts. That this can lead to unfortunate international complications was demonstrated afresh a few years ago. An Iranian pilgrim, of the Shi'ah sect, was overtaken by sickness at a particularly solemn stage of the annual celebration at Mecca. The religious court judged this to be a case of intentional desecration, and the poor wretch was executed. Whereupon the Iranian Government, incensed by what it regarded as an outrage not only against one of its nationals but also against the whole Shi'ah community, broke off diplomatic relations with Saudi Arabia and placed a ban on further pilgrimages to Mecca by its citizens.

The Yemen is another absolute monarchy of patriarchal character. But the puritanical theocratic system of the Wahhabis is rivaled in this case by the no less fanatical sectarian theocracy of the Zaydis. The two countries are thus centuries behind their sister states in political progress. At the same time, however, they are poles apart from each other in the particular orientation of their respective religious doctrines.

Egypt is a constitutional hereditary monarchy. This does not mean, however, that the King "reigns but does not rule." Actually he does a little of both. For he acts through the Council of Ministers, which he appoints and has the right to dismiss—a right that has frequently been exercised. Yet the Council is responsible to Parliament, which is bicameral. Of the Senate, two fifths of its members are appointed by the King and the remainder are elected for periods of ten years. The minimum required age of senators is forty. In 1946 the Senate comprised 147 members. The Chamber of Deputies is an elected body whose members must be at least thirty years of age. Its 1946 membership was 264. The vote for both houses is based on universal male suffrage. Citizens must be twenty-one or over to vote for deputies, and at least twenty-five to vote for senators. The judicial branch consists of National Courts, Mixed Tribunals—which were

modified after the abolition of the so-called Capitulations
in 1937 and are in turn to be abolished in 1949; and the
National Courts of Personal Status, the outgrowth of the
Ottoman Millet System whereby the various religious communities enjoyed a measure of cultural autonomy on a non-
territorial basis. In line with immemorial Near East tradition,
a sense of justice is strongly developed in Egypt as well as
in the other Arab countries. The difficulties in its application
are due largely to the coexistence of several heterogeneous
judicial systems. Furthermore, the prevailing social and political unbalance often makes the judges susceptible to outside influences and pressures of a personal, administrative,
or religious nature, and—not least of all—to the pressure of
excitable public opinion. It is a situation which characterizes
all the more advanced Arab states, that is, those which have
not allowed the administration of justice to remain the
exclusive prerogative of religious courts.

Iraq is a constitutional monarchy, like Egypt. The instrument which limits the power of the Crown and provides
for a democratic government is the Organic Law of 1924.
The legislature is again bicameral, but the entire Senate,
which consists of twenty members, is appointed by the
Crown, each of the "elders" to serve for eight years. Deputies are elected by secret ballot, on the old Ottoman system
of primary and secondary elections, in proportion of one
to every 20,000 of the male population of the country; the
voters must be male and over twenty years of age. Non-
Islamic minorities are required to be represented in the
Chamber. All bills must have the approval of the Crown
and of both Houses of Parliament. Should one of the legislative branches reject a bill, it is then considered in a joint
session which can pass it by a two-thirds majority. The
normal duration of a Parliament is four years. As regards
the administration of justice, conflicts arise first as between
civil and religious law, and second as between the applica-

tion of these laws to settled areas on the one hand and to tribal territories on the other. The special regulations for the tribes have made for frequent evasions of justice; non-tribesmen often seek to prove tribal connections in order to escape punishment for crimes which would not be con-doned by the normal courts. Equalization of treatment under the law is thus one of Iraq's pressing problems.

The new constitution of Transjordan (the name of the country was changed to Jordan in 1949), which became effective on March 1, 1947, vests legislative power "in the National Assembly and the King." The Assembly is bicam-eral. All members of the Senate are appointed by the King, whereas members of the Chamber of Deputies are elected for four years. The King has absolute veto over all legisla-tion. He appoints all members of the Council of Ministers, who are answerable solely to him and not to the National Assembly. In practice an effort is made to obtain representa-tion for the four major elements in the population of the country—settled Muslim Arabs, Beduins, Circassians, and Christian Arabs. But the freedoms which the constitution guarantees in principle are often violated in application.

Both Levant States are parliamentary republics, but they differ from each other in a number of details pertaining to governmental machinery. Lebanon operates on the basis of her constitution of 1926 as subsequently amended on several occasions. Her President is elected for a term of six years by an absolute majority of the legislative body, which is unicameral. Theoretically he may be either Christian or Muslim, but in practice a Muslim would stand little chance of being elected. On the other hand, the Prime Minister is traditionally a Muslim. Deputies are elected for terms of four years by universal male suffrage. Any male citizen of twenty-five or over is eligible. The distribution of deputies is on a confessional basis: thirty Christians and twenty-five Muslims.

The Syrian Republic underwent a coup d'état in March 1949. Until then it had operated on the basis of the constitution of 1930. The President was elected for a five-year term by an absolute majority of the unicameral Chamber of Deputies. He had to be a Muslim, but the Prime Minister could be Muslim or Christian, and a Christian served indeed in that capacity in 1945. The number of Cabinet posts was limited to seven. A two-thirds vote of the Chamber of Deputies was needed for any revision of the constitution. The kind of government that will emerge in Syria after the regime of Chief of State Husni Za'im cannot as yet be foreseen. The country's formal democratic institutions had evidently failed to take root.

Judicial administration in the Levant States is roughly analogous to that of Iraq. Authority is divided between civil and religious courts. Furthermore, there is the same problem in Syria—with her extensive desert areas to the east—in regard to tribal regulations and their occasional abuses, that has been met with already in Iraq. Nor has Syria been any more successful than Iraq in instituting the needed reforms. Any attempt in this direction brings a threat of revolt in the desert.

A description of government in the former British mandated territory of Palestine must await final allocation of its Arab portions. The State of Israel, it should be mentioned in passing at this time, established a Provisional Government on May 14, 1949. The elections of January 1949 gave Israel her Constituent Assembly (Kneset) as provided by the new republic's proclamation of independence.

Throughout the Arab Near East the machinery of government is handicapped as much by the lack of qualified personnel as it is by the various shortcomings in the existing instruments of government. Lack of sufficient time in which these states have been able to practice self-rule is mainly responsible, of course, for this situation. As a result, Cabinet posts have been filled time and again from among the same small ruling circle. New ministries seldom mean much more than reshuffles of the old. The upshot is a sense of confidence on the part of the members of these small and exclusive clubs that they are sure to hold on to some post of Cabinet rank. Being thus relatively secure in their positions, they do not have the same sense of responsibility that ordinarily goes with the need to make good in high office. The public, quickly disabused of its sanguine hopes which the splendid promises of the incumbents had stirred up, soon loses interest and becomes skeptical, or—what is worse—altogether apathetic. Such voices as are raised in opposition proceed to place the blame on the institutions rather than the functionaries. Soon the cry is heard that all the domestic ills are due to new-fangled foreign practices and that the parliamentary system is unsuited to local requirements. The fact is that the system under attack has not had a fair trial and that the institutions cannot become acclimated nor the personnel be developed overnight. Occasionally the opposition may be vigorous enough to turn its guns against the entrenched leaders. This happened, for instance, in the case of the *Black Book* which Makram Ubayd got out in 1943 in his campaign against Nahhas Pasha, who was then Prime Minister of Egypt. But even in that instance the drive was coupled with a bitter attack against Britain, whose pawn Nahhas was accused of being.

Conditions become progressively more discouraging as you go down the line of the governmental hierarchy. Nepotism and corruption are no strangers to deputies. If they reach lower depths here than elsewhere it is largely because of public apathy and the failure of the press to distinguish between special interests and the basic interests of the given country and the region as a whole. Another negative factor is the economic insecurity which goes hand in hand with the lack of tenure that characterizes administrative posts.

Ministerial reshuffles may be followed by large-scale dismissals. This insecurity is particularly evident among minority groups, usually the first to feel the effects of the frequent changes in governmental policy. The Shi'ites and the Kurds as well as the Christians and the Jews of Iraq have had many occasions for complaints and fears, and so also have the Copts of Egypt. The dominant Sunni elements in both these countries have not hesitated to raise religious or ethnic issues if by so doing they could place themselves in a position to further their own private ends. Such situations, to be sure, are not peculiar to the Near East. As is true, however, of so many other political and social aspects of the region's life, these matters are apt to be brought into sharper relief in the Near East than elsewhere.

4. QUESTIONS OF THE FUTURE

Thus, the picture which has been drawn of the present state and temper of Arab society and of its instruments of government is not an encouraging one. It leaves little room for optimism in so far as the immediate future is concerned. As has been indicated, the local states are held back by serious social, economic, and administrative weaknesses. The political superstructure is badly out of balance. Between the individual countries there is an enormous disparity in the tempo of progress, and the region as a whole lags critically behind the Western powers. Comparisons of this sort are always invidious and they may often be misleading. Nevertheless, they can not be avoided, for the simple reason that the Near East is linked to the West by many intricate ties. These can be strained, however, to the point of grave danger by local anti-foreignism as much as by outside imperialism—political, economic, or even spiritual. The inevitable contacts between the Near East and the West may lead to ultimate agreements or to conflicts; conflicts among the local states, or between the region and the interested outside powers, or again among these outside interests. Whether the agreements are to neutralize the conflicts, supersede them, or be overpowered by them will depend in large measure on the degree of strength and genuine independence which the Near East can achieve. Basic to this consideration is the question of Arab unity. For a fragmented and splintered Near East cannot hope to hold its own with the West.

That the region is not united as yet—in spite of the efforts of the Arab League and its solidified stand against Zionism—is clear from the very divergence in the structure and machinery of government within the region. We have seen that the range extends all the way from the most pronounced form of absolute monarchy, in Arabia, to the parliamentary republics of the Levant. Religious differences add their disruptive accent—differences not only between Muslims and the assorted religious minorities, but also those between the individual Muslim sects. Provincial jealousies and grudges are a further and ever-present divisive element, however toned down it may become at any given time.

Another threat to the future of the Near East is implicit in the superficial manner in which Western institutions and ideas have been taken over without due regard for the demands of the indigenous culture. Such concepts as democracy, modernization, and nationalism can have a meaning only if adapted to local molds. But democracy in the Yemen, for instance, is something very different from what the United States or Britain understands by this term—and, on the whole, manages to put into practice. Nor is Arab nationalism strictly comparable to, say, Swiss nationalism, or even to the nationalism of the Yugoslavs. For on the surface Arab nationalism appears to be ethnic, yet its mainspring is religious, at one with the hardy socio-political core of Islam.

Basically it is the same force which prompts the Muslims of India to oppose with violence and bloodshed a united India, because under it the Muslims might be outweighed politically by an ethnically similar but otherwise heterodox majority. In other words, pan-Arabism is in reality an aspect of pan-Islamism, and the failure of the leaders to integrate the two movements has produced many internal conflicts and is certain to sow others. Church, state, and nation cannot be made mutually interchangeable for some purposes and distinctive for other needs. Were the Muslim Arabs of the Near East in the minority, they would oppose in all probability the creation of a pan-Arab state dominated by Christian Arabs.

When you discuss such matters with thoughtful Arabs and ask them whether genuine independence is feasible under such circumstances, they invariably cite some Balkan or Latin-American country in an effort to prove that their own has at least a like capacity for independence. Should you then venture to suggest that Switzerland or Sweden might offer better standards for small states to emulate, you will probably precipitate an embarrassing pause after which a change of subject is definitely in order. Actually, the majority of literate Arabs—not to mention the blissfully ignorant who may ask you to name the Turkish province of which America is a part—believe that their particular country is really more advanced than any Western state. The record of the past and confidence in the future have all but obliterated the reality of the present. Too many seek sustenance in mirages and illusions. And by so doing they present an easier target for Western exploitation. Genuine independence of the Near East—as opposed to relatively hollow forms—should in final analysis be a primary concern of the Western powers as a guarantee of world peace and security. The assistance of these powers is needed and should be extended by them as a matter of enlightened self-interest.

Thus far, however, their conflicting unilateral interests have not stimulated progress in the Near East in a way which might enable the region to take its place as a full-fledged partner, and a further element of balance, in a common enterprise on a global scale.

8. Problems of the Foreign Powers

1. GENERAL PATTERN

It is one of the characteristics of this post-war era that no major power, nor any power which aspires to a major role in international affairs, can today afford to dispense with an active interest in the Near East. The reasons for so decided an orientation in world politics may not always be clear, beyond sundry and stock details, to the respective policy-making bodies, let alone the general public. The moves of more than one government, relative to the region in general and the Arab world in particular, have at times left room for doubt as to whether those in charge had thought through all the implications. It came therefore as no surprise that, at the height of the controversy over the Anglo-American oil discussions in 1944, official Washington was repeating this revealing statement: "We don't quite know what our interests in the Near East are. But they are growing."

Actually, there is nothing very strange about the recent spread of interest in the Near East. The region has always enjoyed considerable attention from cultural and spiritual circles. Neither have approaches of a more worldly sort been lacking in various periods of history, and particularly in recent times. What we are witnessing today, however, is an incomparably greater and more widespread appreciation of the vital place of the Near East in the global balance of things than has ever been possible in the past. And the reasons for this stepped-up cultivation of an essentially old field are not far to seek.

That various conquerors, old and recent, found themselves gravitating toward the Near East in their quest for world power is a familiar fact. It is equally common knowledge that the magnet which drew all of them—the empire builders of long ago as well as the pretenders of yesterday—was the region's position on the face of the globe—a central bridge linking the three continents of the Old World. The relatively recent and man-made waterway of the Suez doubled the capacity of that bridge and multiplied its general significance by an incalculable factor. It was left to the twentieth century to succumb to the spell of the region's oil. Oil, in turn, by powering aerial progress and shrinking the earth's distances, helped to draw attention to yet another local attraction; namely, that no round-the-world, all-weather air route is possible without the use of Near East bases. Here, then, you find concentrated the full complement of geostrategic requirements: central strategic location; convergence of land, water, and air routes; and vital natural resources. But geostrategic thinking is a very new thing, the contribution of an era which has experienced two world wars within the span of a single generation. There has scarcely been enough time to accustom ourselves to the new prominence of the Near East in the light of present global conditions.

It is idle to speculate, as is often done, which of these elements in the region's renewed prominence is the most important: location, communications, or oil? Is the United States interested in the oil alone, while Russia wants oil plus warm-water ports, and Britain all three of these factors and such added political and economic advantages as might be included? The fact is that none of these precious articles is stored in a separate locker, each by itself; they are all interlocked. They cannot be readily sundered. Moreover, these things are not found in a vacuum, but are instead in the physical possession of various local states and territories. They must, therefore, be obtained at a price.

The Near East, as a prime target for international interests, has to be viewed, accordingly, from two angles. One is outside competition for a share in the region's manifold resources; and the other is the local ability to obtain an equitable return. So long as world attention was centered— or dissipated—elsewhere, and the peoples of the Near East were dormant, inarticulate, and all but defenseless, the region was an easy mark for outside exploitation. Today the spotlight plays on the region. Its population has awakened and become vociferous. And the very size of its new-found riches precludes unilateral action by any given power.

Now the indicated intensity of outside competition for the various advantages which environment has bestowed on the Near East adds a further reason why no major power can today afford to ignore this part of the world. This particular additional interest does not derive exclusively from location, oil, or communications; although based on all three, it yet transcends them all. It is, in essence, the interest in world peace and security. Because the region has so singularly been favored by geography, it must pay for the dubious distinction of being the meeting ground of world powers. And because the conflicting needs of these powers run head on into one another in this sector above all others, new wars will be bred here or peace safeguarded. Since wars, like peace, have become indivisible, no country whose lot it is to be a major factor in world affairs can be so improvident as to stay away from this sensitive testing ground and leave to others the power to determine whether it shall be peace or war. Participation in the doings of the Near East has come to be the equivalent of a seat on the world's geostrategic exchange.

The certain prospect of intensified international rivalry

carries with it danger as well as promise for the local population. The danger is that of a global battleground. And the promise is contained in the checks and balances inherent in a situation where so much is at stake. Disagreement among the rival outside powers will benefit the local states temporarily, but such gains can be enjoyed only on borrowed time. Agreement, on the other hand, would be reflected in steady local progress—although on a more measured, less spectacular, scale than the incidental dividends from unbridled competition. Furthermore, a region thus grown stronger and more prosperous would in itself constitute an added check and balance. The greatest threat in the contest over the Near East, as it is now shaping up, lies in a possible reduction of the number of contestants to two. A conflict between two powerful antagonists may degenerate into a private brawl with no holds barred. But three or four evenly balanced rivals meeting on common ground have among them all the elements that make for a society which must coöperate in order to survive.

The attitude of the local population is thus the last major compulsive interest which the foreign powers must bear in mind when operating on Near East soil. Without a wise policy toward the hosts you will not be able to enjoy—openly and above-board—the use of their premises: location, communications, and oil; and you may lose your vote at the table at which world peace and security will be weighed. Such a policy cannot be improvised. It must be based on a painstaking analysis of all the relevant material. And the material is extensive and complex. The legacy of history in this instance is just as embarrassing in its richness as that of geography. The two together have ordained the region to be the main proving ground of the new world order. It is for this reason that the peoples of the Near East are a factor in the international balance today, and may become a more important factor tomorrow.

The principal local group are the Arabs. Because of their commanding position in the community of Islam—here is one example of history refusing to be dealt out—the Arabs cannot be treated in precisely the same way as might be another people of similar size and strength but without comparable socio-political ties outside its own territory. Britain may overestimate, or else choose to overstate, the bearing of her Arab policy on other Islamic groups; but she cannot omit to weigh the matter with the greatest care.

Aside from the Arabs, history has deposited in the Near East a bewildering array of ethnic and religious minorities. They can be used, and have frequently been used, as instruments of policy on the part of foreign powers. France, Britain, Russia, as well as other powers, have not overlooked this opening. These scattered elements will play their part— however passive as a rule—in the future, as they have done in the past. Their role will increase in prominence if conflicts prevail over agreements. Hence a policy regarding the minorities cannot be left to chance any more than a policy concerning the Muslim Arab majority. Thus the whole question of the human factor in the region is an important feature of the broader pattern which underlies the problem of foreign interests in the Near East.

[The account which follows should have been expanded in view of the decisive changes that have taken place since its original writing—notably the partition of India and the emergence of Israel. But limitations beyond the writer's control made a fuller revision impossible. Parts of this and the next chapter are thus dated, the date being 1946. Nevertheless, it is hoped that the statement will serve as a background for what has happened since. Furthermore, policies that seemed slated for discard in 1947 are still largely in force today, although in modified form. A survey and analysis of the most recent events will be given in a later chapter.]

2. BRITISH INTERESTS IN THE NEAR EAST

Among all the outside powers, Britain is unquestionably the one with the greatest individual stake in the Near East. True, her active interest in the region dates no farther back than that of several other foreign countries. But while the others have been intermittent, the British interest has remained continuous and, what is more, has been mounting progressively for over a century and a half. To protect this stake, Britain strained her energies to the utmost in two world wars—both of which were fought in large part on Near East soil and for Near East objectives. To the same end she has been obliged to put down various local uprisings, expend much treasure, weather innumerable political storms —locally as well as at home—and grapple with ceaseless social and economic problems of regional origin. Perhaps the best measure of the region's importance to Britain is this: both the United States and Russia can, of course, maintain themselves as great powers without obtaining a solid foothold in the Near East. Britain obviously cannot. And the fact that Britain must stay on as a Near East power in order to survive as a world power accounts in last analysis for the increased interest in the region on the part of the other major nations.

Briefly, the Near East is to Britain both a means to an end and an end in itself. It is a means to an end primarily because it constitutes a zone of communications between the Mediterranean and the Indian Ocean, and hence the key to the smooth and unimpeded operation of the British Empire life line. This key position is by no means limited to the Suez Canal. That waterway must now share its formerly unrivaled importance with air and overland lines, both of which converge in the Near East. Moreover, the freedom to operate and protect any one of these three means of communication presupposes the freedom of movement and deployment over a large area. The whole region, therefore, and not merely a narrow corridor through it, is a strategic objective. Further, the attitude of the given local populations has become the fourth strategic column of modern times. You cannot protect a land route, a waterway, or an air strip unless you are friendly with, or otherwise safe from, the local people alongside each. And the local people in most of these instances are the Arabs. Their present temper—for purposes of common defense, if not always for purposes of common progress—is such that you cannot be at odds with the Arabs along the Suez, or in Kuwayt, without having to give an accounting to the rest of the Arab world. Finally, the voice of the Arabs reverberates in Bengal and Malaya, and in North Africa and the Dardanelles, not to mention the Russian sections of the Islamic community. The Near East is thus a zone of communications in a very large sense indeed.

More important still, the region is to Britain an end in itself. This is due largely, though not disproportionately so, to the local oil reserves, so necessary to Britain's life as well as her life line. In addition, there are the exports of Egypt, Palestine, and Iraq, each important to Britain's home industries and commerce. And the whole region is a valuable market for British exports, one which will gain in value as the region advances economically and socially. But neither oil nor trade alone, nor yet a combination of both these factors, can account for the outstanding significance of the Near East in the British scheme of things. The strategic factor is paramount. It is today the keystone of the Empire itself. When Mr. Ernest Bevin referred in 1945 to this part of the world as "the throat of the British Empire," he was alluding not merely to the substance which enables modern armies and navies to breathe, but also to the area on the face of the globe where that breath might be choked off most readily.

It is thus clear that the British interest in the Near East, while firmly anchored geographically, has grown in relation to the needs of the Empire until it became central to that Empire's over-all design. The task of tending so substantial a stake and securing it against all contingencies had to be entrusted from the start to British policy. Now just as Britain's interest in the region has been basically stable, though expanding, the policy dedicated to its maintenance has had to be flexible. It has needed overhauling from time to time, in accordance with the changing political conditions in the Near East, the fluctuations in world politics, and the adjustments which Britain has been called upon to make in order to meet these fluctuations. But there has never been a time, since the turn of the eighteenth century, when Britain could be said to be without some form of a positive Near East policy. If her present position in that region still is stronger than that of any other power, that is due in no small measure to the fact that for a century and a half Britain has not failed to appreciate this commitment and to implement it, when the occasion called for it, with all the resources at her command. Today she is resolved to follow the same principle even if she may have to modify her methods. The inherent difficulties are greater, the opposition inside the region and outside appreciably stronger, and her overall strength considerably less of a factor than in the past. On the other hand, she has a reserve of trained personnel which is superior, for this particular purpose, to that of any of her rivals; furthermore, she has shown the necessary foresight to improve and add to the ranks of her human resources charged with the defense of her Near East interests. If all these efforts should prove inadequate in the end—which is by no means a foregone conclusion—it will not be because Britain has lacked a considered policy or has failed to adjust it to the changing needs of the times; it will rather be because the adjustment has been insufficient and has come too late, or because the British Empire has been overtaken by events beyond the control of those responsible for the conduct of its affairs.

Initially, Britain's interest in the Near East was a by-product of her commitment in India. Indian policy dictated infiltration into the coastal lands of Arabia, by way of the Indian Ocean, and the annexation of Aden in 1839. The construction of the Suez Canal made of the Eastern Mediterranean a vital British zone instead of some distant back bay. By the same token the Near East was promoted to a central, as opposed to a tangential, interest. British policy, accordingly, was directed first to the acquisition of a financial stake in the Canal through purchases of shares from bankrupt local interests. This was followed, inevitably, by a gradual penetration of Egypt—at first jointly with France, the other major European shareholder, and since 1882, when Egypt was occupied by British forces, as a strictly British enterprise. France eventually allowed herself to be eliminated as a political rival in Egypt in return for a free hand in Morocco.

The security of the new line of communications, however —which promptly became the Empire's life line—had to be bolstered at its narrowest section. An essential prerequisite in this connection was a stable Near East. Accordingly, it became a prime objective of British policy to prevent further disintegration of the Ottoman Empire, whose Sultan was the legal sovereign in the region. The British went at first so far as to encourage Abdul-Hamid's pretensions to the Caliphate and the pan-Islamic policy which evolved therefrom. For a strong and friendly Sultan enjoying the allegiance of the Islamic world could not only assure stability in the Near East, but might also be able even to check the steady Russian expansion along the Islamic belt, an expansion that threatened Britain's position in Farther Asia. The plan was not an unqualified success, however, since Abdul-Hamid's pan-Islamic propaganda had repercussions among the Muslims of India which proved embarrassing to Britain. From 1880 onwards, therefore, the British became increasingly wary of Turkey, thus leaving the way open to German penetration of that country. But as far as the Near East was concerned, Turkey was able to maintain a semblance of order and surface stability until the onset of the First World War.

The collapse of the Ottoman Empire necessitated a radical readjustment of British policy in the Near East. The governmental vacuum had to be filled. The Arabs insisted that they were ready to fill it themselves. The British, on the other hand, felt that the Arabs were an altogether untried element, politically inexperienced and too retarded socially and economically to establish and maintain self-supporting states, let alone a single Arab state. Above all, however, the British were mindful of their own increasingly critical interests in the region and of the damage which these might suffer in a period of likely chaos. Consequently, Britain decided on a modified form of imperialism: she would keep all the essential controls—except where the French were entrenched—while the Arabs were being guided, at a measured pace, along a course calculated to lead to ultimate independence at some indefinite time in the future.

This policy had, in the British view, the merit of striking a reasonable balance between imperial interests and the new doctrine of national self-determination. But it involved Britain in a series of vague and conflicting promises, among them the McMahon pledges and the Balfour Declaration. The inherent dualism of this policy, moreover, showed itself in contrasted interpretations of its basic features. The British preferred to stress the purity of their motives in launching, say, Iraq on her way to a statehood or the Jews on their way to a national home in Palestine. The affected local elements, for their part, could not see farther than the patent self-interest of their overseers. Furthermore, the Arabs had no patience with a program of deferred self-determination. The new imperialism, in short, was a dual policy to the rulers and a two-faced policy to the ruled. Actually, it made for some mutual benefits on a limited scale. But there was about it a coefficient of paternalism which could not but spell trouble, especially in an age of exaggerated nationalist ideals and slogans.

At all events, the policy was not working right for either side. While it was being tried out—which means primarily the period between the wars—the concurrent French endeavor in the Levant was to the British a source at once of comfort and of embarrassment. France was a moral aid to the British in having to share with them the onus of protecting foreign interests in the region. But French errors of commission had also an adverse bearing on the British position in the neighboring Arab lands. For instead of crediting the British with being more reasonable than the French, the Arabs chose to regard the French practices as a foretaste of what the British, too, had in store for them. Meanwhile, the French, upset and insecure, missed no opportunity to discredit a Western associate whom they suspected and envied.

Yet the British themselves were far from pleased with the results of their policy. It had involved them in constant struggle accompanied by orderly but continuous retreat. The treaty with Iraq, which was signed in 1930, set a pattern for the Anglo-Egyptian treaty of 1936. Transjordan and her Amir would have to be similarly rewarded—not pacified in this instance, since the territory was loyal and submissive—sooner or later. Although these treaties gave Britain the right to maintain small local garrisons, the time could not be far away when even these remnants of direct

British control would have outstayed their welcome. Rampant nationalism and the rising tide of anti-foreign feeling throughout the Near East would surely wash away these offensive reminders of outside dominance. A fresh readjustment of policy was urgently needed. While this was being pondered in London, the second World War broke out.

The course of the war underscored with startling emphasis two facts that were intimately related to Britain's position in the Near East. First, that the geostrategic significance of the region rose in direct proportion to the spread of world conflicts: the more nearly worldwide the conflict, the closer the Near East came to being the absolute global center of gravity. And second, that Britain's account with the Arabs had been overdrawn; with few exceptions they were now either prudently neutral or plainly hostile toward their tutors. The task of mending fences must not be held up pending the outcome of the war. The time to tackle it was right away, while the attention of others still was centered on what to them were more immediate objectives. With such a headstart, the foreshadowed post-war competition could be taken in stride.

Accordingly, the readjustment of British policy which had been on the agenda on the eve of the war was now given high priority. And when the plan was at last unveiled, it looked more like a totally new program than a substantial modification of the old. At a minimum, it set out to cut short by decades the process of controlled evolution which the British policy makers had previously envisioned.

No one thinks, of course, of any interdepartmental agency responsible for the foreign policy of its particular government as a uniformly harmonious body. Various councils are apt to be heard before a given decision is ultimately arrived at. The British files on Arab policy would doubtless make unusually revealing reading in more ways than one. Your colonial administrator, preoccupied with strictly local matters, lacks the perspective—and the relative freedom from direct responsibility—which is the attribute of your councillor on foreign affairs. Aside from these two stands the area expert who is expected to furnish the necessary cultural and historical background. Generally, his voice carries little authority, for the academic and the practical are supposed to be opposing and often mutually incompatible interests. But Britain is too experienced a hand at managing an empire to have neglected the specialist departments altogether. And she is particularly fortunate in having a small but outstanding group of Arab specialists.

The Foreign Office, which must countersign all such decisions, listened to the Arab experts in the days of Kitchener and Allenby and in the period between the wars, but gave its approval to suggestions that came from the colonial wing. The separatism in the Near East that was stimulated in those days wherever it did exist, or was created where it did not exist, was the unmistakable product of colonial thinking and experience. The basic policy was one of purposeful fragmentation: into individual political units calculated to keep alive the differences between state and state, and into distinctive communal groups within each state in order to keep alive the need for continued British assistance. In other words, the gradual evolution of dependent and semi-dependent peoples while the assisting foreign power was taking good care of its own primary interests was a fine principle, provided that such evolution proceeded at a suitable pace and in the assigned track. Separatism was the time-tested instrument of this policy.

The scheme failed because it was founded upon an anachronism. Methods of bygone centuries were now out of date—and, moreover, the Near East was not like some sheltered area in the recesses of Africa. Neither did the substitute treatment by treaty constitute a permanent cure, to judge from the experience of the early part of the Second

World War. The thing to do, then, was to pay more heed to the councils of the Arab experts. They had long opposed fragmentation, on moral as much as on practical grounds. This was no time for indecision. The Arab unity movement, which had the initial advantage of great popular appeal in the local countries, must be given the positive backing of the British authorities.

It would probably make a better story if it could be asserted that unobtrusive scholars had, wholly by their own efforts, scored this signal victory over the diplomats—their confidence somewhat shaken by a long record of failure. But it would not be a true story. The fact is that, unbeknown to themselves, Russia and the United States were partly responsible for the shift in British policy in the Near East. The joint Anglo-Russian occupation of Iran, the subsequent demonstration of what the Iranian trunk line can mean to Russian security, the Tripartite Treaty (among Britain, Russia, and Iran) of January 1942, and the Tehran Declaration (by Churchill, Roosevelt, and Stalin) of December 1943—all these were successive steps in the reëstablishment of Russia as a Near East power. Stalingrad and the Russian victories which followed made the Near East in general, and the Greek Orthodox and Armenian communities in particular, take increasing notice of Russia, while encouraging Russia at the same time to give more and more attention to the vital strategic center to the south. A resurgent Russia, which had not tasted a major victory since Napoleonic times, might not be satisfied with a purely Platonic contemplation of the Near East. Neither would the United States be likely to be so satisfied, what with the Arabian oil, the opportunities for trade, and the realization that a third world war might be hatched in this region. A strong foothold in the Near East by either of these powers might well threaten established British interests. To minimize this threat, it seemed wisest to make sure of the Anglo-Arab ties reinforced through a British-sponsored Arab unity movement.

The new policy, at a maximum, looked to the building up in the Near East of a stable Arab society, organized politically into a confederation of states or any other combination which these countries might choose, the whole group to coöperate in maintaining British interests because they would be also its own interests. There can be no quarrel with the premise of coöperation on a free basis. But it is a sanguine premise when applied to this particular instance, because it presupposes, first, a wholehearted British effort, second, a wholehearted and united Arab effort, and third, the absence of serious opposition from other interested parties. Actually, there has been trouble, in varying degrees, on all three of these counts.

The British set out resolutely to see the scheme through. They were prepared to minimize the surviving part of their commitment to the Zionists—to the vanishing point if necessary—and to withdraw their discreet support of the Kurds. When the pro-Zionist planks in the 1944 platforms of both major political parties in the United States brought angry protests from the Arabs throughout the region, the British were in no way disconcerted. On the contrary, any drop in the American stock in the Near East, while the British stock was climbing, was all to the good. Further, Britain welcomed and backed the various preliminary steps which were to lead to the formation of the League of Arab States; and the new League showed its appreciation by the moderate manner in which its charter addressed itself—in oblique fashion— to the existing foreign interests. Lastly, the British took a strong stand in the Franco-Syrian crisis of May-June 1945, a stand that could be construed as pro-Arab, and was so construed in various local circles.

Three things happened, however, which tended to raise doubts in certain British quarters as to the ultimate value to Britain of her revised Arab policy. One was Egypt's demand for a new treaty with Britain, one that would purge the country of all the remaining vestiges of British political domination. The other was Russia's open entry into the Near East arena. And the third was the renewal of the battle for Palestine with all its multitudinous ramifications.

Britain's Labor Government could not be accused of insincerity in seeking a formula which would be consistent with Egyptian national pride and yet guarantee the protection of the Suez Canal. Egyptian ideas on the subject, however, have left Britain with the impression that the chauvinism of Egypt may not soon be checked. Not only did Egypt want the British troops out of the country within a year—which cannot be regarded as an altogether unreasonable demand—but she insisted also on the "unity of the Nile Valley," that is, exclusive sovereignty over the Sudan instead of an Anglo-Egyptian condominium. Moreover, Egyptian leaders have voiced demands for the Italian colony of Eritrea, thus rivaling Russian claims to the colony; and they also have pressed for the independence of Tripolitania and Cyrenaica; failing that, they want these North African territories to come under the trusteeship of either Egypt or the Arab League. These developments have done more than arouse in Britain Conservative opposition, which feels that Egypt—a very substantial beneficiary of the late war—should be held to the terms of the 1936 treaty. They have, in addition, raised doubts in the minds of the sponsors of the latest British policy in the Near East as to whether an extremist Egypt could be counted upon to cooperate with Britain on a voluntary basis.

Russia's challenge to Britain's overall position in the region will be discussed presently. In so far as Britain is concerned, this challenge, coupled with the ultra-nationalism of the Egyptians, caused the authorities to improvise a substitute line of defense. This was set up in March 1946, when

King George VI, in a treaty with the Amir Abdullah of Transjordan, granted that state "full independence." The meaning of this phrase becomes perfectly clear when the treaty is analyzed in conjunction with an annex to it which gives Britain the right to maintain and even increase the present forces in Transjordan. The meaning of the move as a whole is no less easy to decipher. Britain felt compelled to maintain a physical hold on some central part of the Near East so as to be able to protect her wide-flung interests in the region. A place like Cyprus—which has been suggested as an alternative—could not possibly fill this need, certainly not in times of peace. With the complete withdrawal of the British garrisons from Egypt and Iraq likely to occur soon, Britain had to regroup in another suitable part of the Near East where her welcome promised to last longer. The mandated states of Palestine and Transjordan afforded the only remaining opportunities. And since Palestine could not be viewed as a comfortable spot by any stretch of the imagination, the choice fell—for this reason as well as a variety of others—upon Transjordan.

Why then, the elevation of the country to the status of a kingdom? Surely a state with a population of less than 400,000, including a considerable number of nomads, its administration under the effective control of the British and its defense under their complete control, can be independent in name only. The answer to this puzzle need not be sought farther than Russia. As a mandated territory, Transjordan might come under a joint trusteeship in which Russia would wish to share. Rather than agree to such a division of control, Britain chose to assure herself of unshared control of the country through the expedient of nominal independence.

In thus releasing Transjordan from mandatory supervision while obtaining essentially similar privileges by treaty, Britain had modified once again, but had not reversed completely, her policy toward the Arab world. For this step would seem to constitute a digression from the straightforward course that had genuine Arab unity as its ultimate goal. At least that is the view which some Arab quarters have taken in this connection. Lebanon stigmatized the Anglo-Transjordan treaty as harmful to the Arab cause and lodged her protest to this effect with the Council of the Arab League. The Arabs cannot have forgotten so soon that muddling along and retreat by treaty characterized the British Near East policy in the period between the wars.

If this is a sign that in tending to her long-range commitments Britain has fallen back on day-to-day methods, it would fit in with all the other manifestations of uncertainty and confusion which have come to mark British—and United States—relations with Russia. Once more it becomes clear that the Near East is, and is destined to remain, a sensitive barometer of the political climate the world over. Agreement among the major powers with regard to the Near East can come only as an integral part of a broader pattern of international coöperation. While there is conflict among the foreign interests in the region—British, Russian, and American interests at this particular juncture—the rest of the world cannot be free from strife. The question which must be posed is whether all the avenues that might lead to agreement have been explored. No doubt, the capitals of the world are fully aware of the gravity of the situation. Yet a move such as the elevation of Transjordan, in the manner in which it was effected, can only increase, rather than relax, the existing suspicions and tensions. And the Russian veto on Transjordan's application for admission as member of the United Nations is proof that any speck on the map of the Near East may now be sucked into the vortex of global politics, and thereby may foul the delicate international machinery.

Anglo-American relations in the Near East have been

largely under the shadow of the Russian problem. It can be of small comfort to Britain just now that the United States has the goods and the shipping but the local states have mostly frozen sterling. Nor can the American oil interests in Arabia claim a disproportionate amount of attention for the time being. Such things can be taken care of later, and Britain is not unhopeful that the result will be advantageous to her. The present need—as the British see it—is for agreement with the United States on as broad a front as possible. An Anglo-American bloc in the Near East appears to be the prime objective of current British policy in the region. To insure its harmony, it is necessary to eliminate, or at least neutralize, the Palestine stumbling block. An effort in that direction is now in progress.

The problem of Palestine will be discussed briefly in the next chapter.

3. RUSSIAN INTERESTS IN THE NEAR EAST

The one thing that may safely be said of Russia's interest in the Near East is that, if it is not as vital as Britain's or as acute, it is palpably no less intense. The objects of both countries in this region are much the same: communications, resources, and security. But Britain is in, and is striving desperately to protect what she has got. Russia is just on the outside, storming to get in, and convinced that she has a better right than any outsider to be in. For Britain, the Near East is the key to her position as a world power. Russia, jealous of her own prerogatives as a world power—the more so since their universal recognition is of very recent date—is determined that this hard-won status shall not be challenged. The crossroads of the world, under the control of a rival power, constitute for Russia an ever-present danger of such a challenge. She has long sought to break out of her predominantly land-locked empire, and hence the tri-continental bridge of the Near East has been a magnet to her for many decades. Invariably she has been thwarted by Britain. Today she could easily obtain control over that approach to the bridge which is nearest to her. But she will not be satisfied until she can supervise—or at least help supervise—the traffic at the other ends. And as long as Britain has a controlling voice in the matter, Russia will consider herself threatened.

It would seem to be equally safe to assert that Britain has no aggressive designs against Russia in the Near East. But Britain cannot allow her unique position in that region to be weakened beyond minimum requirements of Empire security. To share that position with Russia, as a compromise measure, would to British thinking be the same as to sanction the liquidation of the Empire. The resulting measures and countermeasures since the end of the recent war have added progressively to an already formidable score of mutual suspicion and distrust. Small wonder, then, that the culmination of the long Palestine dispute was to find Britain and Russia each pursuing determined policies that were poles apart.

The present situation is not basically different from what it was through most of the nineteenth century. The policies of the Labor Government of Britain and those of the Soviet Government collide head on in the Near and Middle East, just as the policies of England under Conservative or Liberal regimes clashed with those of Czarist Russia. Thus the contest goes much deeper than the political and social doctrines of the present generation. The tempo, however, has quickened appreciably and the stakes have grown much larger. In the past, the Dardanelles used to be a prime objective of the Russian policy of expansionism—and hence a favorite preoccupation of a sizable school of historians and strategists. But the recent war, which demoted the Balkans from their front-line position in world politics, also served to demonstrate that the Straits have become a matter of secondary interest in world affairs. Today, the mere freedom of the Straits would not answer Russia's needs as a global power. With the British in control of the exits at either end of the Mediterranean, even a regime of the Dardanelles wholly satisfactory to Russia would by itself amount to no more than the escape from one lake into the confinement of another, although a considerably larger one. Fully alive to the new horizons, Russia thus came out openly with a demand for Tripolitania or Eritrea. In other words, Russia's interests reach out, past the Aegean and the Mediterranean, to the expanses of the Indian Ocean. And the Near East has been ordained by geography to be the logical place where such interests can be staked out. Turkey and Iran retain their traditional importance for Russia—this time, however, as way stations rather than as ultimate objectives.

The oft-mentioned goals of petroleum and warm-water ports, both of which would involve Iran—at least initially—would seem to be essentially secondary Russian interests subsumed under the general strategic heading. Oil experts have pointed out that Russia possesses sufficient petroleum reserves at home. And environment has not been particularly generous to the coastal areas around the Persian Gulf in providing them with natural port facilities. Russian interest in Iranian—and Arabian—oil thus appears to be of a negative kind: not so much to insure home exploitation of these resources as to prevent others from expanding their existing holdings and thus strengthening their present position in the region. Added to this is the long history of Anglo-Russian stalemate in Iran, a constant reminder of Russia's failure thus far to win a conclusive victory in this contest. The same psychological motivation may underlie Russian claims to the Turkish areas of Kars and Ardahan. Because they were once briefly under Russian rule, Russian national pride now insists on their reincorporation in Russia, even though it was an early Soviet Government which voluntarily returned these provinces to Turkey.

The objection may be interposed at this point that it is a hazardous thing to speak of Russian intentions and motives with any degree of confidence. Until about the middle of 1943 such an objection would have been perfectly valid when applied to Russia's Near East policy. Since then, however, there have been enough sundry indications to yield a gradually evolving pattern which is reasonably clear in general outline if not in specific details. In so far as the Arab world proper is concerned, Russia demonstrated her awareness of the fact that you cannot be a factor in the Near East through remote control, by resuming diplomatic relations with Egypt in 1943 (with the same Mr. Novikov as minister who later became Russian Ambassador to the United States) and establishing legations in Iraq and the Levant States in 1944. Thereafter, a policy of calculated political aggression replaced the earlier Russian policy of watchful waiting. The aggression has so far been mostly on the flanks rather than frontal. The demand for a trusteeship over one of the Italian colonies in Northeast Africa and the delay in withdrawing Russian troops in Iran, in violation of explicit commitments, were instances of the new approach. The lines of this advance pointed at, and would intersect in, the heart of the Arab region. Furthermore, moves of a more direct bearing on the Arab world have not been lacking.

In embarking upon an active policy in the Arab Near East, Russia could count at the start on a substantial reserve of accumulated assets—historical, social, ethnic, and psychological. In contrast to Britain and France, the Soviet Union did not have to bear the onus of a long record of past imperialistic practices in an Arab world increasingly lured to nationalism. For the hastily Westernized elements among the Arab youth, Russia had a particularly strong appeal, in that she shared in the Western heritage without apparently duplicating the selfishness of the Western powers. The artisan class could vaguely discern in the Soviet system an answer to the social and economic ills which beset their own countries. And the mass of the fellahin could not possibly be worse off than they were. Then, too, Russia included within her borders some twenty-five million Muslims, many of whom lived in autonomous republics with a predominantly Muslim population. It was not difficult, under these circumstances, to exploit the superficial similarity between Islam and communism. Given eager ears, this similarity could be blown up no less successfully than was done in the stock comparisons between democracy and Islam. And had not even fascism, and Shintoism, scored modest gains along analogous lines?

Of more concrete advantage to Russia than the factors just cited were several of the ethnic and religious minorities in the Near East. Iraq has approximately three quarters of a million Kurds, or about as many as Iran. Another million and a half live in Turkey. Split thus among three states, although they occupy contiguous districts, three million or more of these hardy mountaineers are eager to grasp at any plausible prospect of national unity and autonomy. The Russians, who speak a language related to Kurdish, have long loomed as potential liberators. And Kurdish nationalist leaders have often managed to make the short journey into Russian territory and establish contact with Soviet circles.

Alongside the Kurds, there are close to three million Armenians in the Caucasus and the Near and Middle East. About a quarter million of these are scattered throughout the Arab states, particularly Syria and Lebanon. A like number remain in Turkey and Iran. Christians all, and overwhelmingly members of the Apostolic Church of Armenia—also known as the Gregorian Church—the Armenians of the Near and Middle East have never been completely at ease in these Islamic regions. Their sufferings at the hands of the Turks are a singularly depressing chapter of relatively recent history. Politically, the Armenians are split into the rightist Tashnags, the leftist Hunchags, and the centrist Ramgavars. But the ideal of national unity has a strong appeal for the great majority of the people. This includes, of course, those now living outside the borders of the Armenian Soviet Socialist Republic, and especially those who are dispersed through the Near and Middle East. Furthermore, the Patriarchate of all Armenians has remained in Echmiadzin (twelve miles west of Erivan)—which is now Russian soil—since the fifteenth century. Lastly, the lot of Armenians in Russia has been a gratifying one from all accounts. It was the Armenian Soviet Republic, for instance, which had the necessary authority to sign with Turkey the Treaty of Kars, in October 1921, whereby the now disputed provinces of Kars and Ardahan were ceded to Turkey. All in all, coöperation with Russia appears to be advantageous to the expatriate Armenians in nearby Islamic lands. Even the rightist Tashnags, who strive for a united and independent Armenia and who have been opposed to communism, are now prepared to advocate a temporarily pro-Russian orientation. The other Armenian groups are naturally less tentative on this question. Thousands have already left the Levant for Russian territory, and larger numbers throughout the area hope to follow suit. In these circumstances, Russia has had good reason to count on the Armenian elements in the Near East as an aid in implementing her new aggressive policy in the region.

A further source of possible contacts between the Soviets and the Arab countries have been the small but compact communist cells in the Levant, Palestine, and Iraq. It was for the apparent purpose of facilitating Soviet political penetration of the Near East that the local communist parties reorganized on a thoroughly nationalist basis, abandoning their earlier anti-religious stand. This belated step could not in itself neutralize the prevailing hostility of conservative Muslim circles toward communism. But it made it possible for Arab political leaders to speak openly of turning to Russia whenever actions of the Western powers gave rise to sufficiently determined Arab opposition. Syrian leaders were prompt to avail themselves of this opportunity during their bitter struggle with France in 1945. Similar cries have been raised on other occasions. What is more, the temper of the Arab world during the concluding months of the war and the confusing days which followed did not encourage overconfidence on the part of the Western interests. It would not have been prudent to dismiss all the Arab intimations of possible overtures to Russia as merely idle threats.

Russia was thus, in 1945, in a favorable position to challenge Britain's grip on the Near East. She proceeded, however, to take one major step which cost her a considerable part of the tactical and psychological advantage that she had accumulated in the region. The long dispute over the retention of Russian troops in Azerbaijan—the Iranian province to the northeast of Iraq—was not only the first serious test case faced by the United Nations but also a test of Russian intentions and methods in the Middle and Near East. Had Russia been willing to let the Azerbaijan dispute remain—to all appearances, at least—an internal Iranian problem, the sympathies of the Arab world would probably not have been affected either way. But Russia's disregard of her pledge to remove all her troops from Iranian soil by a stated date promptly showed the whole affair to be a move in the game of blunt power politics. It also aroused fears as regards the next Russian move. Hitherto Russia had had no strong ethnic lever within her borders which she might use against Arab lands. The Armenian communities in the Near East could scarcely be used as an argument for the annexation to Russia of all the states involved. In Azerbaijan, however, the population includes large numbers of Kurds, in addition to the Azeris. Just as the Azeris might clamor for union with the Azerbaijan Soviet Republic, so might the local Kurds be inspired to demand union with the Kurds of Iraq and Turkey. Here then was the prospect of a brand-new method of power politics, namely, the method of ethnic chain reaction. Iraq was understandably worried, and the neighboring countries were also beginning to wonder when their turn might come. The conflict was ultimately shelved, but Russia had lost much of her psychological advantage with the Arabs. The interested minorities were not immediately affected.

Today the attitude of the Arabs toward Russia is predominantly one of fear. Russia's land mass comes down close to the borders of the region and Russia's naked power bulks large in Arab minds. In a trial of strength between Russia and the West—whether over the Near East alone or on a more inclusive scale—the fearsome proximity of Russia would carry great weight with the Arabs. The fact that Britain is spoken of more kindly in the Near East today than she was a year ago is not so much a sign of any direct improvement in Arab-British relations as it is an indication of Russia's ability to inspire forebodings in nearby countries. There can be no doubt that Russia has an accurate estimate of the present situation in the Near East. It is a situation which could lead to something resembling a balance of power. But it would be at best a nervous balance, requiring cool statesmanship on all sides. And the general climate just now is far from temperate.

4. OTHER FOREIGN INTERESTS IN THE NEAR EAST

Aside from these two major foreign interests—the British and the Russian—each of which seeks in its own way to make use of latent local power—there are two other outside interests that cannot be ignored. Both are secondary at the present juncture only because they are overshadowed by their principal rivals. Yet one of them played a part in the past which in its time was second to none, and the other may assume comparable prominence in the near future. The declining foreign element is represented by the French. The one which has rapidly been coming to the fore stems from the United States The American interest in the Near East has been uncoördinated in the past, but it may yet crystallize under the pressure of latest events. An analysis of the United States interest and policy in the Near East will be presented in the concluding chapter of this book.

French influence in the Near East in general and the Levant in particular was at its peak in the 1860's, at which time France was indisputably Europe's senior ambassador in the region. This preëminence was by no means a sudden growth. Rather it was the outcome of centuries of purposeful cultivation. Long before the Ottoman conquest, the term *Franji* had come to mean "Westerner" in Arab lands. Hence no further identification was required when France sought and obtained most-favored-nation treatment in Egypt as far back as 1447. Early in the seventeenth century France established herself as the protector of European Catholics in the Levant, and this protection was extended in due time to certain Christian subjects of Turkey. The establishment of the semi-autonomous Sanjaq of Lebanon in 1864, under a Christian governor responsible directly to the Sultan, was due primarily to resolute French action following the local disorders of 1860.

In order, however, to remain in the forefront in the Near East, France needed to hold her own elsewhere. After 1870, therefore, France was obliged to yield ground to Britain in Egypt and to Germany in Turkey. Her mandate over the Levant, which came to her as part of the settlement imposed after the First World War, was to have served not only her immediate strategic and economic interests in that area, but was to serve also as a means of extending her influence over the region as a whole. The plan miscarried both in its limited and in its broader objectives. With the removal of French troops from the Levant in 1946 went also France's last hope of playing a major role in the affairs of the Near East.

France's failure in the Near East was political. Her strongest weapon in this part of the world has always been cultural. It would thus seem either that she had sought dividends which her type of investment in the region was not capable of producing, or that she had not succeeded in integrating the ends with the means.

It has often been said—most recently by Britain's distinguished Arab expert, H. A. R. Gibb—that the French are outstandingly successful as cultural missionaries because they are genuinely convinced of the importance of French culture as their country's greatest gift to the world. The British certainly lack this idealistic approach, and with Americans the term missionary still carries a highly specialized connotation. Hence it is France, above all other foreign countries, which has long stood in the Near East for the best that the West has to offer. Nor is this view restricted to France's cultural efforts in the Levant. In 1936, for instance, there were 127 French educational institutions in Egypt, with some 2,500 teachers and 40,000 pupils out of the 70,000 attending foreign schools. France's continued participation in the cultural life of the Near East, unencumbered by ulterior political motives, could be invaluable in promoting the kind of Westernization that the region urgently requires. But such participation would call also for the sort of idealism which seems to be at a discount these days. Moreover, it would be asking too much of human nature to expect of the French that they agree, under present circumstances, to subsist in the Near East on idealism alone.

9. The Problem of Palestine

1. THE ORDAINED LAND

Palestine appears to be the fixed epicenter of a world in continuous ferment. Norms established for other lands break down when applied to this minute territory. Palestine is thus an outstanding anomaly, with a natural law and a life of her own. But because she has wielded an influence in world history entirely out of proportion to her size, other lands have come to share intimately in her life. It has, therefore, been one of Palestine's acquired characteristics to have two distinctive histories, one local and the other extra-territorial. The need for synchronizing and integrating these two histories is an unending problem which has increased in complexity with each successive generation. The present problem of Palestine is the cumulative product of many ages. It cannot be understood, let alone attacked with any prospect of an equitable solution, on the basis of surface appearances alone.

At first glance, the current Palestine entanglement might be mistaken for an essentially minor and local conflict—a conflict between two relatively small groups with a total population in the neighborhood of two million, at arms over the political fate of a very small country, approximately the size of Wales or Maryland. Yet one need not probe far to discover that the issue will not confine itself to that small country. It soon proves to have an intimate bearing on the mood and temper of a large and important region, and—beyond that—on the interests and peace of mind of a very large part of the world. The Palestine problem today is accordingly a world issue and a regional issue, as well as a purely local affair. And it is aggravated as much by the strength and depth of the various interests concerned as it is by their mere extent: strategic interests of world powers—in the region as a whole and, hence, inevitably in this its most sensitive spot; spiritual interests of three world religions, which together embrace nearly one half of the world's population; and the intense emotional interests of those who have been drawn directly or indirectly into the center of the turmoil. The most persistent and compulsive of these profound human attachments is traceable to a people whose whole history, and particularly its last twenty-five hundred years, has been an unrelieved anomaly. The manifold perplexities of the present Palestine problem are in considerable measure a consequence and a reflection of the abnormal history of that people.

If a country's natural environment and early cultural background play a prominent part in setting its later historic course, then Palestine is above all other places an ordained land. As the main lane on the tri-continental bridge, Palestine has borne the brunt of that highway's traffic since the dawn of history. Moreover, she was singled out for unusual physical features. Within the forty-five miles which separate the Mediterranean from the Dead Sea, the coastal plain gives way to the hills of Judaea, which rise above 2500 feet and then descend sharply to the lowest depression on the face of the earth, nearly 1300 feet below sea level. And in the 150 miles between Mount Hermon and the mouth of the Jordan the climate ranges all the way from the alpine to the tropical. These startling variations in topography and climate could not but leave their imprint on successive generations of inhabitants. To many of these the Jordan may have been just like any other body of water of comparable, and rather unimpressive, size. With others, however, it made a mark on the heart and the imagination as deep as is the river's course in this lowest rift on the earth's surface. Palestine is not the kind of country that encourages emotional indifference in people.

No one knows when the belief first gained currency that this land was predestined to play a major role in world history through the medium of a people chosen for the task. Tradition dates it to the time of the Patriarchs and lets it mature against the background of Egyptian servitude and the thirst and hunger of the desert. A poignant episode was made to signalize the end of this first period of wandering, some thirty-three centuries ago. Moses, who at long last had brought his people to the gates of the Promised Land, was not to set foot in it himself. He was permitted to see its length and breadth from the top of Mount Nebo, on the other side of the Jordan, but that ascent was to him the journey's end. "And no man knoweth his sepulchre unto this day," for the ideal in quest of which he had spent his life was deemed too great for the leader to be encumbered posthumously by the gratitude of the led. Recollections of this well-remembered narrative have been vivid in the minds of so many recent groups of ragged wanderers come from a grimmer journey and waiting forlornly at the western gate of Palestine, offshore in Haifa harbor. It is such echoes of Biblical times, and countless others like them, that went to make the modern problem of Palestine the powerful human problem that it is—among many other things.

The remarkable—one may again say, anomalous—thing about this original concept of the Promised Land is that the land went on to exceed its promise. Materially poor and politically insignificant, except for brief intervals, it yet possessed the sustenance to nurture great ethical and social principles, born of old traditions and of new experiences.

These elements were forged into a distinctive culture, and the culture nourished a people and kept it united. The people, in turn, paid their debt to land and tradition with increasingly passionate devotion to both. Although this made for the crystallization of a narrower national ideal, universal values were not being neglected. Through Judaism and Christianity, Palestine became a prominent factor in universal history, thus acquiring an extra-territorial status which was henceforth to interfere with the country's normal existence. But a Promised Land that has fulfilled its promise and bequeathed it to the world is not a normal land.

Islam gave the Arabs a dual stake in Palestine, one religious and the other ethnic. In keeping with Islam's substantial debt to both Judaism and Christianity, Jerusalem was now a sacred center to the Arabs, outranked only by the Holy Cities in the homeland of the Prophet. Furthermore, early Arab conquests had deposited in Palestine members of the conquering hosts, and had, in addition, gradually Arabized the conquered. In course of time the land became as effectively Arab as it had been Israelite or Jewish a millennium and a half earlier. This analogy, however, is not quite complete. Throughout the period of independent Arab empires, the country remained, as it has since then, overwhelmingly Arab in population and an Arab spiritual center. And except for the profoundly disturbing interlude of the Crusades—when the promise of the land became an affliction and a melancholy problem with world-wide repercussions—Palestine continued also under Arab political dominance. Yet throughout that period the country was but one of a number of Arab lands; nor was it ever the primary ethnic, political, or spiritual center of all the Arabs. In Davidic times, on the other hand, and in the centuries which followed, Palestine was the one and only home of a distinctive nation and of its religion and culture. It was to be one of the later characteristics of the anomalous life of that group—indeed, one of the striking anomalies of history—that the dispersion which deprived the Jews of their territorial basis served only to tighten the grip which their common and traditional spiritual home exercised over them. And to the extent to which they failed to be accepted as part of the nations amidst whom they were fated to live, Palestine was to them a Promised Land in nostalgic retrospect and the only national home they had ever had.

What bearing, one may ask, do such historical arguments have on the present problem of Palestine? Their precise legal bearing is certainly debatable, and the general construction that may be placed upon them is subject to conflicting interpretations. It is a fact, however, that to Jews and Arabs these are not merely arguments from history but integral parts of living history. Where deep emotions are engaged it is difficult to steer an objective course. But even an attempt at setting such a course must fail if it disregards the subjective elements that underlie the whole problem. Nor will it succeed, on the other hand, if the balancing factors are lost sight of, in whole or in part. One such balancing factor in particular is all too often ignored by the two parties most directly concerned.

For Palestine is not merely a land haunted by history. She is also the victim of geography, in which respect she shares the fate of the entire region. But since the interaction of history and geography has been a peculiarly intimate process in the Near East, Palestine's historic prominence has brought the entailed environmental factor into proportionately sharp relief. What this means is that the present contest between Arabs and Jews is being waged over a terrain which others would not be disposed to leave uncontested should the current issue be settled. What if it be affirmed that Jews, more than any other group, made Palestine historic, or that Arabs have been the numerically dominant element in the country for the past thirteen centuries? It still remains a fact, trite but true, that geography was at work there ahead of either people. And geography has decreed that the career of the Near East shall be closely interlocked with that of the world outside. What is true of the region as a whole applies especially to its epicenter, the Ordained Land.

It is, therefore, scarcely the result of mere chance that throughout her long history there have been few intervals during which Palestine was permitted to order her own affairs. Authority over the country has resided—with the exception of a few centuries in the Davidic era and thereafter—in some center extraneous to it, one, moreover, which controlled larger regional or inter-regional interests: Egypt, Mesopotamia, Persia, or Syria; Rome; successive capitals of the Arab Empire; Turkey; and, lastly, Britain. Has there been a change in the basic conditions to reverse this determined trend? Obviously not. Indeed, such changes as have taken place in most recent times have all tended to enhance the importance of the Near East to the world at large—thus further curtailing the range within which the region could remain essentially independent of foreign entanglements. And once again it is Palestine that holds the most exposed position. Hence it was this country, of all the states of the modern Near East, that remained longest under the jurisdiction of an interested outside power.

Britain, in spite of the role of Greenwich, is not geography's duly appointed plenipotentiary. But geography has made the Near East vital to the fate of the British Empire. Britain's interest in Palestine is on an altogether different plane from that of the Arab or the Jewish interest in the country. But it is hardly less compelling than the others. And in a world made interdependent by so many recent developments, the weightier stake is likely to tip the scales. If it were a question of human feelings alone, the Palestine problem could be narrowed down to the issue of Jewish rights and needs as against Arab rights and needs. Much more, however, is involved today in the Palestine dispute. The chief additional element is the security of the world's most far-flung empire. And if the objection should be raised that such imperialist interests must not be allowed to operate to the detriment of primary human interests, the answer to that might be disappointing, but valid none the less; namely, that the question of British security cannot be divorced today from the very delicate problem of world stability.

This is not to say that British policy with regard to Palestine has been all that could reasonably be expected. In any realistic appraisal of the situation, however, the fact must be brought out that there were three parties to the dispute, and that each had a case which was not to be reduced beyond its critical minimum. For various reasons Britain has been loath to make this fundamental fact sufficiently clear. She has chosen to stress the bilateral—or Arab-Jewish—aspect of the problem instead of being forthright about its triangular bearing. The Arab-Jewish controversy could not have attained its ultimate intensity if either side had posed to itself this question: would all our difficulties be over if our mutual differences were to be composed? And that question might properly have been followed by another: If Britain should withdraw, would not some other outside power be sure to take her place? The answers to these questions might at one time have made it easier for all concerned to arrive at a peaceful solution. As it was, however, the decision was eventually entrusted to war, with each contestant —the British included—called upon to pay a heavy price.

The modern problem of Palestine may thus be described as a tangled web of conflicting interests in a framework of self-deception. At long last it appears to be on its way to a solution. Whatever this may be, aside from the rise of Israel, it should not be amiss to review briefly the three main angles to the dispute. The matter is as yet too inchoate, in any

case, for a comprehensive statement of this incredibly involved problem. A brief glance at the details may help to
distinguish the meaningful from the irrelevant.

2. THE JEWISH ANGLE

Like the Arab and British cases in Palestine, the Jewish
side lends itself to much distortion by the antagonists and
to no little confusion among the adherents themselves. The
confusion gives rise to further distortion, in the manner of
a vicious spiral. It becomes more and more difficult to sort
out the underlying facts. The interested bystander is understandably at a loss to separate truth from fable. And if he
should carry away with him the notion that Zionism is a
sinister force—a not uncommon notion, incidentally—his error would be no more difficult to account for than the
mistake of those who see in the extreme aims of Zionism
a workable remedy for the composite problem of Palestine
and the other issues connected therewith.

Zionism is the most determined constructive effort to
date to solve the age-old and world-wide Jewish problem.
Hitler's attempt to capitalize on the same problem was the
culmination of all the destructive efforts which recorded
history has witnessed. Its success was awesome but incom-
plete. It attained one-third of its stated goal when nearly
every Jew within reach, more than five million in all out
of a pre-war world total of some sixteen million, was ex-
terminated. A completely successful solution of this macabre
sort would require an evil demiurge with absolute power
of life and death the world over. And such power might
mean the destruction of all mankind. The Jewish problem
survived Hitler as it had survived lesser scourges from the
days of the Biblical Haman onwards. But its solution continued to elude humanity; nor was it brought nearer through
acts of inhumanity.

Zionism is an outgrowth of the Jewish problem. It is by no means fully coextensive with it, for the solution which it seeks would be a partial solution applying only to a segment of the group involved. Even under the most ideal conditions Palestine could accommodate only a portion of the remnant of Jewry. A large number of Jews have no direct interest in Palestine. Some of them have an interest in that country that is decidedly negative. Fulfillment of the Zionist ideal, therefore, might considerably diminish, but could not entirely eliminate, the broader Jewish problem. Palestine is central to the Zionist purpose. But it is tangential to the worldwide Jewish issue. This fact must be borne in mind in any comprehensive analysis of the Palestine question.

Zionism in the broadest sense of the term—a desire for the reëstablishment of the Jews in Zion—is as old as the Jewish dispersion, that is, nineteen centuries in its full extent, and twenty-five centuries since its partial inception following the capture of Jerusalem by Nebuchadnezzar in 586 B.C. The Psalmist who plaintively sang of Zion by the waters of Babylon was a genuine Zionist—a cultural as well as a religious Zionist, one may add, to use the terminological refinements of a later age. Religious Zionism has persisted ever since as a spontaneous expression of the feelings of the pious, an expression which found its way into their prescribed daily prayers. Cultural Zionism, on the other hand, drew its strength from without as much as from within. The less welcome the wandering Jews were to participate in the building up and the benefits of the various indigenous cultures, the more constrained they became to fall back on their own inheritance. Since the Hellenistic era there have always been elements among the Jews inclined towards assimilation, yet more often than not the stated price was their human dignity. The long-term result was progressive differentiation, perhaps the basic cause of anti-Semitism. And anti-Semitism is essentially a stepfather to Zionism; cultural anti-Semitism to cultural Zionism, and—most notably—the political anti-Semitism of the nineteenth and twentieth centuries to contemporary political Zionism.

For the idea of a Jewish state is not inherent in the basic content of Jewish culture. Nor is it the natural result of the enforced distinctiveness of large Jewish communities. Significantly enough, the concept in its modern form originated with assimilationist Jews who had discovered that anti-Semitism was being employed as a political weapon, in Central and Western Europe, by supposedly liberal societies—an ever-present source of "bread-and-circus" diversion for the masses. Short of the millennium, they were now convinced, Jews would continue to be segregated and treated as so many straw men—only to be knocked down when convenient. Second-class citizens for the most part, they could not aspire to a normal life while homeless. The solution was a Jewish state.

But why need such a state be established in Palestine out of all the possible places? This is a question that is heard time and again. There are at least two good reasons for the answer of the political Zionists. One is that there are no vacant spaces on the earth, no habitable country not yet inhabited. The other goes to the root of the matter. The Jews have survived as a people because they had a religion and a culture of their own. And to a large extent they have maintained themselves as Jews because they were not permitted to become, say, Germans or Poles, much as they were anxious to be devoted Germans or Poles. The one thing that sustained them through all the centuries has been their tradition. That tradition is tied up inextricably with one particular country, the Holy Land, the Promised Land. It was there that they had established a notable record, a record to whose lasting value the world has not ceased to pay homage. For generations old Jews would go to the Holy Land to die. The time had come for young Jews to seek in Palestine a life that has been denied them elsewhere. Uganda or Biro-Bijian could not similarly attract them. Palestine has been their one continuous spiritual home for more than three thousand years. They could pull up stakes and give up all they had and start again from scratch—in one land only. To expect a comparable sacrifice in the name of some vacuum would be to expect the impossible of human nature.

The false Messianism which bewitched the world at the end of the First World War gave the Zionists the Balfour Declaration as their share of the spurious harvest. Yet the sacrifice for which they had declared themselves ready was exceeded. So was also the anticipated achievement. While political wrangling and bickering went on, they toiled. Their toil bore fruit which they could not but regard as life-giving, not only to themselves but to their neighbors as well. The land was responding to their touch. But more was being accomplished than the reclamation of a neglected land. A people was being regenerated in the process, no longer a downtrodden people living on the grudged charity of others, but a people reclaimed to dignity and decency, transfigured by an ideal.

It is this spiritual and psychological content of Zionism that is the essence of the Jewish case in Palestine, not the intrusive political content. You can deal with political problems and take political losses more or less in stride. But the spiritual element is an intangible that will not respond to ordinary treatment. The Palestine problem is overwhelmingly a human problem, and the Jewish angle in it is perhaps the most difficult of all to gauge.

But if Palestine is not a spiritual vacuum to the Jews, neither is it a political vacuum to others. Intent on their central aim, the Zionists have viewed the concurrent Arab and British interests in Palestine in a subjective, not to say naïve manner. Because their own case drew its main strength from emotion, and because all of that emotional strength was invested in the immediate task at hand, Zionists have lacked the objectivity needed to appreciate the emotions of the one group and the calculations of the other. Not all Zionists, to be sure; for Palestine Zionism has had its full complement of adumbrations. A large minority has fought resolutely and long for agreement with the local Arabs, looking to a bi-national Palestine. And until the cessation of world hostilities, a vast majority of the country's Jews—including most of those who demanded a national Jewish state—were determined to follow a policy of moderation in the pursuit of their respective political aims. Revisionism was excommunicated, and its activist arms—the Irgun Zvai Leumi and the Stern Group—were vehemently denounced. The Zionist community proper kept up for a quarter of a century its own para-military group, the so-called Haganah or "Defense." The British near the end branded this body as subversive, and facile outpourings of certain magazines have sought to disparage the usual view that the Haganah was the arm of a resistance movement. Actually, the group was organized specifically for purposes of defense against Arab terrorism, and it was consolidated during the lawless period of 1936–39, at which time it had at least the moral support of the British. That support became rather more tangible—in that it was expressed by means of British arms and training—in the critical months preceding the victory at al-Alamayn, when a resolute resistance force in Palestine was of obvious interest to the Allies. Later the Haganah had to deplore, but it did not always dare to counteract, the outrages of the Jewish extremists. For it was itself engaged in an organized campaign against the local British authorities, although in taking this step it must have been prepared for the consequence that the British would choose to confuse its own members with the terrorists on the fringe, and that world opinion might not be able to distinguish between the two groups. The reason for this new counsel of desperation is plain enough. For each Jew now settled in Palestine ten were put to death in Europe. There cannot be many among the settlers who did not lose a friend or relative among those killed. The sight of the miserable survivors of the European holocaust who got as far as Haifa only to be turned back to another concentration camp is not a thing to inspire calm or induce composure. In brief, the present mood of the Jewish community in Palestine is bound up directly with the problem of immigration.

This question has loomed increasingly larger ever since it was made an integral part of the framework of the British mandate. A handful of Jews could not aspire to statehood in a country in which they were outnumbered six to one. The underlying human issue became thus entangled with super-imposed political questions. To Jews, whether Zionist or non-Zionist, immigration was an urgent human need; to Zionists it was also a potential weapon; but to the Arabs it was a growing menace. By the end of the Second World War the relative proportions had changed to approximately two non-Jews for each Jew settled in Palestine. Although the absolute Arab increase still exceeded that of the Jews, the reduction in the relative Arab majority was nevertheless startling; to the Arabs, moreover, it was a perfectly under-standable cause for alarm.

Thus matters stood when the end of the war revealed the workings of Hitlerism in all their stunning horror. The fate of the pitiful remnants should not have been made sub-sidiary to political considerations. But it was made so by the British and the Arabs, while prior nationalist pressure of the Zionists must also be included as an accessory before the crime. The survivors themselves had been through too much to have patience with emphemeral political issues. They were beyond worrying about nationalism and sov-ereignty. They had to get away from all that misery and madness and they wanted the reassurance of being in a Jewish community, whatever its political structure or status. It was an elemental craving, and the Jewish settlement in Palestine echoed it to the full. The Zionist angle of the Palestine problem was a minor matter compared to the melancholy aftermath of the European Jewish problem. The other parties to the Palestine dispute, however, had suffered no corresponding shock. The extra-territorial Jewish problem was not directly their problem.

Aside from its urgent humanitarian aspect, the question of Jewish immigration into Palestine loomed large also in a different sense. The most widespread objection to political Zionism—one which was not confined to its closest opponents alone but was shared by many impartial and liberal groups abroad—was due to the disturbing prospect that a majority would thus fall under the rule of a minority. The Zionists were fully aware of this vulnerable point. They knew that the numbers of Jews in need of a home of their own were greater by far than the total Arab population of Palestine. It was no less clear to them, however, that until the Jews had attained a majority in the country, their own argument would fail to carry enough conviction. Accordingly, they had a dual reason for insisting on unrestricted immigration. And, by the same token, the Arabs opposed continued Jewish immigration with ever-mounting vehemence. The British handling of this very issue—admittedly the most serious and difficult element in the situation—served only to add fresh fuel to the smoldering fires. While survivors from Hitler's terror were being interned in Cyprus or returned to Germany, even the most moderate among the Jews of Palestine were finding it impossible to remain composed. The breach with Britain had become incapable of mending.

3. THE ARAB ANGLE

The Arab case in Palestine has its own heavy emotional overlay which tends to crowd out reason. In fact, whereas a sizable segment of the Palestine Jewish community would grant the Arab side equal technical validity with their own —in that they favor a bi-national Palestine—few Arabs seemed to be inclined towards an analogous approach. The term zealot acquired its special connotation in Roman-ruled Palestine. Today it describes accurately the Arab attitude even more than that of the Jews, an attitude which characterizes not only the Arabs of Palestine but the Arab people as a whole. And it retains its peculiar evocative force when applied to the fanatical fringe of converts abroad, whichever side they may be on. Arab zealotry with regard to Palestine is perhaps the outstanding aspect of the Arab case. It may be extraneous to the case itself, but the feeling is there and it cannot be ignored, whatever the inherent merits. Zionists have been all too prone to minimize its bearing on the central issue.

Basic to this passionate feeling of the Arabs is the fact that Palestine has remained under continuous Arab occupation since the seventh century of the present era. They had, until 1948, a large majority in the country and they would not allow it to fall under the political domination of a heterogeneous minority nor suffer the existing numerical ratio to be reversed or seriously modified. Furthermore, Muslim Arabs have an abiding sense of divine right of occupation. Palestine is their inalienable possession because Allah gave them the land, and no Western intruder can take it away. Thus the issue narrowed down ultimately to an article of faith, which the logic of events may violate but cannot compromise. The practical result was intransigence on the part of the believers.

Stated in these terms, and viewed in conjunction with the

Jewish case, the Arab side appears to be an instance of right set against a rival right. The "state Zionists" recognize that the Arabs have an equitable claim to Palestine, but are convinced that their own claim is immeasurably more valid. The Arabs, on the other hand, refuse to concede any validity to the principal Zionist claims and are bent on disproving each of them. And in this excessive zeal the Arabs have injected into the issue a number of excessive arguments which place moderation at an added disadvantage.

To counter the Zionist argument from history, Arabs have sought recourse in theological casuistry whereby Palestine is declared as having been Muslim in faith from Abraham to Jesus. A somewhat different sort of casuistry entered into Ibn Saud's letter to President Roosevelt, dated March 10, 1945. The Palestine Arabs, its argument runs, are the descendants of the Canaanites, an Arab tribe which arrived in Palestine from the Arabian Peninsula "in the year 3500 B.C." Accordingly, Arabs have dwelt in Palestine continuously since that year "without ever leaving the country." The trouble with this argument is that like all little learning it is a dangerous thing. Ibn Saud may know the precise year in which the Canaanites came to Palestine, and so may the Western publicists who supplied him with this information. (The use of B.C., and particularly of A.D., by a good Wahhabi is rank heresy.) Scholars do not. What scholars do know, however, is that Hebrew is a Canaanite language, which Arabic is not; that the survival of any distinctive Canaanite group in Palestine down to the period of the Arab conquest would have been nothing short of a miracle—scarcely to be expected of heathens; and that if the Arabs of Palestine are the descendants of Canaanites, then the Arabs of Egypt, Iraq, and Saudi Arabia—who most certainly lack the same ancestry—have at best a vestigial relationship with the Palestine Arabs. In short, if the argument from history is admitted as valid, an admission which

Ibn Saud appears to have made, it must be decided in favor of the Jews whose direct connection with some of the pre-Islamic rulers of the land is expressly conceded in the letter in question.

There is the further argument from economic and social hardship which the Arabs raise often and trace to the Jewish colonization of the country. In many instances this argument has been carried to curious lengths. The casual reader might easily gain the impression that the so-called process of colonization of Palestine differed little from the proverbial overrunning of some dark continent. Actually, the lands acquired by the Jews were obtained from very willing sellers, who were paid many times the property's value. And the funds with which these purchases were financed did not come from the fabulous international banker—who is always ready to hand in fiction but is either non-existent or definitely uninterested in fact—but were accumulated with the aid of the modest collection boxes which penetrate seldom above the lower middle class. As for the Arabs' professed indifference to the improvements in industrial and agricultural methods, in education and public health, and in the general social level of the country, all of which have followed in the train of the Zionist effort, it strikes one as being on a par with the quaint complaint of the faddist who objects to doctors; he has the right to refuse their assistance, but he can scarcely expect to win universal sympathy on that score.

Further, there is the Arab political habit of keeping a foot in either camp. The insistence on an independent Arab Palestine is voiced with equal vigor by Arabs everywhere, in and out of Palestine. Yet if Palestine is to be a distinctive state, the established Arab states have no greater right to speak for Palestine than a given Latin-American country has to speak on behalf of its neighbors. On the other hand, if the connection of Palestine's Arabs with those of the neighboring countries is so close as to justify group action, there is no compelling reason why Palestine should be a separate Arab state rather than part of a larger political unit. The Arab stake in Palestine cannot be expected to pay double dividends. Actually, of course, there is more than one reason for this ambivalence. For one, the post-war Western policy of separatism prevented the Arab lands from pursuing their natural course. For another, inter-Arab divisive forces discouraged the formation of larger political units. Be that as it may, Palestine has no historical or cultural grounds for the establishment of a separate Arab state in Palestine. She can make a reasonable case, however, for the inclusion of her predominantly Arab portions in some larger Arab unit. The recurrent agitation for a Greater Syria might lead, conceivably, at some future date, to the creation of such a state, or to a federation of several of the territories most immediately concerned. Arab portions of Palestine would constitute a logical part of a Greater Syria.

Yet the prospect of thus checking and reversing the recent tendency towards political fragmentation did not appear to carry with the Arabs the appeal that it would seem to merit. As has already been indicated, unification poses a threat to the existing parochial interests. Furthermore, it might have an untoward bearing on the Arab case as regards Palestine. For if the whole of Palestine were to be merged with several of the neighboring countries, no foreseeable Jewish immigration into Palestine could possibly endanger the Arab majority of the combined unit; the last argument against that immigration would disappear, and a useful political weapon would automatically be blunted.

In the last analysis, then, the one forceful reason which the Arabs could bring to bear against the Jewish case in Palestine was this: they had a majority in the country which was unalterably opposed to Zionist political aims. As long as the country remained an integral political unit, unpartitioned and unattached to some larger federation of Arab states, the Zionist demand would not have the unqualified support of world opinion. Hence unlimited Jewish immigration was as much of a threat to the Palestine Arabs as it was a human and political necessity to the Zionists. Partition of the country into separate Arab and Jewish sectors might be a reasonable compromise in the view of impartial outsiders, in that each part would come under the dominance of its own majority. But it would not satisfy the Arabs, who by then took the position that the political fate of Palestine—with one-thirtieth of the Arab population of the Near East—had a decisive bearing on the very existence of the whole Arab nation. In this camp, too, the moderates no longer dared to raise their voice, although their reasons were very different from those of the Jewish moderates. The prospects for any kind of voluntary agreement between the two communities had long disappeared.

In this crisis, what was the position of the constituted legal guardian of the country?

4. THE BRITISH ANGLE

It is abundantly clear that the power legally in charge of Palestine was not, and could not be, a disinterested party. Britain's policy in the country had been dictated, first and foremost, by her own vital interests in the region as a whole. She must not be expected to view the Jewish-Arab issue with judicial impartiality. On the contrary, a realistic appraisal of the situation must allow for the desirability to the British of a continued Arab-Jewish impasse. To be sure, such utilitarian leanings and practices are repugnant to many Britons. Indeed, vigorous voices have often been raised in opposition. There is also the other extreme wing, however, which has no moral distaste for methods that might enable their country to thrive on strife. A strife-torn Palestine should be easier to control—though only relatively so—than a Palestine whose people are united in a demand for complete independence. Iraq and Egypt had demonstrated very recently that such demands cannot be sidetracked indefinitely. An independent Palestine would not be a comfortable place from which to supervise the British interest in the Near East and fend off other foreign interests which threaten to irrupt into the region.

The central British policy in Palestine has been one of vacillation between these two extremes, with the imperialist end exercising a stronger pull than the opposing idealist end. Accordingly, it has been an irresolute policy, uncertain of its ground, muddling on and stumbling backwards more often than not. In playing for time, much has been sacrificed to expediency. The attempt to harmonize the McMahon promises with the Balfour Declaration was an instance of expedient compromising, as was also the subsequent whittling down of the mandatory commitment to the Jews or the backing of the Arab League. The rising strength of the Arabs throughout the Near East placed a proportionately higher premium on their good will. The resulting policy for Transjordan has been "promote and rule." In Palestine, the bi-national problem became too acute for divide-and-rule tactics. Hence the attempt was made in 1937 to modify them in the direction of "partition and rule." When this proved impracticable at the time, the suggestion to partition the country into self-governing dwarf states, one Arab and the other Jewish, was shelved.

Post-war conditions imposed on Britain the need for a more determined, more consistent, Near East policy than in the past. Palestine was the one feasible base on which such a policy could fall back. A partitioned Palestine would no longer offer the assurance to British interests which seemed implicit in that scheme earlier. Eventually the Arab portion would be merged with some larger Arab unit and the Jewish portion would be built up into a small state free from the moral drawback of an unreconciled Arab majority. Neither section would then be likely to extend a hearty welcome to British interests.

In retrospect, the whole course of British policy in Palestine, with all its twists and turnings, may be said to have stemmed from the perfectly natural objective to serve imperial British interests in a rapidly changing world. The future may show more clearly than can now be seen where Britain had miscalculated. What is abundantly clear, however, even now is that Britain persisted in clinging to her course long after this had proved to lead to a dead end. She refused to act on the constructive recommendations of the Anglo-American Committee of Inquiry because these called for the termination of her mandate. Later she was to remain equally inactive with regard to the United Nations plan, after requesting that body to tackle a problem which she herself had done much to aggravate. Invariably, thus, Britain strove to retain a foothold in that area. The policy continued unaltered until history stepped in and took the play away from the big powers. And it is history that must decide whether Britain had waited too long for the good of all concerned.

10. Major Events Since 1946

1. GENERAL AND PERIPHERAL

The emergence of Israel not only overshadows the other developments of the brief period now under review but is also an epochal juncture in the history of the modern Near East. The Palestine conflict had manifold repercussions, direct or indirect, within the region as a whole. Its effects, moreover, were felt keenly by a number of outside powers, with the result that the United Nations came to be intimately involved. Nevertheless, the Near East drew to itself a share of world attention for other reasons as well, which had nothing or very little to do with the Palestine issue. Britain's over-all position in the region was in the balance. United States interests were assuming concrete shape. Violence in the Yemen attracted the spotlight for a fleeting moment to the most obscure and backward of the local states. And British sponsorship of a Sanusi Government of Cyrenaica marked a new phase in the contest over the former Italian colonies in North Africa.

Indicated changes in the status of India had caused Britain to look with growing solicitude to her possessions in Africa. The economic and industrial potential of East Africa in particular loomed especially attractive. By the end of 1946 British political and strategic thinking was focused on that quarter to such a degree that Africa was being mentioned as a replacement for India and the Far East in the regrouping of the British Empire. As a corollary, the Near East would be relegated to a secondary strategic role in the British scheme of things.

This appraisal of the situation was promptly accepted at its face value by some circles, while others viewed it with due reserve, not to say outright skepticism. In all probability, there were two schools of thought on the subject within the British Government itself. For the time being, however, there was no urgent reason why England should withdraw from "the throat of the British Empire" and repair to the waistline of Africa. At most, the African plan might be regarded as a long-range alternative while promising intermediate economic advantages. But conditions would have to take a drastic turn for the worse before Britain would reconcile herself to abandoning the Near East to outside powers, least of all to Russia. Hence the redoubled efforts to mend local fences by concluding treaties with Arab states, efforts which proved successful in the case of Transjordan but led to failure in Egypt and Iraq. The most authoritative recent comment on Britain's intentions in the Near East is contained in the following excerpt from Foreign Secretary Bevin's address before the House of Commons on January 22, 1948: "In the Middle East we have a long-standing friendship with the Arab. I have repeatedly said to the United States and the Soviet Union that the Middle East is a vital factor to world peace and that, in addition, it is a lifeline for the British Commonwealth."

Owing mainly to persistent Egyptian pressure for a revision of the 1936 treaty with Britain, negotiations between the two governments began in July 1946 and continued intermittently until the beginning of the following year. In the face of mounting strains and pressures Britain was disposed to grant concessions. On the Egyptian side a realistic solution of the common problems was all but ruled out by fanatical nationalist agitation, interparty rivalries, and ceaseless student riots—often artificially induced. The principal point at issue was the future status of the Sudan, the vast and strategically located territory which had been placed under Anglo-Egyptian condominium in 1899. The lately enhanced potential of East Africa had greatly increased the importance of the Sudan to the British Commonwealth. For Egypt's part, the Sudan had been steadily appreciating in economic importance and was a coveted nationalist prize to boot. The "unity of the Nile Valley"—a misleading slogan so long as Ethiopia was not involved—had been made into an article of faith, heresy in regard to it being tantamount to political suicide or worse. The matter was further complicated by the fact that each side could point to the sympathies of some segment of the Sudanese. In these circumstances a final impasse was inevitable. Confronted with the threat of having the issue placed before the Security Council of the United Nations, Foreign Secretary Bevin declared before the House of Commons on May 16, 1947 that "there will be no attempt to appease the Egyptian Government at the expense of the Sudanese people." The matter came up before the Security Council on August 5. The Council was not persuaded that there existed an imminent threat to the peace and it adjourned on August 29 without taking any action.

Whereas in negotiating with Egypt it was one of Britain's objectives to strengthen her position in Africa, her efforts in the instance of Iraq and Transjordan had as their stated purpose "to regularize and express Anglo-Arab friendship," thereby securing British interests in the Near East proper. By working towards a regional bloc and obtaining through treaties the right of maintaining military forces, Britain hoped to eliminate the danger of any other power acquiring dominance in that region. The Anglo-Iraqi Treaty of Alliance, which was signed in Portsmouth on January 15, 1948 and was scheduled to replace the treaty of 1930, was meant to be the first major step in that direction. Once again, however, extreme local nationalism proved to be an insuperable barrier. Mass riots forced the Iraqi Regent, the Amir Abdul-Ilah, to declare on January 21 that the treaty could not be ratified because it did not "realize the national aims of Iraq."

In Transjordan the developments proceeded more closely according to plan. Following a formal statement in the United Nations that Britain, as mandatory, intended to recognize the independence of Transjordan, a treaty was concluded on March 22, 1946 between Great Britain and the Amir of Transjordan whereby his country was acknowledged as a "fully independent State and His Highness the Amir as the sovereign thereof." On May 25, 1946 the Amir Abdullah was accordingly proclaimed king. The treaty went a long way towards insuring for Britain the privileged position in Transjordan that she had hitherto enjoyed as mandatory. An annex consisting of ten articles and considered an integral part of the treaty gave Britain broad military and diplomatic rights. Outside Transjordan there was outspoken criticism in Arab nationalist circles that the document was scarcely a treaty between equals. Two years later, in an effort to strengthen Abdullah's position with the other Arab states, and mindful of the need for a firm alliance with his country to offset the scheduled withdrawal from Palestine, Britain signed a new treaty with King Abdullah on March 15, 1948. The harsher provisions of the older document were modified, but continued British influence was effectively safeguarded. Thus, in spite of the rebuff in Iraq and the consequent abandonment of the plan to negotiate similar agreements with other Arab states, Britain managed to salvage one valuable alliance. The comment was frequently expressed that the mandatory power was about to leave Palestine by the front door only to reappear at the back door, via Transjordan. Like many such quips, this one contains a kernel of truth—in an oversimplified form.

The United States signified her fresh concern with the Near East by means of a drastic move without precedent in the record of her foreign policy outside the Western Hemisphere. In his message to Congress on March 12, 1947 outlining the basis of what was to become known as the "Truman Doctrine," the President warned that if Greece and Turkey should fall under the control of armed minorities supported from the outside, "confusion and disorder might well spread throughout the Middle East." The manifold implications of this dramatic step require no special mention in the present context. It is necessary only to point out in passing that the Near East had thus attained for the first time the kind of place in official American planning that it had long been accorded elsewhere—either as a means for expansion or as the last bastion against expansionism.

The same awareness accounts, among other and generally lesser factors, for the interest which the United States was to take—often in a confused and fumbling fashion—in the Palestine problem, which was rapidly coming to a head. It is reflected also in sundry other moves, some of which involve the more obscure and remote areas of the Near East. A case in point is furnished by the Yemen. On May 4, 1946 an agreement was concluded between the United States and the Yemen looking to the establishment of closer relations between the two countries. A token loan of one million dollars was extended by the United States to the Yemen shortly thereafter. Implicit in the agreement was American recognition of the importance of a state situated on the rim of a globally vital region. That same factor was also responsible for the admission of the Yemen to the United Nations on September 30, 1947. When it is remembered that fifteen years earlier an incomparably more advanced Arab state—Iraq—had experienced considerable difficulty before being admitted to the League of Nations, the shift in emphasis from individual merit to extraneous factors will be readily appreciated.

But the world was soon to glimpse the primitive character

of the new member state. On February 17, 1948 the Yemen's aged ruler, the Imam Yahya, was assassinated in his palace together with three of his sons and a chief adviser, by a group in the charge of a general and the ruler's sixth son. The uprising was put down a few weeks later, and Sayf al-Islam Ahmad, Yahya's eldest son, became his father's avenger and successor.

Another peripheral area, Cyrenaica, calls for brief mention in this survey because of all the former Italian colonies in North Africa it has the closest geographic, ethnic, and cultural ties with the independent Arab states. After protracted bargaining and maneuvering, an Anglo-Italian agreement was reached whereby all Libya would become independent in 1959. In the meantime, Britain would administer Cyrenaica, France would be in charge of the Fezzan, while Italy was to take over the administration of Tripolitania in 1951. This plan was approved by the First (Political) Committee of the United Nations General Assembly on May 13, 1949, against Soviet opposition which sought to establish a collective trusteeship over the former Italian colonies. On May 18, however, the General Assembly failed to approve the resolution of the Political Committee and postponed a decision until a later session.

This indecision of the international body afforded Britain the opportunity to fulfill a wartime pledge while strengthening at the same time the bond of friendship with a dominant element in the area adjoining Egypt on the northwest. On June 1, 1949 the British authorized the Sayyid Idris al-Sanusi, leader of a sect famed for its defiance of the Italian conquerors, to head a government of Cyrenaica independent in internal affairs. The move provoked immediate protests among Egyptian and other Arab nationalists. Some of the critics went so far as to liken this step to Britain's treatment of King Abdullah. At all events, it is clear that London had by no means become apathetic in regard to the Near East.

2. THE FIASCO OF A MANDATE

The fateful period of transition which marked the end of the mandatory regime in Palestine, and the ferment which followed, must be sketched here only in its barest outlines. Calmer days and a truer perspective than can now be enjoyed may in time produce a detached and definitive account out of the enormous and often conflicting detail already available and the data that have yet to come to light. In any case, the scope of this book and the space allotted to it would permit only the listing of the salient features.

The British resolve to hold on to Palestine as long as at all possible had been all along the most serious obstacle to a comprehensive solution of the Palestine problem. One plan or another was constantly on trial or under advisement. With the single exception, however, of the report of the Anglo-American Committee of Inquiry, all such plans had proved to be out of focus. They might affect, favorably or adversely, the Jewish angle or the Arab angle or both. But none touched in adequate measure on the British aspect of what was essentially a triangular issue. In each case the result was doomed to be one-sided and unbalanced.

The Balfour Declaration was a move by and in behalf of British interests which promised also to be of benefit to the Jews in that it bid fair to alleviate the Jewish problem of that time. This last objective, however, was to prove beyond the ability of any one power to accomplish. And it would have taken greater foresight than Western statesmanship could muster at San Remo, in 1920, to anticipate all the melancholy consequences of the Palestine mandate. At all events, circumstances compelled Britain, after several attempts at piecemeal solutions had failed, to change the course by issuing the White Paper of 1939—in effect a pro-Arab approach to the Palestine issue. But this did little to allay fears and promote harmony. Beyond the shelter of a mandate whose provisions she had felt obliged to circumvent, Britain continued in control of the country while the rift between the local communities was growing wider and deeper all the time. This progressive cleavage diverted attention from the mandatory's own interests in the area. Thus to the very end general attention remained centered on the Arab-Jewish conflict. So far as world opinion was concerned, Britain maintained the psychological advantage of the selfless peacemaker striving for the public good.

The report of the Anglo-American Committee was the first instance of an attempted solution of the Palestine issue by an extra-Palestine body which was not exclusively British. Significantly, the proposals reflected a degree of impartiality that had hitherto been wanting. And, no less noteworthy, the report turned out to be just that much labor wasted. The plan to be put forward instead was the federation scheme that came to bear the name of "Morrison-Grady." Ostensibly a joint Anglo-American conclusion, it was in reality a British formula in which an American delegation acquiesced. It was a thinly disguised reaffirmation of British interests in that it provided for the maintenance of effective British controls in a strategic spot of the Near East, increasingly important at a time when one after another of the established Arab states resolved to remove the last remaining vestiges of foreign influence.

By now the local Palestine communities had lost all faith in the policy of the mandatory power. Moderates in either camp were rapidly losing ground while extremists—Arab as well as Jewish—were thriving. Increasing repression on the part of a British administration progressively more helpless and callous gave Jewish terrorists in particular a new lease on a life of unbridled violence, nurtured by a warped sense of political justice. The overwhelming majority of the Jewish Community gave expression to its sense of outrage and shame, but was in no position, psychologically or administratively, to carry out an effective self-purge. The most hideous acts were to be perpetrated in 1947-48—on British hostages, at the Arab village of Dayr Yasin, and on Count Folke Bernadotte—acts of a few which were to cause so much harm and bring infamy to so many. Unhappily, as is so often the case with fanatics impervious to reason, sequence is liable to be mistaken by them for consequence.

With the situation now wholly out of hand, the British came at last to the conclusion that their position in Palestine had become not only intolerable but also untenable. Early in April 1947 Great Britain formally requested a special session of the United Nations General Assembly to consider the Palestine problem. This body set up in May the United Nations Special Committee on Palestine (UNSCOP), consisting of eleven "neutral" representatives, the states chosen being Australia, Canada, Czechoslovakia, Guatemala, India, Iran, Netherlands, Peru, Sweden, Uruguay, and Yugoslavia.

Britain's request was hailed in some quarters as yet another instance of genuine disinterestedness in her handling of a thankless issue. These circles, however, were soon to be disabused. No sooner had the committee held its first meeting, on May 26, than Mr. Bevin, speaking at the conference of the Labor Party on May 29, stated that he personally would not feel bound by any United Nations decision regarding Palestine unless it was unanimous. The same view was officially communicated to the United Nations by Sir Alexander Cadogan on November 20, when he declared that Britain would not take any responsibility for a United Nations settlement that was not acceptable to both Jews and Arabs. This meant no settlement at all, since it was abundantly clear to all concerned, and to Britain most of all, that any solution would have to be imposed.

What lay behind these mutually contradictory moves by Britain which only threatened to obstruct a speedy solution? Various explanations have been advanced. A reluctance to bow to the inevitable, which one member of UNSCOP has described as a case of imperialism dying hard? The hope that continued chaos might yet cause Britain to be invited back so as to restore order? Saving up credits with the Arabs for future use? Fear of Russian infiltration, now that the Soviets, after long and studious silence, had come out in favor of partition? Foreign Secretary Bevin's personal idiosyncrasies? Or perhaps a combination of several such possibilities? Future history may shed light on this whole question. Mr. Bevin's pronouncement, "I will stake my reputation on solving the Palestine problem," is a matter of record. Eventually his policy was branded as a "blustering persistence in error" by the London *Observer*, and as the "quintessence of maladdress" by Mr. Churchill. There was severe criticism within his own party and the House of Commons margin in his favor in January 1949 was the narrowest in his career as Foreign Secretary, with many abstentions. That the Bevin policy on Palestine misfired is now an obvious fact. It is not established, however, that in clinging tenaciously to his set course, to the last possible moment, the Foreign Secretary was trying to be anything else than pro-British, according to his own lights.

At all events, UNSCOP got little aid and comfort from the British authorities in the preparation of its report, which was completed on August 31, 1947. This first truly international investigative body agreed unanimously that the British mandate should be terminated at the earliest possible date. As to the way in which Palestine independence was to be effected, the committee was divided. A minority of three —India, Iran, and Yugoslavia—called for a federal state. One country—Australia—abstained from voting. The remaining seven representatives brought in the majority recommendations which advocated partition of the land into a Jewish and an Arab state, with economic union. Jerusalem would become a permanent trusteeship.

On November 29, 1947 the General Assembly of the United Nations adopted a resolution in line with the partition recommendations of the UNSCOP majority, by a vote of 33 in favor, 13 against, 10 abstentions, with one country absent. Much has since been said to the effect that the outcome was due primarily to United States pressure. Such a view seems to ignore the fact that the committee which had recommended partition by a 7–3 majority was composed in its entirety of representatives whose countries had no domestic grounds for favoring the Zionists. On the other hand, three of the states in question had ample reason for a pro-Arab orientation. Iran is a Muslim land. India, before her own partition, was the home of nearly a third of the world's total Islamic population, and one of the two successor states is Muslim Pakistan; moreover, the Indian delegate was himself a devout Muslim. Lastly, Yugoslavia has her own substantial Muslim minority. It was a foregone conclusion that the proverbial solidarity which characterizes all Islamic communities would in the case of these three members express itself inevitably in a leaning towards the Arab side. The requirement of strict neutrality in the setup of the committee was thus violated in substance, if not technically. And yet, even this so-called "Muslim bloc," which submitted the minority view, agreed with the rest that the Zionist case was not altogether without merit and, in differing from the majority, went no further than to recommend a federal state in Palestine. This recommendation, too, was promptly rejected by the Arab Higher Committee. In short, the initial majority conclusion in favor of partitioning Palestine had been reached in spite of pro-Arab influences. The United States can scarcely be stigmatized for being impressed with this result. That lobbyists on either side were feverishly at work at Lake Success in November 1947 goes without saying and there is evidence to prove it. Nor can there be any doubt that the United States vote was affected largely by domestic considerations. But if there was any concerted United States pressure on other countries to win them over to partition, it could not have been very successful. For it is certainly significant that Greece and Turkey, by then recipients of aid under the "Truman Doctrine," did not hesitate, nevertheless, to cast their votes against the partition resolution. To say that Washington forced the vote would thus seem to be giving to wishful thinking a curious retroactive twist.

If criticism of the United States is in order, it is not because this country imposed her will on others but rather because the government was not itself clear as to what to do. The new United Nations Palestine Commission of five (Bolivia, Czechoslovakia, Denmark, Panama, and the Philippines), set up to administer Palestine during the transition period, soon discovered that little could be done to implement the partition plan while the mandatory authorities were still in the country. Britain had announced that she would terminate her mandate on May 15, 1948. Until two weeks prior to that date the mandatory administration would have no dealings with the Palestine Commission. The borders of Palestine were to remain closed in the meantime. This meant in effect that while the British blockade cut off Jewish arrivals—which on any substantial scale were possible only by sea—Arabs were able to filter in from the neighboring states, inasmuch as a tight control of all the approaches by land was out of the question. Once again, Britain's technical impartiality served designedly as an instrument of pro-Arab policy. Furthermore, three Arab states—Transjordan, Egypt, and Iraq—were receiving British armaments, in fulfillment, it was explained, of previous contractual obligations. Well-equipped Arab armies could mass on the borders of Palestine and volunteers could cross at will, while Jews must wait for supplies until the eve of the mandate's relinquishment. In their case, in short, the mandatory's attitude was by no means benevolent.

Belatedly the United States discovered that she had become a prominent party to a commitment which she was in no way ready to see through. Relations with Britain were seriously impaired. Partnership with Russia in the matter of partition, however different the underlying motives, was a source of increasing discomfort and the cause of mounting criticism. Oil interests were disturbed and military circles apprehensive. The upshot of all this was the United States request, on March 19, 1948, that the Security Council suspend action on the partition plan and substitute a temporary trusteeship.

This was a startling reversal of a policy that had been advocated so ardently and confidently less than three months earlier. Had the trusteeship plan been advanced as an alternative to the partition proposal, few could have failed to view it as a considered and constructive effort. But coming when it did, this about-face by the world's greatest power was a blow to the prestige of the United States and a threat to the very basis of the United Nations.

With international authority at its lowest ebb, Palestine could see only boundless chaos ahead. The last faint hope for an international settlement had vanished. The Arabs had seldom felt more encouraged, the Zionists never more desperately resolved to take their fate into their own hands. The British forces on their way out were impotent, and in some cases unwilling, to prevent the spread of fighting which was rapidly assuming the proportions of a full-scale war. The Promised Land was flowing, though not with milk and honey. The world looked on with mounting apprehension.

On April 16, 1948 the second special session of the General Assembly convened in a half-hearted attempt to tackle the crisis. The only positive result was the decision, taken on

May 14, to send a mediator to Palestine. On that same day the Jews, invoking the partition resolution of the United Nations, proclaimed the establishment of a Jewish state in Palestine, to be called Israel. On March 15, 1949 Great Britain had signed a new treaty of alliance with Transjordan to replace that of 1946. The British were physically out of Palestine. But, in one way or another, they still were very tangibly in the Near East.

3. THE RISE OF ISRAEL

Initial appraisals of the military prospects in the evolving communal war in Palestine leaned heavily towards the Arab side. Aside from the Palestine "irregulars," the Arab forces closing in from three sides bore the banners of five independent states. Three of these armies had had years of training under competent Western instructors. They were supported by heavy equipment which the British were even then replenishing under the formula of prior contractual commitments. The Haganah, on the other hand, its differences with the extremist Irgun and Stern groups temporarily suppressed, had to put its trust in undercover training and in such small arms as had eluded the vigilance of the mandatory regime. Moreover, the Arabs enjoyed overwhelming superiority in potential manpower. In these circumstances, it was felt, the Jews were doomed to be pushed eventually into the sea, in some sectors less than a score of miles away. Many feared an awesome holocaust. Some circles saw in this prospect the promise of a welcome catharsis. A Jewish victory, at any rate, appeared in those early months of 1948 no more credible than a victory by a prominent later contestant of that year, who nevertheless was to confound all predictions on November 2. By that time, however, the other contest, too, had been all but decided—with equally incredible results.

It is simpler, of course, to analyze the outcome in retrospect. Arab strength had been seriously miscalculated, both locally and abroad. Their armies lacked discipline on the whole and, as the battle progressed, internal social and political weaknesses were making themselves felt more and more. The other side had the advantage of superior discipline, unity, unbounded belief in their cause—in addition to the still fresh memory of yesterday's horrors and the stark conviction that in no other way could a brighter tomorrow be wrested. When all this has been said, however, one is left with the feeling that this latest stage in the immemorial history of Palestine somehow eludes sober analysis—just as many earlier stages in the paradoxical career of that unique land have yet to receive a complete explanation.

The initial weeks of open warfare in Palestine—while British troops were still in the country—served as a warning that the ultimate outcome was not at all a foregone conclusion. The Arabs were forced to surrender Haifa, Jaffa, Tiberias, and Safad and they suffered a major defeat in the Emeq (Valley of Jezreel) even before the mandate had been relinquished and the State of Israel proclaimed. With the lifting of the British blockade essential supplies and manpower began to pour in by sea. Time was working to Israel's advantage.

The new state and its Provisional Government were granted immediate *de facto* recognition by the United States, on May 14, three days ahead of their unconditional recognition by Russia. Critics were prompt to brand the American move as precipitate, an accusation to which Washington had left itself exposed by its prior record of fumbling and inconsistency. Recognition by various other states followed in rapid succession.

On May 20 Count Folke Bernadotte was appointed as United Nations Mediator for Palestine. By June 2 he had succeeded in making the combatants agree to a four-week truce, which went into effect on June 11. The Israelis utilized the break in fighting to regroup and strengthen their armed forces and to proceed with the urgent tasks of internal organization. To the Arabs it was a period of slowly developing rifts in a hitherto united front. Only Transjordan's Arab Legion had made a creditable showing in the battle for the walled Old City in Jerusalem. Yet even this well-disciplined army could not render untenable the position of the 100,000 Jews who had been virtually isolated in the modern sections of Jerusalem. The armies of the sister states had not covered themselves with glory. Since the Arab victory that had been so confidently expected was no longer a certainty, King Abdullah was beginning to weigh the possible advantages of henceforward playing a lone hand. He might thus stand a good chance of falling heir to the Arab portions of Palestine.

Meanwhile, another unforeseen development had become a complex factor in the over-all situation. Israel's military successes were attended by a mass exodus of the Arab population. Their numbers swelled rapidly to hundreds of thousands. There is good evidence that Israeli authorities had not counted on any such eventuality. The result can be ascribed directly to alarmist propaganda of the Husayni group which centered about the former Mufti; indirectly to the effects of divisive British policy; and, as the battle progressed, also to the Irgunist massacre at the village of Dayr Yasin. Those Arabs who stayed in their homes have since discovered that they have nothing to fear from the Israeli administration; they now have three representatives in the new Constituent Assembly (*Kneset*). The fate of the misled refugees, however, must now be the joint concern of Israel, the Arab states, and the nations of the world. They are the miserable victims of circumstances for which others must bear the primary responsibility. For Israel the situation is at once a boon and a burden. The withdrawal of the Arabs has unexpectedly left the young country with a relatively homogeneous population and with far more room for the incoming thousands than could possibly have been anticipated. But this windfall is offset to a large degree by moral considerations. The entire problem is bound to test Israeli statesmanship to the utmost.

The expiration of the truce on July 9 was followed by a succession of notable Israeli victories, and a second truce on July 18. While pressing for the new truce, Count Bernadotte was at work on his comprehensive mediation proposals. On September 17 the Mediator was assassinated in Jerusalem by members of the Stern group. In committing this crime against peace and humanity they set back the very cause which they so pathetically espoused. Three days later, the United Nations released to a deeply shocked world the contents of the late Mediator's proposals. Whatever its inherent merits, the plan obviously sought to restore peace to the troubled land by the quickest available means and thus lessen the international tension which the Palestine conflict had brought about.

In brief, the Bernadotte plan recognized the existence of Israel as a sovereign state. But it modified the original United Nations partition scheme in that it would grant the large desert area in the south, known as the Negeb, to the Arabs while compensating Israel with the much smaller area of Western Galilee. For various reasons the plan proved unacceptable to Israelis and Arabs alike. What is particularly significant, however, is the fact that the Bernadotte proposal was promptly endorsed by Britain, soon to be seconded by the United States. The British endorsement was the first intimation by Foreign Secretary Bevin that his government was prepared to reconcile itself to the existence of Israel, thus reversing a policy of long standing and at the same time incurring much Arab displeasure. In a broader sense, however, this was not a capricious departure. For, apart from bowing to the new realities, Britain saw in a Negeb restored to the Arabs—and especially if joined to Transjordan—the prospect of sharing in the control of an area enjoying obvious strategic advantages, not to mention its reputed economic potential.

That the plan did not go through was due in large measure to sweeping Israeli victories in October and December at the expense of the Egyptian forces. By then Transjordan was openly at odds with the other Arab states, refusing to recognize the Palestine Arab Government which had been set up at Gaza, on September 20, under Husayni leadership and the prime sponsorship of Egypt. The inter-Arab rift became particularly serious after Abdullah had permitted a Palestine Arab Congress, meeting in Jericho on December 1, to acclaim him as "King of Palestine," and had named his own Mufti of Jerusalem in place of the increasingly unpopular Amin al-Husayni. In line with these moves, and in anticipation of new holdings on the Palestine side of the Jordan accruing from the eventual peace settlement, the name of Abdullah's country was changed on April 26, 1949 to the "Hashimite Kingdom of Jordan."

On assuming his duties as Acting Mediator, in September 1948, Dr. Ralph J. Bunche set out to effect a general cease-fire followed by the conclusion of a permanent armistice. In both these tasks he was signally successful, thus earning for himself the gratitude and admiration of the parties concerned, and of the whole community of the United Nations whose prestige he did so much to restore. In a series of bilateral agreements, he first produced an armistice between Egypt and Israel, on February 24, 1949, with the other Arab states gradually following suit. The last armistice agreement, between Israel and Syria, was signed on July 20. A fresh impetus was thus given to the peace talks conducted under the aegis of the United Nations Conciliation Committee—represented by France, Turkey, and the United States—

which hitherto had been holding sessions without any appreciable results.

On January 25, 1949, Israel held elections for her Constituent Assembly (*Kneset*) of 120 members. The largest number of votes went to the *Mapai* Labor Party, headed by Prime Minister David Ben Gurion, which obtained 46 seats. The second largest vote, yielding 19 seats, was polled by the sharply leftist labor group known as *Mapam*. Four seats were won by Communists, one of them an Arab. In view of the oft-voiced suspicion that many of the immigrant ships intercepted by Britain during the last months of her mandate included numerous Communist agents, these results—which reflect some 85 per cent of the entire electorate—appear highly instructive. No less significant is the fact that *Mapam* had refused the Communists' bid to present a joint slate. Two seats were won by the Arab Democratic Party.

On January 29, 1949, world acceptance of the accomplished fact in Palestine was underscored by Great Britain when she granted *de facto* recognition to the State of Israel. Two days later United States recognition of Israel was given *de jure* status. On May 11 Israel became the fifty-ninth member of the United Nations, by a vote of 37 to 12, with 9 abstentions. In the space of one year the new state had fought its way, against seemingly insurmountable odds, to full diplomatic status among the countries of the world. But Israel's problems at home, and with them the joint problems of the Near East as a whole, are as yet a long way from being settled.

4. THE AFTERMATH

The emergence of Israel constitutes the end of one era and the start of another. The parties most obviously affected are, of course, the new state itself and the neighboring Arab nations which have sought to block it. In each instance, but most especially in Israel, many new issues have to be met. Relations between the individual Arab states face drastic revision, and intra-regional alignments are in the inchoate stage. The policies of the outside powers in regard to the Near East are in the process of revision. A sharp picture of the evolving pattern may not be discernible for some time to come. In any case, there is room here only for a provisional sketch done in rough outline.

Israel's immediate problem is the establishment of relations with her Arab neighbors on a friendly basis. The question of the refugees and the necessary boundary issues are sure to tax the conscience and the wisdom of the negotiators. The future status of Jerusalem threatens to be a source of many complexities—local and international, political and religious, practical and psychological. Israeli economy will be strained to the breaking point by the gigantic task of absorbing the flow of immigration, which in two years has swelled the total population by a third. New capital must be attracted, against the handicap of the investor's inherent distrust of a basically controlled economy. In this connection the role of the *Histadrut*, or General Federation of Jewish Labor, may prove to be a determining factor. For this body not only embraces over three-fourths of all organized labor in Israel but is at the same time also the owner-manager of some 20 per cent of the country's commerce, industry, and trade. This dual function on such a large scale offers an unusual opportunity for pioneering developments in capital-labor relations.

Among the other problems that confront the new state is the pressure of marginal elements on the right and on the left. The heirs of the extremist Irgun are now regrouped under the *Herut* (Freedom) Party, which won 14 seats in the January elections. Remnants of the former Sternist group could gain only a single seat. Altered circumstances have greatly weakened the appeal of these elements to the community as a whole. But their potential capacity for making headway among malcontents is by no means negligible. On the far left, though not at the Communist extreme, stands the *Mapam* faction, which is critical of the West and sympathetic, without being actually addicted, to Russia. Their voice cannot be entirely ignored in charting Israel's foreign relations. Lastly, the United Religious Front—the nation's third strongest party, which at present commands 16 seats in the Assembly—is likely to pose more than one acute problem. Since Israel and religion have a common association that reaches back to remote Biblical times, the issue of church and state is certain to contribute its full share of perplexities.

To the Arab states the aftermath of the Palestine war would seem to be far more portentous than to Israel. Their relative disadvantage is in large measure psychological, which makes it all the more difficult to overcome. Defeat is seldom easy to accept. But it is cruelly disillusioning when the people had been nurtured all along on spurious accounts of incessant victories. When the truth begins to penetrate at long last, it threatens to expose all the weaknesses from which the respective countries have suffered. In this instance, two things above all others have been made glaringly clear: the flimsy foundations of the Arab League; and the urgent need for social and political reform inside the individual states.

When the Arab League was founded, it was a question whether its negative basis of united opposition to Zionism would stand the test of time and prove sufficient to outweigh the existing divisive factors. The defeat by a severely handicapped opponent reactivated all the old rivalries, with their intrigues and bickering and mutual recriminations. Egypt's leadership in the Arab League made that body especially vulnerable in view of the Egyptian record on the battlefield. The respectable showing by Abdullah's Arab Legion placed

Jordan temporarily in the limelight and revived the king's old ambitions for a Greater Syria, or—alternatively—for the Fertile Crescent scheme, with Hashimite Iraq included. The difficulty with either of these plans is that each revolves around the poorest and numerically weakest among the Arab states. Furthermore, Abdullah himself has little following and is strongly disliked in Saudi Arabia and in Egypt, aside from being opposed by influential Syrian circles.

Disaffection in Egypt first led to the assassination, on December 4, 1948, of the Cairo Chief of Police. On the 28th of that same month a member of the fanatical Muslim Brotherhood (*Ikhwan al-Muslimun*), which the authorities had dissolved three weeks earlier, shot and killed the Prime Minister, Mahmud Fahmi Nuqrahi Pasha. The leader of the Brotherhood, Shaykh Hasan al-Banna, was shot and killed in turn on February 12, 1949. These acts of violence are symptomatic of Egypt's thoroughgoing internal weakness and may presage far more serious disorders unless drastic steps are taken to deal concretely with the age-old accumulation of domestic ills.

Syria's restlessness led to a coup d'état on March 30–31, 1949, directed by Colonel Husni Za'im, who has a record of pronounced authoritarian leanings. Democratic institutions were suspended and all political parties abolished, with no evident demurrer or regret on the part of the general public. This apathy in a republic was a mute indictment of political practices existing even in the most advanced Arab states. Tension developed promptly not only with Jordan—this being the answer of the new Chief of State to Abdullah's Greater Syria scheme—but also with Iraq and Lebanon. The strain was eased in time, but the general situation remains delicate, not to say explosive. On the other hand, there have been signs of a possible *rapprochement* with Turkey, long the target of Syrian nationalist attacks on account of her annexation of Alexandretta (Hatay). In short, inter-Arab unity and ethnic Arab nationalism bid fair to be supplanted by new alignments and by a greater emphasis on state nationalism.

The Republic of Lebanon appears to regard the latest happenings in Egypt and Syria as a sharp warning that extreme nationalism in any form must not be allowed to get out of hand. On July 8, 1949, Lebanon executed Antun Saadi, leader of the totalitarian Syrian Popular Party, who was charged with instigating an armed rebellion. Twelve of his associates were also condemned to death. At the same time, however, the prevailing nervousness reacted also on more orthodox political parties, such as the powerful Falange. This atmosphere of general uneasiness may foreshadow far-reaching changes throughout Arab world. An evolutionary advance could mean a gradual solution of the most pressing needs.

The over-all situation in the Near East requires, lastly, a reorientation of the policies of outside powers towards the region. Britain has always been realistic enough to try a new approach once the last hope of upholding the old had gone. Her recognition of Israel and her more recent moves in Cyrenaica are proof that a revision of British policy in the Near East has been taking place. Britain's main objectives in that region today may be described as defense of her own position and blocking the spread of Communist influence. Russia's support of the partition plan for Palestine and her friendly initial moves towards Israel have been variously interpreted. The most plausible explanation, however, would seem to be that to Russia partition was the most practical means of getting the British out of the country. There might well have been also the further hope that Israel would prove receptive to Communist policies. If that was a factor, Russia must by now have realized her miscalculation. The results of the January elections in Israel cannot have been encouraging to Moscow. Perhaps this is the reason why anti-Zionist trends have recently been reported from Czechoslovakia, Hungary, and Rumania.

So far, the latest overt moves of the major powers in the Near East have been so many straws in the wind. The situation today is more fluid than it has been in years. The world in general has not quite rid itself of the fatalistic feeling that this civilization, at least, is doomed and that we are living in the twilight which precedes the darkness of the apocalypse. The current difficulties of the Near East are in a very real sense a reflection of the unsettled state of the world. Stability in that region would be an important contribution towards world stability. For that reason, among others, a grave responsibility rests upon the United States.

11. The United States, the Near East, and the Future

1. INTERESTS

Walter Lippmann has reminded us recently that a dynamic nation cannot be an isolationist nation; that to maintain a world position, a nation must have a solvent foreign policy; and that a foreign policy cannot be solvent unless it brings into balance the nation's foreign commitments and the nation's power to meet them.

Commitments are founded on interests. The degree to which a nation may be prepared to enter into extraneous commitments must depend, in the final analysis, upon the importance which that nation attaches to its outside interests.

Foreign interests of nations, large and small, obviously cannot be considered as fixed quantities. They vary with the constantly changing conditions—political, strategic, economic, and social. The policy designed to protect such interests is thus subject to frequent readjustments. Where new interests have sprung up, specific policy has to be devised, consistent with the nation's general foreign policy. What is not variable, however, is the need for maintaining commitments and policy in equilibrium. For the end result cannot be left to chance. Nor can hastily improvised means insure the end desired.

The United States has today very significant interests in

the Near East. The foreign policy required to maintain them is as yet unformed. It is a fact that the interests in question are too recent to have produced at this early stage a far-sighted policy, at once self-consistent and mature. But the same interests are also too critical to allow much time for experimenting with policy or for entrusting it to hit-or-miss methods. The question is whether we have taken or are taking the steps calculated to develop an adequate policy. Before this question can be answered, however, another must first be posed: What are the essential interests of the United States in the Near East?

Limited or specialized United States activities in the region go back in some instances to the beginning of the nineteenth century. The familiar "to the shores of Tripoli" evokes memories of resolute operations, in 1803–04, by the country's young navy against the Tripolitan corsairs who had been preying upon American shipping in the Mediterranean.

American missionaries arrived in the Levant in 1820. By 1834 the mission had an Arabic printing press in Bayrut which was to prove of immense value in facilitating educational work in the whole area. Because of its primary emphasis on native traditions and culture, this American religious-educational enterprise bore unexpectedly rich fruit. Since it was free from any political taint whatsoever, it came to enjoy a reputation and a response which the concurrent, and competing, French effort could not bring forth. Steady progress was crowned in 1866 by the opening in Bayrut of the Syrian Protestant College, which in course of time attained the status of a general and justly celebrated university. The part which this institution has played in raising the level of Arab cultural and national activities, thanks both to its direct impact on the students and the subsequent influence of its graduates, cannot be exaggerated. What is more, this particular American investment—"an investment in international good will," to cite the motto of the Near East College Association—was in a broader sense, too, bread cast upon the waters. The good will of the Arabs was extended to the United States as a whole, following especially the proclamation of the Wilsonian principle of national self-determination. And the Arabs, for their part, had earned, by their warm response to the university's efforts, the genuine devotion of its sponsors and staff to the success of the Arab national cause. It should also be borne in mind that, aside from the American educational personnel with field experience in the Near East, this country has few sources on which it can depend for informed advice on Arab affairs. The advice that is thus available, if not always objective, has almost invariably been sympathetic to Arab aspirations.

American archaeological activity in the Near East dates back to the year 1838. It was in that year that Edward Robinson began his journeys in Palestine for the purpose of studying the geography, topography, and archaeological remains of the Holy Land. In the course of the century following Robinson's first campaign, American archaeologists have contributed their full share to the international undertaking which has had as its object the unearthing and interpretation of the region's priceless treasures of the past. The modern Near East owes to this joint effort much of the knowledge which it now has of its own background. This has proved to be a source of pride and gratification to the various local states—Egypt and Iraq, Palestine and the Levant.

To round out this brief review of sporadic American interests in the region prior to the war, mention has to be made of our trade with the Near East: imports, consisting in the main of unprocessed agricultural products; and exports, chiefly of automobiles and other machinery. In this field of international relations with the Near East, the

United States occupied a relatively minor place, especially when compared with Britain's. All in all, the pre-war concern of the United States with the Near East was for the most part religious, educational, archaeological, and humanitarian. The commercial interest was for a long time insufficient to attract unusual attention from political circles.

The inception of practical United States interests in the Near East on a large scale dates back to the discovery of extensive oil fields in the region. Determined opposition by this country to the San Remo disposal of the Mosul oil fields eventually gained for American companies a one-quarter share in that concession. American holdings in the Near East were enlarged considerably in the 1930's, but direct government participation in the enterprise, to parallel Britain's, was still lacking. The prodigious drain on our domestic petroleum reserves which was brought about by the Second World War finally made the oil of the Near East an urgent concern of national United States policy. An attempt was made in 1944 to give the country a direct stake in Arabian oil in the form of a government-financed pipe line from the Arabian fields to some Mediterranean outlet. For a variety of reasons that attempt failed. Meanwhile, the national need for insuring an adequate future oil supply has been growing progressively more acute. The whole question has been dealt with at greater length in a previous chapter.

The events of the recent war, while they enhanced the importance of adequate petroleum reserves, also served to bring out other factors. These additional factors have already been discussed. Their combined effect is to make of the Near East a global center of gravity. It remains only to inquire how each factor relates to the direct interests of the United States. Aside from oil, the Near East has a strong claim on world interest by reason of position, world communications, and the region's potential bearing on war or peace. The strategic position is unquestionably of far greater significance to either Britain or Russia than it is to the United States. World communications, on the other hand—and especially air communications—cannot be judged on any such relative basis. If any single power has the right of veto over them, they cease to be world communications and become a dangerous world monopoly. Or, to put it differently, if the Near East is the key to vital world communications, the control of that region's communication facilities must be an international concern. This is one reason, then, why no major power today can afford to dispense with an active interest in the Near East. It applies to the United States with as much cogency as it does to Russia or Britain.

Another interest in the Near East which the major powers have in common is the interest in world peace and security. Resting on the three dominant factors of position, oil, and communications, this interest obviously transcends all others. The United States cannot surrender by default her right to determine whether it shall be peace or war any more than can Russia or Britain. That such a decision may be made in the Near East has been amply demonstrated by recent events. It is in that region that Britain and Russia have been bitter rivals for many years, and it is there that this rivalry is more acute now than ever. Without the moderating influence of a third great power, the outcome is likely to be war. If a basis for peace and coöperation is to be discovered, the prospects for arriving at it are heightened by the presence of other vitally interested parties. The United States has vital interests in the Near East owing to her need for oil and her concern about world-wide air routes. She is in fact a vitally interested party. She has also precisely the same interest in peace as have all the other powers. Accordingly, our full-fledged participation in the affairs of the Near East would be by no means a matter of taking on the thankless task of mediator. It should be a matter of enlightened, and urgent, self-interest.

2. POLICY

These multiple interests of the United States in the Near East did not develop slowly, in a process of orderly evolution. They overtook us, so to speak, without prior warning. President Roosevelt's dramatic meeting with Arab leaders in February 1945 in Egyptian territorial waters was perhaps the first general intimation to this country that the region had assumed a position requiring a long-range commitment on our part. And the rapidly growing feeling that we had more at stake in the Near East than mere oil reserves was given substance in President Truman's Army Day address of April 6, 1946. Yet a clear appreciation of our commitment in the Near East, with all its manifold implications, has not been in evidence. Hence there could be no purposeful policy to marshal our power behind that commitment.

This statement needs to be qualified. Over a period of years we have had a succession of policies bearing on the Near East. Our protest against the indicated exclusion of American business interests from sharing in the development of the Mosul oil fields was an instance of policy. The American-British Convention of 1924 regarding the Palestine mandate was another such instance. The plan to finance and operate a pipe line from the Arabian oil fields presupposed a policy of some kind. And our recognition of the independence of the two Levant States in 1944 was yet another instance of policy. We have thus had various individual policies. But we have lacked a single comprehensive policy towards the region as a whole. A policy, that is, carefully considered and duly integrated, based on a thorough analysis and full understanding of our own interests, the local interests, and the competing foreign interests. One, moreover, which would be representative of our government as a body, instead of reflecting the wishes of this or that department or agency—not to speak of the sympathies of the legislative or executive branch of the government. Finally, any considered United States policy in the Near East should form an integral part of the country's general foreign policy. These fundamental requirements have not been met to date. They have been neglected or ignored. What we have had has been a series of disjointed fragments of policy with regard to the Near East, in place of the uniform and coördinated effort that is needed. That is why, to go back to Walter Lippmann's statement, ours has not been a solvent undertaking in that region.

The political divisions which prevail in the Near East today should not blind us to the underlying cultural and psychological unity of the region as a whole. Unifying forces invariably come to the fore in the Near East when foreign interests are involved. Whatever the differences among the individual states, or the domestic conflicts within any one state, they will be readily subordinated—by the Muslim Arabs, and usually also by the Christian Arabs—to the primary need for a common front against an intrusive pressure or threat of pressure. This sense of ethnic solidarity is strengthened among the Muslim Arabs—who constitute an overwhelming majority of the region's population—by the traditional community of religious interests. In short, the far-reaching interdependence of the local states and territories imposes on the interested foreign power the obligation to approach the entire region as a unit. To deal with one local state is to invite the intimate participation of the rest. And to pursue an economic objective in one part of the region is to be involved in the political life of the whole Near East. The modern Near East is much like a feather bed: you cannot punch it in one spot without causing it to bulge out in several other places. Hence any foreign policy in the Near East which is not a comprehensive regional policy is an invitation to bankruptcy.

What kind of regional policy should the United States adopt in pursuing her interests in the Near East? It would scarcely be unjust to the British to describe their course in the region as one of increasingly more considerate imperialism. Public opinion in this country would not willingly approve any form of imperialism, however enlightened. Even though our practices may not always stay within the bounds prescribed by our institutions, we are geared to democracy psychologically as well as functionally. And just as we seek to honor the democratic ideal at home, we are inclined to favor it abroad. Thus, while we appreciate the close kinship which exists between ourselves and democratic Britain, we are inclined to draw comfort from the belief that, given Britain's commitments, we would attempt to practice abroad what we preach at home. Therefore, the instinctive answer of most Americans to the question just posed would be, "Of course, our policy in the Near East should be in harmony with our democratic ideal." This would seem to be also the genuine belief of the official bodies responsible for the planning and conduct of our Near East affairs.

It appears, however, that having arrived at this view, we have gone on to allow our wish to run away with our judgment. We are genuinely interested in the principle of a democratic, prosperous, and independent Near East. The region's prosperity, we admit, is not quite yet around the corner, although it may not be far away. But we somehow take for granted that the corner has already been turned both as regards full independence and essential democratic progress. The facts of the case do not justify such assumptions.

Some Near East countries have taken over many Western concepts and institutions. It has proved to be a hasty process of adoption, not accompanied by meaningful assimilation of the new elements on the part of the adoptive states. The resulting weaknesses and abuses will under ordinary conditions be condoned at home and go unnoticed abroad. The real test occurs when internal strains have brought on a severe crisis. At such times a change in government may bring with it the collapse of the underlying institutions, which turn out to have been little more than hollow forms. This is precisely what happened recently in Syria. Until March 1949 that state, together with neighboring Lebanon, was cited with pride and satisfaction as one of the two Arab states which, as parliamentary republics, pointed the way to political progress in the whole region. Yet when Syria succumbed in that month to a military coup d'état, the democratic institutions went out, undefended and unlamented.

Democracy in the Near East is not as yet a reality, not even in the relatively advanced and progressive states. The existing constitutional monarchies lag farther behind, while Saudi Arabia and the Yemen make no pretense of being anything other than absolute regimes. It may well be that democracy in the Western sense, with all necessary allowances for the disproportion between institutions and practices, is not the ideal system for the Arab states; or that it may be applicable in the end, but must be allowed enough time to develop and strike root. One must not overlook the fact that the ancient Near East developed a kind of democracy of its own thousands of years before the West. At any rate, by assuming the existence of a democratic Near East today, we are only helping to postpone the essential political and social reforms without which that region cannot look forward to genuine peace and security.

We have been equally naïve, sentimental, or inconsistent, as the case may be, in the matter of the independence of the various Near East states. The fact that we are genuinely committed to the goal of their independence should not cause us to confuse the ideal with its actual attainment. A truly independent Near East would seem to offer the best promise of stability in the region, and would thus contribute to the peace and stability of the world. But by encouraging in the Near East states an inflated sense of self-importance we are indirectly retarding the desired achievement. Foreign aid, which is so urgently needed, may be belittled and even declined if the prospective recipient is pampered into the erroneous belief that such assistance is really gratuitous.

It follows that our policy towards the Near East should be based on a thorough understanding of the present social and political conditions in the region. It should be realistic and strive neither to overplay nor to underestimate the current state of the region's development. A level appraisal of the situation cannot but prove advantageous, in the final analysis, to both sides. It is likewise a matter of mutual interest that our stake in the Near East be maintained. The cry is often raised that unless we support the established regimes, at all costs, communism will sweep the entire region. The truth would seem to be that if the Near East turns to ideologies that are repugnant to the vast majority of its population, it will be mainly our fault in seeking to perpetuate conditions that no group can tolerate indefinitely. In other words, it is our task to facilitate evolutionary changes in the region if chaos, violence, and resort to panaceas are to be avoided.

The third basic requirement of an effective United States policy in the Near East is that it must be an independent policy. For a variety of reasons we have hitherto deferred largely to the British in this matter. This pronounced dependence on Britain could not be really advantageous to ourselves. It has not been in the best interests of the region. And, to the extent to which it encouraged unilateral moves, it has not worked to the ultimate advantage of Britain.

Our ready deference to Britain in the Near East is due primarily to historical circumstances. When our own interests first drew us to that region, we found that Britain had already leased the most attractive premises for her own occupancy and had taken out options on a majority of the others. We were obliged either to sublease or pay a heavy premium to Britain for the acquisition of direct rights. In the case of Saudi Arabia, economic opportunities still happened to be open; but even here Britain's political influence set definite limits to our economic initiative, inasmuch as economy and politics are very closely interlocked throughout the region. Confronted with the eclipse of French influence in the Near East, and in the face of Russian expansionism pointing unmistakably towards this strategic center, Britain eventually came to view the growing United States interest with more satisfaction than apprehension.

For our part, we cannot begrudge the British the many advantages of their prior start. Nor can the British be blamed for capitalizing on their greater experience or for hoping to prolong indefinitely a highly useful form of partnership. But there was in this situation the danger that our interests and policy in the Near East could develop only with British approval. Our attitude towards the local countries would have to harmonize with Britain's attitude. In short, we should have to underwrite Britain's policy in a region vital not only to her but also to us and to others.

This is not to imply that on any number of major issues we would not have arrived independently at the same conclusion as the British. Our agreements with our principal ally would most likely have outnumbered the disagreements. But a decision freely arrived at is not a decision that has been imposed. It is inconceivable, for instance, that we would have embraced on our own initiative the Morrison-Grady plan for Palestine which would give Britain control through federalization while we footed the bill. Genuine Anglo-American coöperation might have led to a solution in Palestine without resort to arms. As it was, the issue caused a severe strain in the mutual relations of the two countries. It was only after the Palestine situation had got out of hand, threatening a world-wide crisis, that a balanced Anglo-American policy in the region became at long last a distinct possibility.

The fourth and last condition for a constructive American policy in the Near East is that, aside from being regional, realistic, and independent, it must also be consistent. The Palestine problem in particular saw us vacillating and foundering, with the result that the situation in the Near East progressed from bad to worse while the prestige of the United Nations sank to its lowest depths. Fortunately for all concerned, the explosion that followed was primarily a local blast. Another explosion in the Near East might not remain confined to that region alone.

3. PERSONNEL

An important reason for our deficient foreign policy in the Near East is the lack of adequate personnel. A country's foreign commitment is dictated by the country's domestic needs and the requirements of its international position. But that commitment must be guided, in the last instance, by the nature of the foreign area in which it is to be maintained, the special local conditions, and the rival interests of other foreign powers which converge in that same area.

The task of furnishing the necessary information about the foreign scene falls to the area specialists. They contribute the basic intelligence—process it, to use the jargon of the recent war—and keep it up to date. In due time, this material is deposited within reach of those who frame foreign policy. Between the area specialists and the ultimate policy makers there may be many intermediate stages; the original material may thus be subjected to progressive attenuation. The eventual policy does not always reflect the best judgment of the specialists. The final framer of regional policy may choose to ignore a set of facts which obstruct the path to an expedient conclusion, while the specialist is often at a loss to account for the reasoning which led to the policy. At all events, the end result depends largely on the ability and competence of the analysts all along the line. They carry a grave responsibility.

It would be grossly unfair to the Near East personnel of our State Department and the agencies associated with it to hold the rank and file accountable for the insolvency of our present policy in the Near East. The fault lies with the system rather than with the individuals; and beyond that, with the course of our general foreign policy in the decades preceding the recent war. In a period of "live alone and like it" we were content to leave other countries alone, especially those of the remote Near East. Hence, we had no need for specialized Near East personnel. Nor were the staffs of our consulates and legations encouraged to acquire even a semblance of area knowledge. Before a representative of the United States Government had spent enough time in the Near East to be able to ask for a glass of water in the vernacular, he would be transferred to some wholly dissimilar center. Hence he did not make any effort to learn. Our foreign personnel, with rare exceptions, was on a strictly itinerant basis.

When in the course of the war our Near East interests suddenly became vital national interests, we found ourselves, accordingly, without trained and experienced men and women to handle our growing commitment in that region. Competence in this highly complex field cannot be developed overnight. One does not generally study during one's college years such things as Arabic, Islamic civilization, or the social and economic history of the Near East. Furthermore, these are extremely taxing subjects, each requiring a lifetime of devoted application. And, unlike

Britain or Italy or France, we had no colonial empire which could absorb the surplus of such devotees.

In recent years, while our stake in the Near East has been steadily growing, the system under which the necessary area work has to be carried on has not been subjected to anything like a corresponding expansion and modernization. The number of "geographic desks" is still smaller than the number of countries which they are expected to cover. And the diversified knowledge which each desk man is supposed to possess would be little short of encyclopedic. Moreover, a recent transfer from Farther Asia might suddenly be placed in charge of a Near East field entirely obscure to him or vice versa; as if the required skills at any level, save the purely mechanical one, were interchangeable. Finally, the specialist departments assembled and developed during the war have been broken up. The fragments that remain are hamstrung by over-administration and the stultifying emphasis on form in place of substance. Small wonder, then, that the person who does not mistake the scissors-and-paste technique for constructive research on world affairs has little incentive to stay on. The entire setup has been a sad anachronism.

It does not require great vision to realize that policy which does not rest on facts—all the relevant facts—can be only a stab in the dark; that the handling of significant facts by amateurs leads to amateurish results; and that where international relations are concerned, dependence on such results is—in the words of an international expert of a century and a half ago—"worse than a crime; it is a mistake." The Second World War was rehearsed in Manchuria, Ethiopia, and Spain. If in the 1930's we had possessed enough bedrock information about those countries, we might have been less complacent about the progress of events. Today the seeds of war are perhaps being planted—or the chances for peace may await the proper initiative—in Iran, Saudi Arabia, or

Palestine. We cannot leave the diagnosis of such trends to some otherwise admirable person, whose chief recommendation may be the fact that he spent three years teaching in an American school in the Near East—where he failed to master the mysteries of the Arabic alphabet. We cannot set our sights too high in this respect. Nor can we afford to leave gaps in our coverage of the whole field. The least that we should gain from such an effort would be a better understanding of the world we live in. It could not be less than a sound investment in international stability.

Private institutions cannot be expected to train and develop the needed personnel. The faint efforts in this direction that are now being made in Washington may at best produce stopgaps. They may also lure us into a false sense of security. Schools sponsored by commercial interests, missionary interests, or the present interests of the State Department, can do no more than produce graduates in the image of the sponsors. And, in all candor, that would not be a reassuring image.

If the foregoing statement seems too strong, any doubter should be quickly disabused of his misgivings by a glance at what other countries have been doing. Britain's Near East experts do not need further introduction. Yet Britain has been losing no time in adding to her already impressive group of Near East personnel through an intensive training program which seeks to attract the most promising prospects in the United Kingdom. As against this, the Near East experts worthy of the name whom this country could assemble today would probably be outnumbered by the secretariat of an average-size British legation in the Near East. As for Russia, her personnel program aimed at the Near East appears to be, from such accounts as are available, even more intensive than Britain's.

When we take up a given Near East problem with Britain—or when the time comes to sit down to a similar discussion in an international conference—the council which will carry the greatest weight is likely to be the council fortified by the largest battery of indisputable facts. Britain's adult policy in this respect has already paid rich dividends in Anglo-American discussions, and cannot fail to do so in the future. It is ultimately a question of perhaps the most honorable kind of international competition that can be engaged in: competition in the coöperative quest for truth. Without entering this competition, we cannot hope to lay the foundation for an independent United States policy in the Near East. And if we fail to develop such a policy, we shall have missed a unique opportunity to enhance the prospect for world peace and security.

4. OPPORTUNITY

The Near East today is not the home of a major political power. It is, however, by reason of its position and its natural resources, and especially by reason of the fact that vital interests of the world's leading powers converge here and clash, the global center of gravity. It includes, moreover, a spiritual center sacred to one half of the population of the world. The region as a whole, therefore, is a sensitive barometer of the mood and temper, the problems and prospects, of a world whose fate has become indivisible but whose nations are not yet united. The anxious watchman looks thus to the Near East for a sign of what tomorrow may have in store.

Because Armageddon now carries a meaning never revealed to a seer of the past, he who dares to think of its banishment would seem to be reaching out for the millennium. Yet these two opposite extremes are not very far apart in the Near East. And it may well be decided in this region of immemorial visions which of the two shall prevail.

The United States is now on the scene in common with other great powers. The cold war that is in progress may determine the immediate future of the world. The one encouraging sign is that this is a many-sided contest and not just a bitter two-power struggle. With several parties vitally concerned, including the small local states, there still is hope that the negative balance of power may give way to the positive balance of common interests. So long as we take our proper share of responsibility, the small nations may yet be able to develop their strength to the full measure of their inherent capacities. A great deal depends, therefore, on how conscious the United States is of her vital opportunity.

History has had more practice in the Near East than elsewhere in the world. The region is thus a suitable stage for setting the course of future history. The Near East—which long ago evolved the concept of a society transcending ethnic and political boundaries—has demonstrated also, in the millenniums in which it has functioned as an enduring cultural factor, the essential interdependence of past and present, East and West, idealism and realism. It is a deep conviction of that interdependence that the nations of the world must have before they can become truly United Nations. And that conviction is very close to the surface in the Near East today.

Appendix.   Suggested Reading

Of making many books there is no end.
Ecclesiastes, 12:12

The gentle critic who used the above words to describe literary activity in the ancient Near East—at a time when the term manufacture had as yet nothing to do with mechanical processes—might well have proved neither gentle nor critical if confronted with today's accumulated literature on the Near East as a whole. The gathering of the relevant titles alone would impose a staggering effort. Needless to add, no one can be expected to have digested more than a fraction of the total output on any one of the scores of subjects which make up the entire field. Accordingly, no two lists of suggested introductory reading about this region are likely to correspond. Each would be bound to contain subjective selections. Since omission has to be the rule and inclusion the exception, no value judgment is implied by the omissions. The titles set down below refer to books, periodicals, and articles which I would have noted if the American Foreign Policy Library, of which this book is a part, had not set out to spare the reader the encumbrance of even a minimum of footnotes. In virtually every instance these publications are richly annotated so that any reader who wishes to delve deeper into a particular subject need not want for more specialized guides. At all events, adequate documentation in the present case would have taken up more space than the text itself.

1. BACKGROUND MATERIAL

The study of the ancient Near East is an ever progressive and expanding subject. No single comprehensive work in this field could therefore lay claim to universal endorsement. The most up-to-date treatment that can reasonably be expected of any one author is probably to be found in Ralph Turner, *The Great Cultural Traditions* (2 vols., New York and London: McGraw-Hill, 1941). This work affords an excellent orientation as to the environmental factor and a valuable synthesis of the various cultural aspects. W. F. Albright, *From Stone Age to Christianity* (Baltimore: The Johns Hopkins Press, 1940), traces expertly the development of religious ideas in their proper historical context. Millar Burrows, *What Mean These Stones?* (New Haven: American Schools of Oriental Research, 1941), gives a thoughtful analysis of the promise as well as the limitations of archaeology in its bearing on Biblical studies. On the emergence of democratic ideas, see E. A. Speiser, "Some Sources of Intellectual and Social Progress in the Ancient Near East," in *Studies in the History of Culture* (Menasha, Wisconsin: American Council of Learned Societies, 1942), and Thorkild Jacobsen, "Primitive Democracy in Ancient Mesopotamia," *Journal of Near Eastern Studies*, vol. II (Chicago, 1943). For the exact sciences note Otto Neugebauer, "The History of Ancient Astronomy: Problems and Methods," same journal, vol. IV (Chicago, 1945).

Out of the very extensive literature on Islam mention may be made of H. Lammens, *Islam* (translated by E. Denison Ross, London: Methuen, 1929) and *Whither Islam?* (edited by H. A. R. Gibb, London: Gollancz, 1932). The socio-political basis of Islam has been analyzed most recently by Arthur Jeffery, "The Political Importance of Islam," *Journal of Near Eastern Studies*, vol. I (Chicago, 1942). A very recent contribution of significance is H. A. R. Gibb, *Modern Trends in Islam* (Chicago, 1947).

On the Arab empires there is Philip K. Hitti, *History of the Arabs* (London: Macmillan, 1937). In the matter of the recent history of Arab lands there can be no substitute for Arnold J. Toynbee, *The Islamic World* (London: Oxford University Press, *Survey of International Affairs*, 1925, vol. I, published in 1927). My own manifold indebtedness to this work is herewith gratefully acknowledged. The standard work on the development of the Arab nationalist movement is George Antonius, *The Arab Awakening* (U. S. edition, Philadelphia: Lippincott, 1939; original edition, London: Hamish Hamilton, 1937, recently reprinted). This book is particularly valuable for its treatment of the early stages of the nationalist movement and for its appendix containing the King-Crane Report. T. E. Lawrence's personal impressions of the Arab Revolt scarcely need special mention. The McMahon correspondence is now presented officially in Command Paper 5957 and discussed in Command Paper 5974 (both London, 1939). Other documents bearing on British-Arab relations are given in the appendices to M. V. Seton-Williams, *Britain and the Arab States* (London, 1948).

For the period between the wars there is no better account of year-to-year developments in the Near East than is given in the successive volumes of the *Survey of International Affairs* (edited by A. J. Toynbee and published by the Royal Institute of International Affairs, or Chatham House, founded in 1920). Very little space can be devoted here to works on the individual countries. On Egypt there is *Great Britain and Egypt (1914–1936)*, published by the just-cited Royal Institute of International Affairs, and A. E. Crouchley, *The Economic Development of Egypt* (London: Longmans, 1938). A brief summary is presented by Frank H. H. Roberts, Jr., *Egypt and the Suez Canal* (Washington: The Smithsonian Institution, War Background Studies, No. 11, 1943). Charles Issawi, *Egypt: An Economic and Social Study* (London, 1947) is a notable work by an Egyptian

writer. *The Anglo-Egyptian Sudan* has been treated by
H. A. MacMichael (London: Faber and Faber, 1934). For
Arabia there is the *Admiralty Handbook* on this area, issued
for unrestricted use in 1920 and K. S. Twitchell, *Saudi
Arabia* (Princeton, 1947). Other sections of the Near East
have been expertly treated under the same auspices, and
widespread enjoyment of these handbooks is only a question
of their release by the Admiralty. Nor would the interested
reader wish to miss H. St. J. B. Philby, *Arabia* (New York:
Scribner, 1930). For Southern Arabia we have Freya Stark,
The Southern Gates to Arabia (London: John Murray,
1936) and H. Ingrams, *Report on the Social, Economic and
Political Conditions of the Hadhramaut Colonial Office*
(London: H. M. Stationery Office, 1936). Important yet
little known material concerning the Persian Gulf area is
contained in C. V. Aichison, *Collections of Treaties, En-
gagements and Sanctions Relating to India and Neighbour-
ing Countries* (Government of India, vol. XI, Persian Gulf,
Delhi, 1931). A collection of similar documents pertaining
to the whole region has been made by Helen Miller Davis,
*Constitutions, Electoral Laws, Treaties of States in the Near
and Middle East* (Durham, 1947).

On Iraq there is the model study by Philip W. Ireland,
Iraq (New York: Macmillan, 1938). The most penetrating
work on the Levant States is of post-war date: A. K.
Hourani, *Syria and Lebanon* (London: Oxford University
Press, 1946).

It is not surprising that the literature on Palestine is more
voluminous by far than on any other part of the region.
Much of it has appeared since the end of the war. Only the
barest sampling of the available material can here be attempted. A particularly significant work on the subject, in
that it contains a wealth of economic data not available elsewhere, carefully coördinated with the relevant socio-political material, is *Palestine: Problem and Promise*, by Robert

E. Nathan, O. Gass, and D. Creamer (Washington: Public Affairs Press, 1946). The same Press has issued (1944) the statement by Carl J. Friedrich on *American Policy Toward Palestine*, which is pro-Zionist in its bearing. The Arab position has been stated by J. M. N. Jeffries, *Palestine, The Reality* (London: Longmans, 1939). A painstaking analysis of the British administration of the country is offered by Paul L. Hanna, *British Policy in Palestine* (Washington: Public Affairs Press, 1942). An account of the problem from the point of view of the soil conservationist is given by Walter Clay Lowdermilk, *Palestine, Land of Promise* (Harper, 1944). Out of the many official British publications, the one which has particular current interest is the *Report of the Palestine Partition Commission* (Command Paper 5854, London, 1938). Publications of the United Nations are already now, and promise to be increasingly in the future, sources of important material on Palestine. The full report of the United Nations Special Committee on Palestine, to cite one example, was published at Lake Success in 1947.

Events leading up to the recent war in Palestine, and the developments during that struggle and since then, have produced an additional library of respectable proportions, and more books are coming off the presses all the time. The following is merely a sample listing. Esco Foundation, *Palestine: A Study of Jewish, Arab, and British Policies* (2 vols., New Haven, 1947) is the most exhaustive account from a moderate Zionist angle, with contributions by twenty Christian and Jewish scholars. Chaim Weizmann, *Trial and Error* (New York, 1949) is significant as the autobiography of the first President of the State of Israel. Perhaps the most incisive account of the workings of the Anglo-American Committee of Inquiry is that by Richard Crossman, *Palestine Mission* (New York, 1947). The corresponding story of UNSCOP is told by Jorge García-Granados, *The Birth of Israel* (New York, 1948). As examples of the pro-Arab approach may be cited R. B. Williams-Thompson, *The Palestine Problem* (London, 1946) and Nevill Barbour, *Palestine: Star or Crescent?* (New York, 1947). Finally, there is James Parkes, *A History of Palestine* (New York: Oxford University Press, 1949), which starts with the earliest times but brings the account down to the very latest developments.

The general history of the region is the subject of Carl Brockelmann's *History of the Islamic Peoples* (New York, 1947), and, still more recently, of G. E. Kirk's *A Short History of the Middle East* (Washington, 1949).

Turning now from history and politics to special disciplines, we have such contributions as A. Bonné's *Economic Development of the Middle East* (London, 1945), Doreen Warriner's *Land and Poverty in the Middle East* (London, 1948), and *Arabian Oil*, by R. F. Mikesell and H. B. Chenery (Chapel Hill, 1949).

In regard to broader treatments of the Near East and discussions of particular phases of the region's life, there are the pertinent sections of André Visson, *The Coming Struggle for Peace* (New York: Viking, 1944), objective and lucid but rather cursory. Arab nationalism has been investigated by W. E. Hocking, *The Spirit of World Politics* (New York, 1932), and Hans Kohn, *Nationalism and Imperialism in the Hither East* (London: Routledge, 1932). A valuable study of social conditions in the region is Hans Kohn, *Western Civilization in the Near East* (New York: Columbia University Press, 1936). A symposium on various aspects of the modern Near East is presented in *The Near East, Problems and Prospects* (University of Chicago Press, 1942), edited by Philip W. Ireland. Among the contributors to this volume is the distinguished British Arabist, H. A. R. Gibb, who is also the author of a very thoughtful analysis in *International Affairs*, vol. XX (London, October 1944), entitled "Middle Eastern Perplexities."

As examples of important specialized articles—the number

of which could be multiplied almost at will—may be cited "Conflict over Palestine" (New York, *Information Service*, published by the Federal Council of the Churches of Christ in America, October 7, 1944); Grant S. McClellan, "Palestine and America's Role in the Middle East" (New York, *Foreign Policy Reports*, July 1, 1945); James M. Landis, "Middle East Challenge" (*Fortune*, September 1945); Robert J. Barr, "Postwar Trade Prospects in Egypt, Iraq, Palestine" (Washington: *Foreign Commerce Weekly*, June 30, 1945); and E. DeGolyer, "Preliminary Report of the Technical Oil Mission to the Middle East" (*Bulletin of the American Association of Petroleum Geologists*, July 1944).

Finally, it should be pointed out that the best over-all sampling of recent publications as they appear may be found in the book review section of the *Middle East Journal* (Washington, since 1937), which also carries excellent bibliographies.

2. CURRENT DEVELOPMENTS

It is a fairly accurate measure of the unusual interest which the Near East has aroused lately in this country that considerable space is now devoted to the region in our quarterlies, monthlies, weeklies, and dailies and that the subject receives also a corresponding share of radio time. But there is no ready rule to indicate how much of this large total output is informed and significant. The quality of the given statement varies obviously from writer to writer and from speaker to speaker. Usually, however, the spoken word is less reliable than the signed written statement—always excepting outright propaganda. The various Town Meetings and Round Tables, for instance, have done little to raise the general level of thinking and information on the Near East. And the radio commentators—with a few outstanding exceptions, which it would be invidious to list but which most listeners can pick out for themselves—have failed on the whole to add to their reputations on the strength of their pronouncements upon a subject to which they are clearly strangers.

In regard to periodical publications, some are plainly "slanted" and must therefore be approached with caution. It goes without saying, for example, that the material published by the *Institute of Arab American Affairs* (New York) is bound to be pro-Arab, and that the pamphlets and bulletins issued by the *American Zionist Emergency Council* (New York) cannot but be pro-Zionist. Yet acquaintance with the various partisan claims is essential to an adequate understanding of the issues involved; and moreover, each side sponsors statements by interested outsiders in addition to releases by members of its regular staff. Jewish auspices, however, do not imply necessarily sponsorship of a Jewish state in Palestine. Thus the monthly *Commentary* (New York), which is published by the American Jewish Committee, has published articles reflecting diverse points of view on controversial political issues, articles giving the British side as well as the bi-national angle, and either friendly to Zionism or critical of it. Furthermore, The American Council for Judaism (New York) gets out an *Information Bulletin* which is vigorously anti-Zionist.

In spite of all this top-heavy emphasis in the periodicals, the current problems of the Near East are not restricted to Palestine. Yet the reader who seeks balanced data on the subject is all but limited to the dispatches in the daily press. His other possible sources rarely show more than an intermittent awareness of the region. Perhaps the best coverage outside of newspapers is to be found in the publications of the Foreign Policy Association (New York), particularly the *Foreign Policy Bulletin* and the *Foreign Policy Reports*. Occasional items of importance in this connection find their way into *Foreign Affairs*, the quarterly review of the Council on Foreign Relations. The *Nation* and the *New Republic* may be relied upon sporadically to present incisive treatments of some selected topic bearing on the Near East. *The Middle East Journal* (1906 Florida Ave., N. W., Washington, D. C.) has established itself, since its appearance in January 1947, as an indispensable medium of comment and information about the whole region.

The annual edition of the well-known British reference work, *The Statesman's Year Book*, is probably the best general source of information on vital facts about the Near East as well as the world at large. It is not, however, the last word on the subject. Some of its material is antiquated, partly because it goes back to statistics of several years ago, and partly also because cabinets and newspapers often change so quickly in the Near East that no annual can keep up with such data. For those who have access to British periodical publications, the weekly *Economist*, and the weekly editions of *The Times* of London and the *Manchester Guardian* are likely to provide valuable information and suggestive opinion about the Near East.

For day-to-day coverage of developments in the region and of outside relations with the region there are no better sources than the *New York Times* and the *New York Herald Tribune*. To be sure, careful comparison may disclose that these papers do not always present all the relevant news fit to print. Supplementary reading of the *Christian Science Monitor* often proves to be a rewarding experience. The same may be said of several other newspapers. But the regular study of the first-named paper for a period of the past ten years or so is certain to disclose the steady growth of interest in the Near East and the increasing realization of the region's importance in so far as the United States is concerned.

INDEX

INDEX

Zionism, Zionists, 67, 199–205, 223, 225; and Colonel Lawrence, 53; issue dominant in Near East, 54; repercussions, 54, 67, 71, 107, 108, 161; and Arabs, 57, 108, 161, 207–210; claim to Palestine, 69–71, 201–202; as viewed in King-Crane Report, 71; and Britain, 74–84, 178, 210–212; varieties of political opinion, 79, 203; and United States, 107, 178; cultural, 200; religious, 200; political, stimulated by anti-Semitism, 201; spiritual and psychological content, 202

Zionist Organization, 69, 79

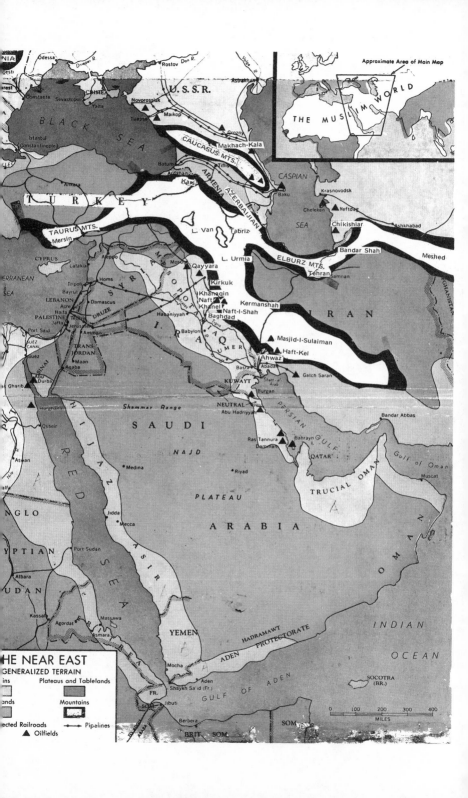

Approximate Area of Main Map

THE MUSLIM WORLD

U.S.S.R.

Odessa
Rostov   Don R.
Dnieper R.
Constanta
Sevastopol
Yalta
CRIMEA
Istanbul
(Constantinople)
BLACK   SEA
Novorossisk
Tuapse
Maikop
Grozny
Makhach-Kala
CAUCASUS MTS.
Batumi
Tiflis
Ankara
Astrakhan
Volga R.
Krasnovodsk
CASPIAN
Baku
Neftdag
Cheleken
Chikishlar
Ashkhabad
Meshed

TURKEY
TAURUS MTS.
Mersin
Kars
ARMENIA
AZERBAIJAN
L. Van
Tabriz
L. Urmia
ELBURZ MTS.
Bandar Shah
SEA
Tehran
samnan

CYPRUS
Latakia
Aleppo
Mosul
Qayyara
Kirkuk
Kermanshah
I R A N
Bandar Abbas

MEDITERRANEAN
SEA
Tripoli
Homs
Bayrut
LEBANON
Haifa
Acre
Damascus
DRUZE
Habbaniyyah
Khanaqin
Naft
Khanel
Naft-I-Shah
Masjid-I-Sulaiman
Haft-Kel

PALESTINE
Jaffa
Tel Aviv
Jerusalem
Amman
Baghdad
Babylon
Tigris
Ahwaz
Abadan
Gatch Saran
Port Said
SUEZ CANAL
Suez
TRANS-JORDAN
Maan
Aqaba
SINAI
Babylon
SUMER
Basra
Shatt-al-Arab
KUWAYT
Burgan
PERSIAN GULF

Abu Durba
Gharib
Morghais
Quseir
Shammar Range
Abu Hadriyya
NEUTRAL
Ras Tannura
Dammam
Bahrayn
QATAR
Gulf of Oman
Muscat

S A U D I
N A J D
Medina
Riyad
Aswan
Nile

ANGLO
EGYPTIAN
SUDAN
Atbara
Kassala
Agordat
Massawa
Asmara
Port Sudan

P L A T E A U
A R A B I A
TRUCIAL OMAN
O M A N

RED   SEA
HIJAZ
ASIR
Jidda
Mecca

YEMEN
HADRAMAWT
ADEN PROTECTORATE
INDIAN
OCEAN

Mocha
Shaykh Sa'id (Fr.)
Aden
FR.
SOM.
Jibuti
GULF OF ADEN
SOCOTRA
(BR.)

SOM.
Berbera
BRIT. SOM.

THE NEAR EAST
GENERALIZED TERRAIN

Plains
Lowlands
Selected Railroads
▲ Oilfields

Plateaus and Tablelands
Mountains
Pipelines

0   100   200   300   400
MILES